SELECTED POETRY AND PROSE

THE
OTHER VOICE
IN
EARLY MODERN
EUROPE

A Series Edited by Margaret L. King and Albert Rabil Jr.

RECENT BOOKS IN THE SERIES

Chiara Matraini

SELECTED POETRY AND PROSE

A Bilingual Edition

*Edited and Translated
by Elaine Maclachlan*

*With an Introduction
by Giovanna Rabitti*

THE UNIVERSITY OF CHICAGO PRESS
Chicago & London

Chiara Matraini, 1515–1604 (?)

Elaine Maclachlan is an independent scholar who previously was a lecturer at Harvard University, Smith College, and Tufts University. Her published translations include Fabio Luca Cavazza's *The Italian Paradox: An Exit from Communism*, Carla Lonzi's *Spit on Hegel*, and a number of Chiara Matraini's poems.

Giovanna Rabitti teaches Textual Studies of Italian Literature in the Department of Languages at the University of Sassari. She has done extensive work on Italian women's writing as a genre in relation to the principal canon of literature, as well as textual studies of individual authors (Chiara Matraini, Vittoria Colonna, Laura Battiferri). She has published articles on autobiographies and on travel literature and is preparing a critical edition of a part of Pietro della Valle's *Viaggi* (Travels).

The University of Chicago Press, Chicago 60637
The University of Chicago Press, Ltd., London
© 2007 by The University of Chicago
All rights reserved. Published 2007
Printed in the United States of America

16 15 14 13 12 11 10 09 08 07   1 2 3 4 5

ISBN-13: 978-0-226-51084-2 (cloth)
ISBN-13: 978-0-226-51085-9 (paper)
ISBN-10: 0-226-51084-0 (cloth)
ISBN-10: 0-226-51085-9 (paper)

The University of Chicago Press gratefully acknowledges the generous support of James E. Rabil, in memory of Scottie W. Rabil, toward the publication of this book.

Library of Congress Cataloging-in-Publication Data
Matraini, Chiara, 1515–1604?
[Selections. English & Italian. 2008]
Selected poetry and prose / Chiara Matraini ; edited and translated by Elaine Maclachlan ; with an introduction by Giovanna Rabitti. — A bilingual ed.
p. cm. — (The other voice in early modern Europe)
English and Italian.
Includes bibliographical references and index.
ISBN-13: 978-0-226-51084-2 (cloth : alk. paper)
ISBN-13 978-0-226-51085-9 (pbk. : alk. paper)
ISBN-10: 0-226-51084-0 (cloth : alk. paper)
ISBN-10: 0-226-51085-9 (pbk. : alk. paper)
I. Maclachlan, Elaine. II. Title.
PQ4630.M263A2 20008
858'.309—dc22
2007033067

⊗ The paper used in this publication meets the minimum requirements of the American National Standard for Information Sciences—Permanence of Paper for Printed Library Materials, ANSI Z39.48-1992.

To my beloved Dan, and in memory of my beautiful sister Nancy

CONTENTS

ACKNOWLEDGMENTS

This book would not have been possible without the help and assistance of many people. In particular, I would like to thank Giovanna Rabitti for her introduction to this book and for her immense contribution to the study of Matraini's work. I also thank Natalia Costa-Zalessow for the translation of the introduction and for her invaluable help in my own translations. The staffs of the Widener Library of Harvard University, the Biblioteca Nazionale di San Marco in Venice, and the Biblioteca Capitolare Feliniana in Lucca were most helpful. Additional valuable assistance in translation was provided by Janet Smarr, Susan Tarcov, Cinzia Rucellai, Laura Licata, Paula Phipps, Antonio Morena, Cinzia Scafetta, and Paolo de Ventura. A generous grant from the National Endowment for the Humanities (NEH) enabled me to complete the translations.

Thanks to Liz Wilson, Katie Angelou, and Dan Duryea for their typing skills. My sincere gratitude goes to Al Rabil for the encouragement that got the book started and his great patience in seeing it through to the end. For her unflagging encouragement and support, I thank my friend Ellen Miller.

The publication of any book is a significant accomplishment, but so much more so for a recovering stroke victim. My 1996 stroke ended my teaching career and took away my spoken Italian and much of my freedom of movement. However, my ability to read and write in both English and Italian, and my passion for Chiara Matraini, remained intact. I began this book in 2000 after the conference "Strong Voices, Weak History: Medieval and Renaissance Women in Their Literary Canons" in Philadelphia where I met Al Rabil. The progress has been slow, but here I am at the end of my book. I encourage anyone who has had a stroke to believe that they can improve with help and to persevere in making their own dreams a reality.

Elaine Maclachlan

THE OTHER VOICE IN
EARLY MODERN EUROPE:
INTRODUCTION TO THE SERIES

Margaret L. King and Albert Rabil Jr.

THE OLD VOICE AND THE OTHER VOICE

In western Europe and the United States, women are nearing equality in the professions, in business, and in politics. Most enjoy access to education, reproductive rights, and autonomy in financial affairs. Issues vital to women are on the public agenda: equal pay, child care, domestic abuse, breast cancer research, and curricular revision with an eye to the inclusion of women.

These recent achievements have their origins in things women (and some male supporters) said for the first time about six hundred years ago. Theirs is the "other voice," in contradistinction to the "first voice," the voice of the educated men who created Western culture. Coincident with a general re-shaping of European culture in the period 1300–1700 (called the Renaissance or early modern period), questions of female equality and opportunity were raised that still resound and are still unresolved.

The other voice emerged against the backdrop of a three-thousand-year history of the derogation of women rooted in the civilizations related to Western culture: Hebrew, Greek, Roman, and Christian. Negative attitudes toward women inherited from these traditions pervaded the intellectual, medical, legal, religious, and social systems that developed during the European Middle Ages.

The following pages describe the traditional, overwhelmingly male views of women's nature inherited by early modern Europeans and the new tradition that the "other voice" called into being to begin to challenge reigning assumptions. This review should serve as a framework for understanding the texts published in the Other Voice in Early Modern Europe series. Introductions specific to each text and author follow this essay in all the volumes of the series.

TRADITIONAL VIEWS OF WOMEN, 500 B.C.E.–1500 C.E.

Embedded in the philosophical and medical theories of the ancient Greeks were perceptions of the female as inferior to the male in both mind and body. Similarly, the structure of civil legislation inherited from the ancient Romans was biased against women, and the views on women developed by Christian thinkers out of the Hebrew Bible and the Christian New Testament were negative and disabling. Literary works composed in the vernacular of ordinary people, and widely recited or read, conveyed these negative assumptions. The social networks within which most women lived—those of the family and the institutions of the Roman Catholic Church—were shaped by this negative tradition and sharply limited the areas in which women might act in and upon the world.

GREEK PHILOSOPHY AND FEMALE NATURE. Greek biology assumed that women were inferior to men and defined them as merely childbearers and housekeepers. This view was authoritatively expressed in the works of the philosopher Aristotle.

Aristotle thought in dualities. He considered action superior to inaction, form (the inner design or structure of any object) superior to matter, completion to incompletion, possession to deprivation. In each of these dualities, he associated the male principle with the superior quality and the female with the inferior. "The male principle in nature," he argued, "is associated with active, formative and perfected characteristics, while the female is passive, material and deprived, desiring the male in order to become complete."[1] Men are always identified with virile qualities, such as judgment, courage, and stamina, and women with their opposites—irrationality, cowardice, and weakness.

The masculine principle was considered superior even in the womb. The man's semen, Aristotle believed, created the form of a new human creature, while the female body contributed only matter. (The existence of the ovum, and with it the other facts of human embryology, was not established until the seventeenth century.) Although the later Greek physician Galen believed there was a female component in generation, contributed by "female semen," the followers of both Aristotle and Galen saw the male role in human generation as more active and more important.

In the Aristotelian view, the male principle sought always to reproduce itself. The creation of a female was always a mistake, therefore, resulting from

---

1. Aristotle, *Physics* 1.9.192a20–24, in *The Complete Works of Aristotle*, ed. Jonathan Barnes, rev. Oxford trans., 2 vols. (Princeton, 1984), 1:328.

an imperfect act of generation. Every female born was considered a "defective" or "mutilated" male (as Aristotle's terminology has variously been translated), a "monstrosity" of nature.[2]

For Greek theorists, the biology of males and females was the key to their psychology. The female was softer and more docile, more apt to be despondent, querulous, and deceitful. Being incomplete, moreover, she craved sexual fulfillment in intercourse with a male. The male was intellectual, active, and in control of his passions.

These psychological polarities derived from the theory that the universe consisted of four elements (earth, fire, air, and water), expressed in human bodies as four "humors" (black bile, yellow bile, blood, and phlegm) considered, respectively, dry, hot, damp, and cold and corresponding to mental states ("melancholic," "choleric," "sanguine," "phlegmatic"). In this scheme the male, sharing the principles of earth and fire, was dry and hot; the female, sharing the principles of air and water, was cold and damp.

Female psychology was further affected by her dominant organ, the uterus (womb), *hystera* in Greek. The passions generated by the womb made women lustful, deceitful, talkative, irrational, indeed—when these affects were in excess—"hysterical."

Aristotle's biology also had social and political consequences. If the male principle was superior and the female inferior, then in the household, as in the state, men should rule and women must be subordinate. That hierarchy did not rule out the companionship of husband and wife, whose cooperation was necessary for the welfare of children and the preservation of property. Such mutuality supported male preeminence.

Aristotle's teacher Plato suggested a different possibility: that men and women might possess the same virtues. The setting for this proposal is the imaginary and ideal Republic that Plato sketches in a dialogue of that name. Here, for a privileged elite capable of leading wisely, all distinctions of class and wealth dissolve, as, consequently, do those of gender. Without households or property, as Plato constructs his ideal society, there is no need for the subordination of women. Women may therefore be educated to the same level as men to assume leadership. Plato's Republic remained imaginary, however. In real societies, the subordination of women remained the norm and the prescription.

The views of women inherited from the Greek philosophical tradition became the basis for medieval thought. In the thirteenth century, the supreme Scholastic philosopher Thomas Aquinas, among others, still echoed

2. Aristotle, *Generation of Animals* 2.3.737a27–28, in *The Complete Works*, 1: 1144.

Aristotle's views of human reproduction, of male and female personalities, and of the preeminent male role in the social hierarchy.

ROMAN LAW AND THE FEMALE CONDITION. Roman law, like Greek philosophy, underlay medieval thought and shaped medieval society. The ancient belief that adult property-owning men should administer households and make decisions affecting the community at large is the very fulcrum of Roman law.

About 450 B.C.E., during Rome's republican era, the community's customary law was recorded (legendarily) on twelve tablets erected in the city's central forum. It was later elaborated by professional jurists whose activity increased in the imperial era, when much new legislation was passed, especially on issues affecting family and inheritance. This growing, changing body of laws was eventually codified in the *Corpus of Civil Law* under the direction of the emperor Justinian, generations after the empire ceased to be ruled from Rome. That *Corpus*, read and commented on by medieval scholars from the eleventh century on, inspired the legal systems of most of the cities and kingdoms of Europe.

Laws regarding dowries, divorce, and inheritance pertain primarily to women. Since those laws aimed to maintain and preserve property, the women concerned were those from the property-owning minority. Their subordination to male family members points to the even greater subordination of lower-class and slave women, about whom the laws speak little.

In the early republic, the *paterfamilias*, or "father of the family," possessed *patria potestas*, "paternal power." The term *pater*, "father," in both these cases does not necessarily mean biological father but denotes the head of a household. The father was the person who owned the household's property and, indeed, its human members. The *paterfamilias* had absolute power—including the power, rarely exercised, of life or death—over his wife, his children, and his slaves, as much as his cattle.

Male children could be "emancipated," an act that granted legal autonomy and the right to own property. Those over fourteen could be emancipated by a special grant from the father or automatically by their father's death. But females could never be emancipated; instead, they passed from the authority of their father to that of a husband or, if widowed or orphaned while still unmarried, to a guardian or tutor.

Marriage in its traditional form placed the woman under her husband's authority, or *manus*. He could divorce her on grounds of adultery, drinking wine, or stealing from the household, but she could not divorce him. She could neither possess property in her own right nor bequeath any to her children upon her death. When her husband died, the household property passed not to her but to his male heirs. And when her father died, she had no claim to any family inheritance, which was directed to her brothers or more remote male relatives. The effect of these laws was to exclude women from civil society, itself based on property ownership.

In the later republican and imperial periods, these rules were significantly modified. Women rarely married according to the traditional form. The practice of "free" marriage allowed a woman to remain under her father's authority, to possess property given her by her father (most frequently the "dowry," recoverable from the husband's household on his death), and to inherit from her father. She could also bequeath property to her own children and divorce her husband, just as he could divorce her.

Despite this greater freedom, women still suffered enormous disability under Roman law. Heirs could belong only to the father's side, never the mother's. Moreover, although she could bequeath her property to her children, she could not establish a line of succession in doing so. A woman was "the beginning and end of her own family," said the jurist Ulpian. Moreover, women could play no public role. They could not hold public office, represent anyone in a legal case, or even witness a will. Women had only a private existence and no public personality.

The dowry system, the guardian, women's limited ability to transmit wealth, and total political disability are all features of Roman law adopted by the medieval communities of western Europe, although modified according to local customary laws.

CHRISTIAN DOCTRINE AND WOMEN'S PLACE. The Hebrew Bible and the Christian New Testament authorized later writers to limit women to the realm of the family and to burden them with the guilt of original sin. The passages most fruitful for this purpose were the creation narratives in Genesis and sentences from the Epistles defining women's role within the Christian family and community.

Each of the first two chapters of Genesis contains a creation narrative. In the first "God created man in his own image, in the image of God he created him; male and female he created them" (Gn 1:27). In the second, God created Eve from Adam's rib (2:21–23). Christian theologians relied principally on Genesis 2 for their understanding of the relation between man and woman, interpreting the creation of Eve from Adam as proof of her subordination to him.

The creation story in Genesis 2 leads to that of the temptations in Genesis 3: of Eve by the wily serpent and of Adam by Eve. As read by Christian theologians from Tertullian to Thomas Aquinas, the narrative made Eve responsible for the Fall and its consequences. She instigated the act; she deceived her husband; she suffered the greater punishment. Her disobedience made it necessary for Jesus to be incarnated and to die on the cross. From the pulpit, moralists and preachers for centuries conveyed to women the guilt that they bore for original sin.

The Epistles offered advice to early Christians on building communities of the faithful. Among the matters to be regulated was the place of women. Paul offered views favorable to women in Galatians 3:28: "There is neither Jew nor Greek, there is neither slave nor free, there is neither male nor female; for you are all one in Christ Jesus." Paul also referred to women as his coworkers and placed them on a par with himself and his male coworkers (Phlm 4:2–3; Rom 16:1–3; 1 Cor 16:19). Elsewhere, Paul limited women's possibilities: "But I want you to understand that the head of every man is Christ, the head of a woman is her husband, and the head of Christ is God" (1 Cor 11:3).

Biblical passages by later writers (although attributed to Paul) enjoined women to forgo jewels, expensive clothes, and elaborate coiffures; and they forbade women to "teach or have authority over men," telling them to "learn in silence with all submissiveness" as is proper for one responsible for sin, consoling them, however, with the thought that they will be saved through childbearing (1 Tm 2:9–15). Other texts among the later Epistles defined women as the weaker sex and emphasized their subordination to their husbands (1 Pt 3:7; Col 3:18; Eph 5:22–23).

These passages from the New Testament became the arsenal employed by theologians of the early church to transmit negative attitudes toward women to medieval Christian culture—above all, Tertullian (*On the Apparel of Women*), Jerome (*Against Jovinian*), and Augustine (*The Literal Meaning of Genesis*).

THE IMAGE OF WOMEN IN MEDIEVAL LITERATURE. The philosophical, legal, and religious traditions born in antiquity formed the basis of the medieval intellectual synthesis wrought by trained thinkers, mostly clerics, writing in Latin and based largely in universities. The vernacular literary tradition that developed alongside the learned tradition also spoke about female nature and women's roles. Medieval stories, poems, and epics also portrayed women negatively—as lustful and deceitful—while praising good housekeepers and loyal wives as replicas of the Virgin Mary or the female saints and martyrs.

There is an exception in the movement of "courtly love" that evolved in southern France from the twelfth century. Courtly love was the erotic love between a nobleman and noblewoman, the latter usually superior in social rank. It was always adulterous. From the conventions of courtly love derive modern Western notions of romantic love. The tradition has had an impact disproportionate to its size, for it affected only a tiny elite, and very few women. The exaltation of the female lover probably does not reflect a higher evaluation of women or a step toward their sexual liberation. More likely it gives expression to the social and sexual tensions besetting the knightly class at a specific historical juncture.

The literary fashion of courtly love was on the wane by the thirteenth century, when the widely read *Romance of the Rose* was composed in French by two authors of significantly different dispositions. Guillaume de Lorris composed the initial four thousand verses about 1235, and Jean de Meun added about seventeen thousand verses—more than four times the original—about 1265.

The fragment composed by Guillaume de Lorris stands squarely in the tradition of courtly love. Here the poet, in a dream, is admitted into a walled garden where he finds a magic fountain in which a rosebush is reflected. He longs to pick one rose, but the thorns prevent his doing so, even as he is wounded by arrows from the god of love, whose commands he agrees to obey. The rest of this part of the poem recounts the poet's unsuccessful efforts to pluck the rose.

The longer part of the *Romance* by Jean de Meun also describes a dream. But here allegorical characters give long didactic speeches, providing a social satire on a variety of themes, some pertaining to women. Love is an anxious and tormented state, the poem explains: women are greedy and manipulative, marriage is miserable, beautiful women are lustful, ugly ones cease to please, and a chaste woman is as rare as a black swan.

Shortly after Jean de Meun completed *The Romance of the Rose*, Mathéolus penned his *Lamentations*, a long Latin diatribe against marriage translated into French about a century later. The *Lamentations* sum up medieval attitudes toward women and provoked the important response by Christine de Pizan in her *Book of the City of Ladies*.

In 1355, Giovanni Boccaccio wrote *Il Corbaccio*, another antifeminist manifesto, although ironically by an author whose other works pioneered new directions in Renaissance thought. The former husband of his lover appears to Boccaccio, condemning his unmoderated lust and detailing the defects of women. Boccaccio concedes at the end "how much men naturally surpass women in nobility" and is cured of his desires.[3]

---

3. Giovanni Boccaccio, *The Corbaccio, or The Labyrinth of Love*, trans. and ed. Anthony K. Cassell, rev. ed. (Binghamton, N.Y., 1993), 71.

WOMEN'S ROLES: THE FAMILY. The negative perceptions of women expressed in the intellectual tradition are also implicit in the actual roles that women played in European society. Assigned to subordinate positions in the household and the church, they were barred from significant participation in public life.

Medieval European households, like those in antiquity and in non-Western civilizations, were headed by males. It was the male serf (or peasant), feudal lord, town merchant, or citizen who was polled or taxed or succeeded to an inheritance or had any acknowledged public role, although his wife or widow could stand as a temporary surrogate. From about 1100, the position of property-holding males was further enhanced: inheritance was confined to the male, or agnate, line—with depressing consequences for women.

A wife never fully belonged to her husband's family, nor was she a daughter to her father's family. She left her father's house young to marry whomever her parents chose. Her dowry was managed by her husband, and at her death it normally passed to her children by him.

A married woman's life was occupied nearly constantly with cycles of pregnancy, childbearing, and lactation. Women bore children through all the years of their fertility, and many died in childbirth. They were also responsible for raising young children up to six or seven. In the propertied classes that responsibility was shared, since it was common for a wet nurse to take over breast-feeding and for servants to perform other chores.

Women trained their daughters in the household duties appropriate to their status, nearly always tasks associated with textiles: spinning, weaving, sewing, embroidering. Their sons were sent out of the house as apprentices or students, or their training was assumed by fathers in later childhood and adolescence. On the death of her husband, a woman's children became the responsibility of his family. She generally did not take "his" children with her to a new marriage or back to her father's house, except sometimes in the artisan classes.

Women also worked. Rural peasants performed farm chores, merchant wives often practiced their husbands' trades, the unmarried daughters of the urban poor worked as servants or prostitutes. All wives produced or embellished textiles and did the housekeeping, while wealthy ones managed servants. These labors were unpaid or poorly paid but often contributed substantially to family wealth.

WOMEN'S ROLES: THE CHURCH. Membership in a household, whether a father's or a husband's, meant for women a lifelong subordination to others. In western Europe, the Roman Catholic Church offered an alternative to the ca-

reer of wife and mother. A woman could enter a convent, parallel in function to the monasteries for men that evolved in the early Christian centuries.

In the convent, a woman pledged herself to a celibate life, lived according to strict community rules, and worshiped daily. Often the convent offered training in Latin, allowing some women to become considerable scholars and authors as well as scribes, artists, and musicians. For women who chose the conventual life, the benefits could be enormous, but for numerous others placed in convents by paternal choice, the life could be restrictive and burdensome.

The conventual life declined as an alternative for women as the modern age approached. Reformed monastic institutions resisted responsibility for related female orders. The church increasingly restricted female institutional life by insisting on closer male supervision.

Women often sought other options. Some joined the communities of laywomen that sprang up spontaneously in the thirteenth century in the urban zones of western Europe, especially in Flanders and Italy. Some joined the heretical movements that flourished in late medieval Christendom, whose anticlerical and often antifamily positions particularly appealed to women. In these communities, some women were acclaimed as "holy women" or "saints," whereas others often were condemned as frauds or heretics.

In all, although the options offered to women by the church were sometimes less than satisfactory, they were sometimes richly rewarding. After 1520, the convent remained an option only in Roman Catholic territories. Protestantism engendered an ideal of marriage as a heroic endeavor and appeared to place husband and wife on a more equal footing. Sermons and treatises, however, still called for female subordination and obedience.

THE OTHER VOICE, 1300–1700

When the modern era opened, European culture was so firmly structured by a framework of negative attitudes toward women that to dismantle it was a monumental labor. The process began as part of a larger cultural movement that entailed the critical reexamination of ideas inherited from the ancient and medieval past. The humanists launched that critical reexamination.

THE HUMANIST FOUNDATION. Originating in Italy in the fourteenth century, humanism quickly became the dominant intellectual movement in Europe. Spreading in the sixteenth century from Italy to the rest of Europe, it fueled the literary, scientific, and philosophical movements of the era and laid the basis for the eighteenth-century Enlightenment.

Humanists regarded the Scholastic philosophy of medieval universities

as out of touch with the realities of urban life. They found in the rhetorical discourse of classical Rome a language adapted to civic life and public speech. They learned to read, speak, and write classical Latin and, eventually, classical Greek. They founded schools to teach others to do so, establishing the pattern for elementary and secondary education for the next three hundred years.

In the service of complex government bureaucracies, humanists employed their skills to write eloquent letters, deliver public orations, and formulate public policy. They developed new scripts for copying manuscripts and used the new printing press to disseminate texts, for which they created methods of critical editing.

Humanism was a movement led by males who accepted the evaluation of women in ancient texts and generally shared the misogynist perceptions of their culture. (Female humanists, as we will see, did not.) Yet humanism also opened the door to a reevaluation of the nature and capacity of women. By calling authors, texts, and ideas into question, it made possible the fundamental rereading of the whole intellectual tradition that was required in order to free women from cultural prejudice and social subordination.

A DIFFERENT CITY. The other voice first appeared when, after so many centuries, the accumulation of misogynist concepts evoked a response from a capable female defender: Christine de Pizan (1365–1431). Introducing her *Book of the City of Ladies* (1405), she described how she was affected by reading Mathéolus's *Lamentations:* "Just the sight of this book . . . made me wonder how it happened that so many different men . . . are so inclined to express both in speaking and in their treatises and writings so many wicked insults about women and their behavior."[4] These statements impelled her to detest herself "and the entire feminine sex, as though we were monstrosities in nature."[5]

The rest of *The Book of the City of Ladies* presents a justification of the female sex and a vision of an ideal community of women. A pioneer, she has received the message of female inferiority and rejected it. From the fourteenth to the seventeenth century, a huge body of literature accumulated that responded to the dominant tradition.

The result was a literary explosion consisting of works by both men and women, in Latin and in the vernaculars: works enumerating the achievements of notable women; works rebutting the main accusations made against women;

4. Christine de Pizan, *The Book of the City of Ladies,* trans. Earl Jeffrey Richards, foreword by Marina Warner (New York, 1982), 1.1.1, pp. 3–4.

5. Ibid., 1.1.1–2, p. 5.

served the cause of reexamining the issue of women's nature by placing domestic issues at the center of scholarly concern and reopening the pertinent classical texts. In addition, Barbaro emphasized the companionate nature of marriage and the importance of a wife's spiritual and mental qualities for the well-being of the family.

These themes reappear in later humanist works on marriage and the education of women by Juan Luis Vives and Erasmus. Both were moderately sympathetic to the condition of women without reaching beyond the usual masculine prescriptions for female behavior.

An outlook more favorable to women characterizes the nearly unknown work *In Praise of Women* (ca. 1487) by the Italian humanist Bartolommeo Goggio. In addition to providing a catalog of illustrious women, Goggio argued that male and female are the same in essence, but that women (reworking the Adam and Eve narrative from quite a new angle) are actually superior. In the same vein, the Italian humanist Mario Equicola asserted the spiritual equality of men and women in *On Women* (1501). In 1525, Galeazzo Flavio Capra (or Capella) published his work *On the Excellence and Dignity of Women*. This humanist tradition of treatises defending the worthiness of women culminates in the work of Henricus Cornelius Agrippa *On the Nobility and Preeminence of the Female Sex*. No work by a male humanist more succinctly or explicitly presents the case for female dignity.

THE WITCH BOOKS. While humanists grappled with the issues pertaining to women and family, other learned men turned their attention to what they perceived as a very great problem: witches. Witch-hunting manuals, explorations of the witch phenomenon, and even defenses of witches are not at first glance pertinent to the tradition of the other voice. But they do relate in this way: most accused witches were women. The hostility aroused by supposed witch activity is comparable to the hostility aroused by women. The evil deeds the victims of the hunt were charged with were exaggerations of the vices to which, many believed, all women were prone.

The connection between the witch accusation and the hatred of women is explicit in the notorious witch-hunting manual *The Hammer of Witches* (1486) by two Dominican inquisitors, Heinrich Krämer and Jacob Sprenger. Here the inconstancy, deceitfulness, and lustfulness traditionally associated with women are depicted in exaggerated form as the core features of witch behavior. These traits inclined women to make a bargain with the devil—sealed by sexual intercourse—by which they acquired unholy powers. Such bizarre claims, far from being rejected by rational men, were broadcast by intellectuals. The German Ulrich Molitur, the Frenchman Nicolas Rémy, and the Italian Stefano Guazzo all coolly informed the public of sinister orgies and midnight pacts with the devil. The celebrated French jurist, historian, and political philosopher Jean Bodin argued that because women were especially prone to diabolism, regular legal procedures could properly be suspended in order to try those accused of this "exceptional crime."

A few experts such as the physician Johann Weyer, a student of Agrippa's, raised their voices in protest. In 1563, he explained the witch phenomenon thus, without discarding belief in diabolism: the devil deluded foolish old women afflicted by melancholia, causing them to believe they had magical powers. Weyer's rational skepticism, which had good credibility in the community of the learned, worked to revise the conventional views of women and witchcraft.

WOMEN'S WORKS. To the many categories of works produced on the question of women's worth must be added nearly all works written by women. A woman writing was in herself a statement of women's claim to dignity.

Only a few women wrote anything before the dawn of the modern era, for three reasons. First, they rarely received the education that would enable them to write. Second, they were not admitted to the public roles—as administrator, bureaucrat, lawyer or notary, or university professor—in which they might gain knowledge of the kinds of things the literate public thought worth writing about. Third, the culture imposed silence on women, considering speaking out a form of unchastity. Given these conditions, it is remarkable that any women wrote. Those who did before the fourteenth century were almost always nuns or religious women whose isolation made their pronouncements more acceptable.

From the fourteenth century on, the volume of women's writings rose. Women continued to write devotional literature, although not always as cloistered nuns. They also wrote diaries, often intended as keepsakes for their children; books of advice to their sons and daughters; letters to family members and friends; and family memoirs, in a few cases elaborate enough to be considered histories.

A few women wrote works directly concerning the "woman question," and some of these, such as the humanists Isotta Nogarola, Cassandra Fedele, Laura Cereta, and Olympia Morata, were highly trained. A few were professional writers, living by the income of their pens; the very first among them was Christine de Pizan, noteworthy in this context as in so many others. In addition to *The Book of the City of Ladies* and her critiques of *The Romance of the Rose*, she wrote *The Treasure of the City of Ladies* (a guide to social decorum for women), an advice book for her son, much courtly verse, and a full-scale history of the reign of King Charles V of France.

WOMEN PATRONS. Women who did not themselves write but encouraged others to do so boosted the development of an alternative tradition. Highly placed women patrons supported authors, artists, musicians, poets, and learned men. Such patrons, drawn mostly from the Italian elites and the courts of northern Europe, figure disproportionately as the dedicatees of the important works of early feminism.

For a start, it might be noted that the catalogs of Boccaccio and Alvaro de Luna were dedicated to the Florentine noblewoman Andrea Acciaiuoli and to Doña María, first wife of King Juan II of Castile, while the French translation of Boccaccio's work was commissioned by Anne of Brittany, wife of King Charles VIII of France. The humanist treatises of Goggio, Equicola, Vives, and Agrippa were dedicated, respectively, to Eleanora of Aragon, wife of Ercole I d'Este, duke of Ferrara; to Margherita Cantelma of Mantua; to Catherine of Aragon, wife of King Henry VIII of England; and to Margaret, Duchess of Austria and regent of the Netherlands. As late as 1696, Mary Astell's *Serious Proposal to the Ladies, for the Advancement of Their True and Greatest Interest* was dedicated to Princess Anne of Denmark

These authors presumed that their efforts would be welcome to female patrons, or they may have written at the bidding of those patrons. Silent themselves, perhaps even unresponsive, these loftily placed women helped shape the tradition of the other voice.

THE ISSUES. The literary forms and patterns in which the tradition of the other voice presented itself have now been sketched. It remains to highlight the major issues around which this tradition crystallizes. In brief, there are four problems to which our authors return again and again, in plays and catalogs, in verse and letters, in treatises and dialogues, in every language: the problem of chastity, the problem of power, the problem of speech, and the problem of knowledge. Of these the greatest, preconditioning the others, is the problem of chastity.

THE PROBLEM OF CHASTITY. In traditional European culture, as in those of antiquity and others around the globe, chastity was perceived as woman's quintessential virtue—in contrast to courage, or generosity, or leadership, or rationality, seen as virtues characteristic of men. Opponents of women charged them with insatiable lust. Women themselves and their defenders—without disputing the validity of the standard—responded that women were capable of chastity.

The requirement of chastity kept women at home, silenced them, isolated them, left them in ignorance. It was the source of all other impediments. Why was it so important to the society of men, of whom chastity was not required, and who more often than not considered it their right to violate the chastity of any woman they encountered?

Female chastity ensured the continuity of the male-headed household. If a man's wife was not chaste, he could not be sure of the legitimacy of his offspring. If they were not his and they acquired his property, it was not his household, but some other man's, that had endured. If his daughter was not chaste, she could not be transferred to another man's household as his wife, and he was dishonored.

The whole system of the integrity of the household and the transmission of property was bound up in female chastity. Such a requirement pertained only to property-owning classes, of course. Poor women could not expect to maintain their chastity, least of all if they were in contact with high-status men to whom all women but those of their own household were prey.

In Catholic Europe, the requirement of chastity was further buttressed by moral and religious imperatives. Original sin was inextricably linked with the sexual act. Virginity was seen as heroic virtue, far more impressive than, say, the avoidance of idleness or greed. Monasticism, the cultural institution that dominated medieval Europe for centuries, was grounded in the renunciation of the flesh. The Catholic reform of the eleventh century imposed a similar standard on all the clergy and a heightened awareness of sexual requirements on all the laity. Although men were asked to be chaste, female unchastity was much worse: it led to the devil, as Eve had led mankind to sin.

To such requirements, women and their defenders protested their innocence. Furthermore, following the example of holy women who had escaped the requirements of family and sought the religious life, some women began to conceive of female communities as alternatives both to family and to the cloister. Christine de Pizan's city of ladies was such a community. Moderata Fonte and Mary Astell envisioned others. The luxurious salons of the French *précieuses* of the seventeenth century, or the comfortable English drawing rooms of the next, may have been born of the same impulse. Here women not only might escape, if briefly, the subordinate position that life in the family entailed but might also make claims to power, exercise their capacity for speech, and display their knowledge.

THE PROBLEM OF POWER. Women were excluded from power: the whole cultural tradition insisted on it. Only men were citizens, only men bore arms, only men could be chiefs or lords or kings. There were exceptions that did not disprove the rule, when wives or widows or mothers took the place of men, awaiting their return or the maturation of a male heir. A woman who attempted to rule in her own right was perceived as an anomaly, a monster, at once a deformed woman and an insufficient male, sexually confused and consequently unsafe.

The association of such images with women who held or sought power explains some otherwise odd features of early modern culture. Queen Elizabeth I of England, one of the few women to hold full regal authority in European history, played with such male/female images—positive ones, of course—in representing herself to her subjects. She was a prince, and manly, even though she was female. She was also (she claimed) virginal, a condition absolutely essential if she was to avoid the attacks of her opponents. Catherine de' Medici, who ruled France as widow and regent for her sons, also adopted such imagery in defining her position. She chose as one symbol the figure of Artemisia, an androgynous ancient warrior-heroine who combined a female persona with masculine powers.

Power in a woman, without such sexual imagery, seems to have been indigestible by the culture. A rare note was struck by the Englishman Sir Thomas Elyot in his *Defence of Good Women* (1540), justifying both women's participation in civic life and their prowess in arms. The old tune was sung by the Scots reformer John Knox in his *First Blast of the Trumpet against the Monstrous Regiment of Women* (1558); for him rule by women, defects in nature, was a hideous contradiction in terms.

The confused sexuality of the imagery of female potency was not reserved for rulers. Any woman who excelled was likely to be called an Amazon, recalling the self-mutilated warrior women of antiquity who repudiated all men, gave up their sons, and raised only their daughters. She was often said to have "exceeded her sex" or to have possessed "masculine virtue"—as the very fact of conspicuous excellence conferred masculinity even on the female subject. The catalogs of notable women often showed those female heroes dressed in armor, armed to the teeth, like men. Amazonian heroines romp through the epics of the age—Ariosto's *Orlando Furioso* (1532) and Spenser's *Faerie Queene* (1590–1609). Excellence in a woman was perceived as a claim for power, and power was reserved for the masculine realm. A woman who possessed either one was masculinized and lost title to her own female identity.

THE PROBLEM OF SPEECH. Just as power had a sexual dimension when it was claimed by women, so did speech. A good woman spoke little. Excessive speech was an indication of unchastity. By speech, women seduced men. Eve had lured Adam into sin by her speech. Accused witches were commonly accused of having spoken abusively, or irrationally, or simply too much. As enlightened a figure as Francesco Barbaro insisted on silence in a woman, which he linked to her perfect unanimity with her husband's will and her unblemished virtue (her chastity). Another Italian humanist, Leonardo Bruni, in advising a noblewoman on her studies, barred her not from speech but from public speaking. That was reserved for men.

Related to the problem of speech was that of costume—another, if silent, form of self-expression. Assigned the task of pleasing men as their primary occupation, elite women often tended toward elaborate costume, hairdressing, and the use of cosmetics. Clergy and secular moralists alike condemned these practices. The appropriate function of costume and adornment was to announce the status of a woman's husband or father. Any further indulgence in adornment was akin to unchastity.

THE PROBLEM OF KNOWLEDGE. When the Italian noblewoman Isotta Nogarola had begun to attain a reputation as a humanist, she was accused of incest—a telling instance of the association of learning in women with unchastity. That chilling association inclined any woman who was educated to deny that she was or to make exaggerated claims of heroic chastity.

If educated women were pursued with suspicions of sexual misconduct, women seeking an education faced an even more daunting obstacle: the assumption that women were by nature incapable of learning, that reasoning was a particularly masculine ability. Just as they proclaimed their chastity, women and their defenders insisted on their capacity for learning. The major work by a male writer on female education—that by Juan Luis Vives, *On the Education of a Christian Woman* (1523)—granted female capacity for intellection but still argued that a woman's whole education was to be shaped around the requirement of chastity and a future within the household. Female writers of the following generations—Marie de Gournay in France, Anna Maria van Schurman in Holland, and Mary Astell in England—began to envision other possibilities.

The pioneers of female education were the Italian women humanists who managed to attain a literacy in Latin and a knowledge of classical and Christian literature equivalent to that of prominent men. Their works implicitly and explicitly raise questions about women's social roles, defining problems that beset women attempting to break out of the cultural limits that had bound them. Like Christine de Pizan, who achieved an advanced education through her father's tutoring and her own devices, their bold questioning makes clear the importance of training. Only when women were educated to the same standard as male leaders would they be able to raise that other voice and insist on their dignity as human beings morally, intellectually, and legally equal to men.

THE OTHER VOICE. The other voice, a voice of protest, was mostly female, but it was also male. It spoke in the vernaculars and in Latin, in treatises and dialogues, in plays and poetry, in letters and diaries, and in pamphlets. It battered at the wall of prejudice that encircled women and raised a banner announcing its claims. The female was equal (or even superior) to the male in essential nature—moral, spiritual, and intellectual. Women were capable of higher education, of holding positions of power and influence in the public realm, and of speaking and writing persuasively. The last bastion of masculine supremacy, centered on the notions of a woman's primary domestic responsibility and the requirement of female chastity, was not as yet assaulted—although visions of productive female communities as alternatives to the family indicated an awareness of the problem.

During the period 1300–1700, the other voice remained only a voice, and one only dimly heard. It did not result—yet—in an alteration of social patterns. Indeed, to this day they have not entirely been altered. Yet the call for justice issued as long as six centuries ago by those writing in the tradition of the other voice must be recognized as the source and origin of the mature feminist tradition and of the realignment of social institutions accomplished in the modern age.

We thank the volume editors in this series, who responded with many suggestions to an earlier draft of this introduction, making it a collaborative enterprise. Many of their suggestions and criticisms have resulted in revisions of this introduction, although we remain responsible for the final product.

PROJECTED TITLES IN THE SERIES

also female models, most notably Vittoria Colonna. She belonged to a small but growing tradition of women writers who made independent lives for themselves. Though encouraged by male literati, she was also apparently rejected by some. Lodovico Domenichi, who was first her mentor, included her poetry in an anthology he published in 1556 but then omitted her from a better-known one in 1559. Perhaps it was this rejection that led to her only departure from Lucca for three years to Genoa (1562–65). She returned apparently a much more confident and mature writer, as her later prolific output in both poetry and prose reveals, fashioned now in more religious (and orthodox) dress. She published a final book of poems, most of them new, in 1597, seven years before her death, after a long life of struggle for self-discovery. The rediscovery of her as a writer took much longer.

HISTORICAL CONTEXT

When Chiara Matraini appeared on the literary scene, the Renaissance in Italy had already reached its highest point. The first part of the sixteenth century had seen a great flourishing of poetry. It seems that everyone who could write had to be able to compose a poem. While in the preceding century humanists, whose language was Latin, predominated, now poets in the Italian language were the stars. Literature had become more popular, not only because it was written in Italian but above all because it was easier to obtain—printing presses were mushrooming. There was no political unity in Italy, but a literary unity was achieved by following the rules proposed by Pietro Bembo (1470–1547), who launched Petrarch (1304–74) as the model for poetry, setting the trend of Petrarchism, and Boccaccio (1313–75) as a model for prose.

Women benefited from this particular change. Lacking the rigorous humanistic education given to boys, they could compose in Italian and be admired. Moreover, ladies of highly placed, even ruling, noble families, such as Vittoria Colonna and Veronica Gambara (1485–1550), set an example. The first book of lyric poems written by a woman to be published in Italy was Colonna's *Rime*, in 1538,[1] but her work was not the first by a woman to appear in print. That distinction goes to Antonia Pulci, whose *sacre rappresentazioni*, or mystery plays,

---

1. Dionisotti considered the appearance of Colonna's *Rime*, which went through several editions, as the spark that lit the flame of a feverish poetic activity among Italian women. But he believed this to be only a Renaissance phenomenon without continuity, which is not correct. The problem was that the writers who came later were completely neglected by critics. See Carlo Dionisotti, *Geografia e storia della letteratura italiana* (Turin: Einaudi, 1967), 183–204.

had appeared in incunabula between 1490 and 1495.[2] Colonna became a role model to women who wanted to distinguish themselves. Thus poetry was cultivated by ladies of the nobility, by well-off women, as well as by courtesans, with excellent results. These women were admired by learned men of their time. A testimony in point is the publication of the first anthology of Italian women poets, edited by Lodovico Domenichi, *Rime diverse d'alcune nobilissime et virtuosissime donne*, published in 1559,[3] that contains poems of fifty-three women.

The second half of the sixteenth century, whose greatest poet was Torquato Tasso (1544–95), saw a shift in literary style, brought about by the newly imposed limitations of the Counter-Reformation; the *Index of Prohibited Books* and the Inquisition had a crippling effect on Italian culture, as Galileo's case demonstrates. Not only authors were persecuted, but printers and booksellers as well.

Chiara Matraini's active literary life coincided with this difficult period. But she cultivated the Petrarchism that was in vogue when she started writing, even if it was no longer so fashionable when she republished her revised work. Perhaps for this reason she did not receive the attention she deserved. Women poets of the high Renaissance fared better.

BIOGRAPHY

According to baptismal records now in the archives of the city's Duomo (Cathedral of San Martino), Chiara Matraini was born in Lucca on June 4, 1515, to Benedetto Matraini and his wife, Agata (or Agnese) Serantoni.[4] The following year she lost her father and was placed under the guardianship of her paternal uncle, Rodolfo. The Matraini family, by now well established, had come to Lucca from Borgo di Matraia, a nearby locality, around 1350. Originally the members of the family were modest weavers, but with time their social condition improved to the point of making them relatively influential. Public records mention the appointment, in 1453, of a Lorenzo Matraini, dyer, to the council of the city of Lucca. Unfortunately, and this is true in part for Chiara as well, all that is known about the Matrainis deals with their pub-

---

2. See the introductory paragraphs of Natalia Costa-Zalessow, "Le *Fantasie poetiche* di Virginia Bazzani Cavazzoni," *Esperienze letterarie* 27, no. 2 (2002): 57–75. Some doctrinal writings of Catherine of Siena were published in Bologna in 1475, but it is not a work of literary invention as was that of Antonia Pulci.

3. Lodovico Domenichi, *Rime diverse d'alcune nobilissime et virtuosissime donne* (Lucca: Busdraghi, 1559).

4. Not on June 14, 1514. See Giovanna Rabitti, "Linee per il ritratto di Chiara Matraini," *Studi e problemi di critica testuale* 22 (1981): 155.

lic life. Based on archival material, some events in which they participated can be reconstructed, but nothing has been found that sheds light on the family environment or on the personalities of the individual members.

Very little is known about Chiara's nearest relatives. We know only the names of her parents, while a little more emerges about her older brother Luiso and her uncle Rodolfo. They, in fact, took part in what is known as the Moto degli Straccioni (revolt of the ragamuffins), the 1531 rebellion which forced the ruling members of the oligarchic republic of Lucca to grant the lower nobility and middle class (consisting mainly, but not only, of weavers and dyers) regular access to public office. To find Chiara's relatives among the leaders of this political faction is in itself meaningful, while the failure of the revolt, as could have been expected (given the rigidity of the political system), was particularly traumatic—the defeat was complete and the ensuing punishments in 1532 were very harsh. This left a profound mark not only on the family history but also on the personal formation of Chiara, the future writer, about whose education nothing is known.

Even before the exploits of the ragamuffins, some unusual events occurred within the family that strike our imagination and presumably had an even stronger impact on the young and ambitious Chiara Matraini. In 1526 her brother Luiso, who since 1523 had been a member of the Council of Lucca, was banned from all public office upon his sentencing for sodomy. The good name of the entire family was compromised. On May 4, 1531, when Rodolfo was appointed to the council, its members did not fail to hint at this scandal in their declared motivations for choosing him: "he [Rodolfo] was very influential among several of those people and, so that the bad ones of his family, who were not few, would be less bitter, seeing that one of them was entering government . . ."[5] At the end of the revolt, Luiso was imprisoned, together with Filippo (son of Lunardo) Matraini, his cousin. Filippo succeeded in escaping but remained banished from Lucca, condemned to death by default. Luiso died in prison, in pitiable physical conditions, in April 1535. The famous and powerful Rodolfo was not harmed, but he retired to private life. Other members of the extended Matraini clan were also condemned, either to death or to prison.[6]

While these events were unfolding, Chiara was just beginning to face

---

5. "egli [Rodolfo] poteva assai con diversi di quella gente e perché quei cattivi del suo casato, che non erano pochi, s'invelenissero meno, vedendo che uno de' loro n'entrava in governo." Marino Berengo, *Nobili e mercanti nella Lucca del Cinquecento* (Turin: Einaudi, 1965), 126–27.

6. For more details see Berengo, *Nobili e mercanti*, and Gherardo Sergiusti, *Sommario de' Successi della Città di Lucca*, ed. Riccardo Ambrosini and Albarosa Belegni (Pisa: Edizioni ETS, 1997), 107–11, for a list of all of those condemned.

adult life. She was eleven years old when her brother was condemned for sodomy and sixteen when the revolt was crushed. At the age of fifteen, in 1530, that is to say, in a period when her family seemed destined for achievement, she was wedded to Vincenzo Cantarini, to whom uncle Rodolfo handed over a dowry of 300 *scudi*, which later became an object of contention. The fact that Chiara had entered into another family circle a year before the Matrainis found themselves at the peak of their political mishaps (1531–32) did not diminish the emotional impact that the political affair had on her, not only because it all happened so fast, but above all because she was and always remained—contrary to local tradition—strongly attached to her paternal family as well as its last name, which she never renounced.[7] Perhaps her new Cantarini family was disappointed, not having foreseen the possibility of such a total defeat of their newly acquired Matraini relatives.[8]

From 1533, the year of the birth of her son Federigo, until the 1540s, Chiara's life went on in complete anonymity. In 1542 she was already a widow, and although we cannot truly determine the beginning of her "metamorphosis," from this moment on her life gained the freedom to assume a public dimension. In 1547, the thirty-two-year-old widow made people talk about her. An anonymous town chronicle, *Vita di Gherardo Sergiusti P.L. celebre col nome di Gherardo Diceo* (Life of Prof. Gherardo Sergiusti famous under the name of Gherardo Diceo),[9] is preserved in the library of Lucca. Although it is quite biased, it contains some verifiable facts. It describes colorfully and in detail the stormy and scandalous passion of Chiara (already known as a poet and musician) for Bartolomeo Graziani, the unfaithful husband of Elisabetta, daughter of Gherardo Sergiusti—famous in his day as a historian.[10] Because of Sergiusti's fame, the affair of the two lovers, who openly lived together, was severely condemned in 1547, but not everyone shared such an opinion, as Pietro Pera states in his *Miscellanea lucchese:*

7. These ties were reciprocal, for both her brother and her mother (in 1551) named her as their main heir.

8. Berengo (*Nobili e mercanti*, 152) mentions a Giuliano Cantarini (but does not identify him further), who was first on the side of the conspirators, in contact with Lorenzo Matraini, a priest, but who later betrayed them by revealing one of their plans.

9. P. L. = Pubblico Lettore (Public Lecturer), for Sergiusti was professor at the University of Bologna.

10. Part of this chronicle, *Vita*, was published in Sergiusti, *Sommario*, 135–48, but only up to the year of his death in 1542. (The text of the *Vita* is found in the manuscript *Miscellanea lucchese*, Biblioteca Governativa di Lucca, MS 1574.) Therefore the section regarding Matraini and Graziani was not included. On January 29, 1542, Bartolomeo Graziani, defined as the rich but eccentric son of Luca, married Elisabetta Sergiusti, who had a dowry of 800 *fiorini* (F.) and a trousseau of 200 F. She bore him at least one child (144–45).

Besides poetry, Matraini delighted in music and played the spinet and sang very pleasantly, so that the youths of Lucca, attracted by her gracefulness, went to converse in her house, where at times they spent a good part of the night singing, playing music, and merrymaking, which caused a lot of murmuring and slander, since the contemporary habit of free conversation was unknown in those days, and in the *Vita* of M[esser] Gherardo Sergiusti an unfavorable description was given of this excellent woman.[11]

In fact, the *Vita* explicitly states that Bartolomeo Graziani had "established in his house, in order to satisfy the wicked widow,"[12] an academy where "not only during all hours of the day, but also at night, they laughed, made jokes, used foul language thousands of times, and engaged in an infinite number of indecent things (because many young secular men, who had come from Pisa to Lucca during vacation, went there)."[13] The *Vita* may even include a clue as to the possible assassin of Graziani, who was murdered sometime between 1547 and 1553, most likely by his wife's brother and one of his friends. But it reads like a Renaissance *novella*, in which Elisabetta, the innocent wife, and her brother Nicolao are depicted as victims, as opposed to Graziani, the bewitched, Chiara the evil woman, and a friend of theirs turned traitor. Undoubtedly, all of this is very suggestive, but it is also dangerously close to fiction, and given the uncertainty of the information, it should suffice that I have mentioned it.

However, one particular aspect of this story, which is definitely true, emerges with clarity. In that period, in the late 1540s and early 1550s, Chiara was heading toward literary activity and cultivated her passion for music and for poetry through the contact she had established with the educated young men of Lucca and Pisa. Evidence of these years, of the love affair with Graziani as well as of his murder, can be found in her *Rime e prose* (Poems and Prose), published in 1555,[14] which is her remarkable first literary work. From this moment on Matraini's life ran on a double track. The public one

11. "Oltre la poesia, dilettossi la Matraini della musica e suonava la spinetta e cantava d'ottimo gusto, di modo che la gioventù lucchese, allettata dalla sua grazia, andava a far conversazione a casa sua, ove alle volte passava buona parte della notte in canti e suoni e allegria; lo che, non essendo in quei tempi l'usanza presente del libero conversare, diede motivo a varie mormorazioni e maldicenze, e nella vita di M. Gherardo Sergiusti di questa eccellente donna ne viene fatto uno svantaggioso ritratto." *Miscellanea lucchese*, MS 1547, c. 397, as quoted in Rabitti, "Linee per il ritratto," 142.

12. "missa in casa sua, per satisfare la scelerata vedova." Rabitti, "Linee per il ritratto," 142.

13. "la notte, non che il giorno da tutte l'ore a ridere, burlare, dir mille sporcitie e fare infinite cose disoneste (perché vi andavano molti giovani secolari, che di Pisa erano venuti a Lucca nelle vacantie)." Rabitti, "Linee per il ritratto," 142.

14. Chiara Matraini, *Rime e prose* (Lucca: Busdraghi, 1555).

is delineated by her documented literary friendships with the polygraphs and editors of Italian and Latin literary works, Benedetto Varchi (1503–65), Lodovico Dolce (1508–68), and above all Lodovico Domenichi (1515–64, active in mid-century Lucca), who helped the poetess start a planned literary "self-promotion." These literati served as a support to her editorial "launch." In 1556, a year after the publication of her first book, her translation from Latin[15] (not the original Greek) into Italian of an oration attributed to Isocrates, *A Demonico*[16] (Letter to Demonicus), was published in Florence, while her entire *canzoniere*, the *Rime* of 1555, were included in the anthology *Rime di diversi signori napoletani e d'altri*, edited by the well-known Lodovico Dolce. Moreover, selected compositions by her were included in the anthology *Delle rime nuove di diversi eccellentissimi autori*, edited by Lodovico Domenichi in 1556, and in the collection of poems by Tito Giovanni Scandianese, *La fenice*.[17]

Practically nothing is known about the other track, her private life, just as is the case with her early years. Nevertheless, a few important events in Matraini's life can be reconstructed, thanks to some preserved letters and to various allusions found in her works. She most likely met Cesare Coccapani in 1560 when he came to Lucca, having been appointed a judge for a limited time.[18] He was from Carpi and his family enjoyed a good relationship with the ruling Este family. (It should not be forgotten that Matraini's cousin had found refuge in Reggio Emilia when he fled Lucca.) A new love ensued, or at least a long-lasting, intense spiritual and intellectual friendship, attested by the few letters exchanged between the two that have come down to us in a seventeenth-century copy.[19] Not much more is known about what happened to Matraini in the decade 1560–70. Ascertained are only a trip to Genoa (c. 1562–65) and an ongoing, passionate, dragged-out litigation (partially overseen by Coccapani while she was away from Lucca) between Chiara and her son Federigo, who did not want to give up his mother's dowry. For her that money meant the only possibility of economic independence, and in a letter to Coccapani she asks for advice on how to proceed: "how I should go about

---

15. This means that she had mastered Latin, but we do not know whether she had studied it with a teacher or was self-taught.

16. Titles are frequently given in abbreviated form. See list of Matraini's publications for full titles.

17. Tito Giovanni Scandianese, *La fenice* (Venice: Giolito, 1557).

18. Coccapani returned to Lucca as a judge in 1592–93. See Rabitti, "Linee per il ritratto," 149.

19. This correspondence was partially published for the first time in Rabitti, "Linee per il ritratto."

expediting and bringing to a good conclusion the litigation to free my dowry and my inheritance and my interests from the hands of my son so adverse to me."[20] Although few, these words reveal her feelings toward her son.

In the other letters addressed to Coccapani, the voice of Chiara is strong. She discloses to him her true feelings and desires—her complete dedication to literature, accompanied by a yearning to reach perfection and literary immortality:

> It will never happen, as far as possible, that I give up that beautiful and honored exercise. . . . I delight in it by nature, and if God does not take away my intellect, I will never give it up. And if my hands and my tongue were tied, I would follow it just the same with my mind. And if it were that one could not reach it without suitable wealth, and if it were possible for me, by depriving myself of all possessions, to become perfect in it, I would gladly abandon my own nourishment to obtain that life that always lives.[21]

She also expresses her desire to compete with the good writers and therefore to be judged the way they are judged, not complimented just because she writes better than most women:

> I frankly believe that you compliment me in your heart as well as with your words because I am a woman, for women generally express themselves poorly in their writings. But I, who want to write beyond what is common to women delighting in composing poetry, or to men who have composed or written commendably, don't believe that my work should be read in this manner, without finding defects or contradictions.[22]

20. "che modo avrei da tenere a dar presto e bene spedizione alla mia lite a cavar la mia dote e le mie eredità e i miei interessi di mano del mio e a me tanto contrario figliuolo." Rabitti, "Linee per il ritratto, 151.

21. "Questo non sarà mai per tempo nessuno, che per quanto mi sia possibile, io tralasci quel bello e onorato esercizio . . . io me ne diletto tanto per propria natura, che se Dio non mi priva della mente non sono mai per abbandonarlo. E quando mi fossero legate le mani e la lingua, seguireilo in ogni modo con il desiderio. E se non fosse che senza convenevoli facoltà non vi si potesse attendere, e mi fusse possibile, per divenir priva di tutti i beni di fortuna, divenir in esso perfetta, io volontariamente abbandonerei il proprio vitto per acquistar quel vivere che sempre vive." Rabitti, "Linee per il ritratto," 150.

22. "Credo bene che mi lode nel core come nelle parole, per esser donna, le quali alla comune bassamente sogliono parlare ne' loro scritti; ma io che oltre il comune uso delle donne che si dilettano di comporre, e degli huomini che lodevolmente hanno composto o scritto vorrei comporre e scrivere, non mi par che sieno le cose mie da esser così assolutamente giudicate, senza menda o contradizione." Rabitti, "Linee per il ritratto," 152.

She confesses to him that she had no formal education. Moreover, her liter-
ary aspirations were suffocated by the environment surrounding her (obvi-
ously a hint at Lucca, where she was branded a wicked woman). Thus she was
unable to do as much as she wanted to, not simply because she is a woman,
as some will have it. From her personal case she passes to the impersonal and
attacks all those who consider women to be imperfect creatures incapable
of doing well in letters or sciences, producing a poignant little manifesto in
defense of women, full of bitterness, reflecting her own personal desperation,
vented freely because it is not meant for print:

> It is not as some have said or still say, driven by malignity expressed
> together with their ignorance, that woman is of such imperfection
> that she is not capable of any science or art . . . and that which they
> [women] do not accomplish in these fields is only because they were
> never given a chance; they are always kept within the house, occupied
> in menial work, and men dare tell us that only that woman merits praise
> whose deeds and praise do not leave the walls of her home.[23]

The year 1576 can be considered the beginning of the last period of
Matraini's life. Having returned to Lucca, now protected from gossip by her
age, she set out to recast herself as an acceptable stereotype—that of a moral
and wise woman. Her project to have an altar erected in the Church of Santa
Maria Forisportam, the church of the neighborhood where she was born
and where she wanted to be buried, is of that year. The chapel was to have
a complex painting in which the Cumaean Sibyl, bearing Matraini's like-
ness, points out to Emperor Augustus the apparition of the Madonna with
baby Jesus in her arms. The painting was done by Alessandro Ardenti and
can now be seen in the Museum of Villa Guinigi in Lucca under the title *La
Sibilla Cumana* (The Cumaean Sibyl). Her obvious intention to recast herself
is reflected in her literary productions, published from 1581 to 1590, which
are all strictly religious: *Meditazioni spirituali* (Spiritual Meditations, 1581),
Considerazioni sui sette salmi penitenziali (Considerations on the Seven Penitential
Psalms, 1587), and *Vita della Vergine* (The Life of the Virgin, 1590). Only in
her very last years, when she had achieved an assured literary reputation

---

23. "non è come alcuni hanno già detto o dicono, mossi da malignitade espressa insieme con
tutta ignoranza, che la Donna sia di cotanta imperfezione, che non sia capace di ciascuna scienza
e arte . . . e quello che in tali esercizi non fanno è solo perché non s'è loro dato occasione, essendo
tenute sempre rinchiuse e occupate in bassi esercizi, osando gli uomini dirci che quella Donna
solamente merita d'esser lodata, i cui fatti e le cui lodi non escono dalle mura della sua casa."
Rabitti, "Linee per il ritratto," 153–54.

(which was even publicly recognized by Aldo Manuzio the younger in two letters), did Matraini's moderately but tenaciously transgressive nature reappear with the publication of her *canzoniere* (in 1595 and 1597), a true personal monument to herself. The fruit of her more audacious years, although mostly rewritten, almost "sanitized," is still eloquent enough to constitute a real sum of the poet's uncommon life. In 1602 she published *Dialoghi spirituali* (Spiritual Dialogues), a work written earlier, as will be seen.

Chiara Matraini died most likely in 1604, after having signed her fourth will in which she is referred to as very ill. She left her possessions to the Matraini relatives and did not mention her son. He must have died earlier, for a sonnet, poem 53 in the 1597 edition, alludes to his death. He signed his last will in 1571 and named his cousin Carlo as his heir, without mentioning his mother. He probably died between 1571 and 1575.

Matraini was buried in the chapel erected by her in Santa Maria Forisportam, where the simple inscription *S[epoltu]ra di Chiara Matraini* can still be seen, her only monument, which she did not want to share with anyone, for in her last will she specified that her tomb must be sealed in such a way that no one else could be buried there ("non si possa sotterrare altri").

LITERARY CAREER AND RELIGIOUS WORKS

Chiara Matraini's literary works reflect the author's private life, which cannot be disregarded even if it is not directly expressed or fully known. They too are divided into distinct aspects (the nucleus of the 1550s and the works published after 1575), even if in reality the same undercurrent runs throughout Matraini's entire literary production. It must be kept in mind that all of her works exist only in printed form; nothing, or almost nothing, in manuscript form has come down to us, and there are no autographs. Her first publication appeared in 1555, *Rime e prose* (Poems and Prose), which consists of her first *canzoniere amoroso* (poems describing a love story) and two prose selections: a letter addressed to an unidentified man (indicated only as M. L.) in defense of amorous subject matter, and the *Orazione dell'arte della guerra* (Oration on the Art of War), a rhetorical exercise in defense of the strategic capacity of a *condottiero* (Renaissance army leader), regardless of the outcome of the battle, written in praise of man's cognitive qualities.

The fundamental role of prose in the context of Matraini's books will be discussed later. The lyric part, however, is the main body of this volume and is a true *canzoniere* in the traditional sense—a depiction of a love story from its beginning (falling in love and praise of the beloved) to its end (death of the beloved and a religious conclusion). The poems of 1555 were inspired by the tragic love affair with Bartolomeo Graziani, which came to an end with his mysterious murder. These events left a clear and indelible mark even under the leveling of Matraini's imitation of Petrarch, for she reveals her complete dedication to him, as in poem A 17,[24] while in poem A 14 she delineates love's perplexing joys and torments. Yet it was a harmonious love that bound her and her beloved. Later on she laments his death and the envy and deceits of others, the suffering she had to bear—victim of misfortune (the opposite of what was said about her in the anonymous *Vita*).

The poem A 82 (see below, chap. 1) contains precise references to the violent death of her beloved:

> Pure, eternal, joyous, and noble soul,
> you who, ending your life in your mid years,
> have flown among the blessed spirits,
>   [Chiara, eterna, felice, e gentil alma,
> che, fornito il tuo corso a mezzo gli anni,
> volata sei fra l'anime beate,][25] (lines 1–3)

> So, feeling your deadly pain
> in a horrible vision black and deadly,
> I saw you leave your mortal body
> to a merciless serpent, intent only
> on your destruction, wherefore it stung your heart,
> and your life was ended that very next day,
> and the serpent was contented. Oh, merciless, bitter fate!
> Oh, pitiless, unrelenting Death!
> [perch'io, sentendo il tuo mortale affanno,
> in orribil visione, atra e funesta,
> vidi farti lasciar la mortal vesta
> a cruda serpe irata e nel tuo danno
> intenta solo, ond'il cor morse, e spenta
> fu la tua vita il dì poscia, e contenta
> si rimase ella. O cruda, acerba sorte!
> O dispietata, inesorabil Morte!] (lines 73–80)

---

24. From here on the poems referred to will be preceded by A, B, C, to indicate the three different editions, 1555, 1595, and 1597, respectively.

25. Matraini's poems cited in this introduction are included in this anthology. For convenience both Italian texts and English translations by Elaine Maclachlan are provided here as well.

Here the tragic and violent events are filtered and assume the guise of a vision, while Matraini's own pain is expressed as a foreboding:

> A deeper pain or a more fierce, horrible fate
> (miserable me) Heaven could not show to me
> than this, alas, which the heart foresaw so deeply.
>   You know that I said so; and what you once tried
> to deny to me, you felt one moment near death,
> distant to your faithful eyes.

> [Più grave doglia o fiero, orribil caso
> (misera) non poteva il Ciel mostrarme
> di questo, ohimè, che tanto il cor previde.
>   Tu 'l sai s'io 'l dissi; e quel che di negarme
> cercasti un tempo, un punto in ver' l'occaso
> lontan sentisti alle tue luci fide.] (lines 21–26)

What hurts Chiara most is that the murderer went unpunished:

> Now for his inflamed fury, our traitor
> and enemy triumphs and rejoices
> as Nero did, in the high burning of Rome.
>   But if the just anger of God cannot
> control the burning and cruel Monster, what shall
> we say? For surely God sees and hears it.

> [Or dell'ardente suo furore il nostro
> nemico traditor trionfa e gode,
> qual fea Neron ne l'alta arsion di Roma.
>   Ma se di così ardente e crudel Mostro
> la giust' ira di Dio l'ardir non doma,
> che direm noi? Ch'ei pur lo vede ed ode.] (A 86, lines 9–14)[26]

In the *canzone* A 66 (see below, chap. 1), the naming of the river Lappato, which runs between Pescia and Lucca, reveals a clue:

> In a green woodland
> in the sweet summer breezes
> I saw two noble shepherds, in love,
>   walking alone with pleasure

---

26. For full poem, see below, chap. 1.

by a green riverbank,
singing joyously of their happy loves.

. . . .

How full of mirth
in that happy day
was the well-born, adventurous lover:
    the source of the brook Lappato knows this,
who heard from all around
thanks given devoutly and piously.

[In un verde boschetto,
a la dolce aura estiva
vidi due innamorati almi pastori
    soli andar con diletto
sopr' una verde riva,
cantando lieti i lor felici amori.

. . . .

Quanto di gaudio pieno
in quel felice giorno
fosse il ben nato, aventuroso amante
    del bel Lappato il seno
sallo, che d'ogn'intorno
grazie render sentio devote e sante.] (lines 1–6, 40–45)

Disguised in this pastoral setting in the countryside of Lucca, the nymph's love, which makes the *chiara fonte* turn into *una fiamma al mondo eterna e rara*, is a testimony of Matraini's own passion:

then the proud Nymph,
who was in his heart,
came alone to meet him along the lovely riverbank;
    by a sweet desire she was
drawn to him, and as a gift
she came to give him her heart.
Oh, what a happy Love:
it made me change from what I was,
transforming me from a clear fountain
into an eternal and rare flame of the world.
    [la Ninfa altera
che nel suo core stassi,

venne sola a incontrar lungo il bel rio,
    che da un dolce desio
di lui portata, in dono
veniva a darli il core.
O che felice Amore,
ond' io mi trasformai da quel ch'io sono,
facendomi di chiara
fonte, una fiamma al mondo eterna e rara.] (lines 56–65)

But the autobiographical cipher is accompanied by other ciphers common to Renaissance poetry, such as the powerful gaze of the beloved's eyes, called "lights," "flames," or "suns." These intertwine and give the collection of poems a moderately "experimental" form. Structure and language are such that the poems, rather than being rigidly separated into parts by a planned division, flow like a continuous current, marked by varied elaborations of basic leitmotifs. The collection gives the overall impression that one is reading a *canzoniere* written *in vita* (while the beloved was alive), in spite of the fact that it was published after the death of Graziani. There is also a prevalence of poetic exercises and philosophical observations, next to a rendering of the author's own story as a writer, with references to her more or less prestigious cultural relationships, as if the *canzoniere* were reflecting that censured literary salon which Chiara, surrounded by students from Lucca and Pisa, animated in those ill-famed late 1540s and early 1550s in the sleepy (but not asleep) Lucca.

Matraini's subsequent works, above all her 1556 translation of Isocrates' oration *A Demonico*, dedicated to Giulio de' Medici, son of Alessandro de' Medici, and the reappearance of her poems in various anthologies, among which the reprinting of her entire *canzoniere* in the 1556 anthology edited by Lodovico Dolce stands out, show her determination to obtain a dignified place in the literary establishment, for which even the choice of subject matter was a qualifying element. Advised, encouraged, and aided by Lodovico Domenichi, she was careful not to entrust her image to a simple amorous inspiration but to broaden her interests to include classics and philosophy.

The beginning was promising, for Matraini started out with a balanced mixture of secular and spiritual themes that paid close attention to the possibilities offered by mid-sixteenth-century literature written in Italian as a means of communication, as opposed to that written in Latin used by the humanists. But it was a departure that did not follow the intended path. Partly due to Chiara's personal problems, partly perhaps due to the poor reception of her efforts on the part of the well-established men of letters, her publications came to a sudden stop. Moreover, she lost the help of Lodovico Domenichi, who died in 1564, but their relationship probably ended earlier, for he did not include her in the first anthology dedicated entirely to women poets, *Rime diverse d'alcune nobilissime et virtuosissime donne,* which he edited and published in Lucca in 1559. By excluding her he meant either to condemn her to oblivion or to put her at a disadvantage compared with the women poets he included.

Matraini's voice was silent for a long time. Only in 1581 was her third work, *Meditazioni spirituali* (Spiritual Meditations), published in Lucca. This period, when she returned to Lucca from Genoa and recast herself in a new role beyond that of a writer, has already been discussed. To understand the meaning of this text, one must examine the subtle and thorny problem of Matraini's religiosity. Although the subject would merit a vaster inquiry, it should be enough to point out that Chiara had ties to heretical groups, attested by Luccan friendships (Lucca was one of the cities most sympathetic to the reformist message), as well as by Matraini's great veneration of Vittoria Colonna, who was involved with the Viterbo group and was in favor of a spirituality not approved by the Roman church. It is evident from Matraini's stylistic choices and strategies of self-representation that she considered Colonna not only a literary model but a true role model (for her image, her spirituality, her life).

The years that separate Colonna from Chiara Matraini are important for various reasons, one of the most important being that the strict new rules set by the Council of Trent that separated the two halves of the sixteenth century placed limits on tolerance and opportunity. Matraini, who lived during the Counter-Reformation, found herself obliged to recast her own image. Her very wise choice of returning to the publishing scene with a book of religious inspiration and continuing for a long time in that direction assumes a programmatic value. The context of her *Meditazioni spirituali* is prudently directed toward a safe orthodoxy. The first meditation, on confession and repentance, is followed by others on the capital sins and on the necessity to remedy one's faults. In accord with her inclination to combine prose and verse, each prose section is followed by a concluding sonnet. It is a complex book full of "extraliterary" value and unique for the appearance, on the title page, of her married name, Chiara Cantarini de' Matraini, a solitary homage to the city's tradition that a woman use her husband's last name. Other texts followed, from which her desire to take up exemplary themes emerges even more clearly.

Considerazioni sui sette salmi penitenziali (Considerations on the Seven Penitential Psalms) represent Matraini's attempt to weigh in on a subject that had constituted, ever since Petrarch had tried his hand at it, a true benchmark for a writer. Moreover, in 1583, Flaminio Nobili, also from Lucca, had published a similar comment (*I sette salmi penitenziali con una breve e chiara sposizione*),[27] while Laura Battiferra Ammannati's *I sette salmi penitenziali*[28] had appeared earlier, in 1564.

On a similar track is her *Vita della Vergine* (Life of the Virgin), a subject dear to Matraini and exquisitely orthodox.[29] The text is followed by "Annotations" written by Giuseppe Mozzagrugno, the rectory priest of the Church of the Salvatore, in Lucca. This work was Matraini's most popular, and rightly so, given its fine combination of a sincere profession of faith and of a familiarity with the Scriptures, accompanied by a few conscious borrowings from the apocryphal texts, sources for Mary's childhood. It was republished in the seventeenth century.

The possibility of returning to secular literature, forty years after the first publication of her poems, came with the reappearance of her *canzoniere* in 1595, but she could not hide the signs of her long activity dedicated to other literary genres, mainly religious and meditative. While the 1555 edition reflected the restless and vivacious animator of literary salons, this new version is a programmatic depiction of a mature and wise lady.

Matraini's literary career actually ended here. Her last publication, *Dialoghi spirituali*, which appeared very late, in 1602, shows all the signs of belonging to the silent years of 1560–80. The intertextual ties that bind this work to her *Meditazioni spirituali* are very obvious. It consists of four dialogues (a genre widely used in the Renaissance for its immediateness, or conversational style), a *Narrazione* (Narration) by the author to an imaginary academy of curious people (*Accademia dei Curiosi*), three sermons, and various poems. The concepts, and at times even the expressions that characterize the course of repentance (theme of the *Narrazione*), are absolutely identical to those of the *Meditazioni*, as is also the fictional doubling of the narrating "I" which has the noble role of a guide, as well as the humble role of the person who must cleanse herself of sin.

---

27. Flaminio Nobili, *I sette salmi penitenziali con una breve e chiara sposizione* (Venice: Nicolini, 1583).

28. Florence: Giunti. The poetry of Laura Battiferra has been published bilingually in "The Other Voice" series, which includes Battiferra's rendering of the first penitential psalm (Psalm 6). See Laura Battiferra degli Ammannati, *Laura Battiferra and Her Literary Circle*, ed. and trans. Victoria Kirkham (Chicago: University of Chicago Press, 2006), 223–29.

29. A complete translation of this text has appeared in "The Other Voice" series: Vittoria Colonna, Chiara Matraini, and Lucrezia Marinella, *Who Is Mary? Three Early Modern Women on the Idea of the Virgin Mary*, ed. and trans. Susan Haskins (Chicago: University of Chicago Press, 2007).

Obviously, common to both works are the stages leading to a progressive purification through the perception of the capital sins. But in the *Dialoghi* [30] a more conspicuous propensity toward an open narrative style is evident. The road to salvation is a kind of "flight" under the tutelage of a guide who, from above, points out the world below with its ugliness caused by sin (recalling Dante's *Divine Comedy*). There is also a greater expressive immediacy, almost an urgency, which makes the author mention Martin Luther by name, followed by the obligatory condemnation. In the dialogues themselves, these characteristics are combined with a flattering self-description under the name of "Theophila," a cultured woman who guides "Philocalio," the young son of her friend Cangenna, toward love of true knowledge. Although fiction, the work draws from real life, for Cangenna Lipomeni (or Lippomani) is not a fictional person but Matraini's friend. The book, which ends with a poem dedicated to Santa Chiara (Saint Clare), is a wisely put together text, not much different from her preceding work, most likely a double to the *Meditazioni* but less useful as a project of self-redemption and therefore put aside. It docs not really matter whether its late publication was the result of a precise wish to make it known or of a simple desire to continue publishing, along the lines of the last appearance of her *canzoniere* that came out in Venice in 1597. At any rate, what matters is the obsessive continuity of Matraini's intention to rise stubbornly from the ashes even of a public auto-da-fé, a phoenix excessively faithful to herself.

REWRITING: A LIFELONG ENDEAVOR

Matraini's *Rime e prose* reappeared (unauthorized) in 1595, to be followed by a definitive (authorized) edition two years later. But actually the three editions of 1555, 1595, and 1597 are three different versions reflecting the different stages of the author's literary career. All three versions contain poems and prose which have to be looked at separately. As far as the *canzoniere* is concerned, the reader might easily be misled by the collection's opening sonnet which contains only slight variations. Most of the rest of the poems underwent a radical change.

The original 1555 edition contains 99 compositions, while the 1595 version was reduced to 77, only 24 of which are the same, chosen from among the later, more meditative or spiritual, less amorous poems, as if Matraini

---

30. See also Janet Smarr, *Joining the Conversation: Dialogues by Renaissance Women* (Ann Arbor: University of Michigan Press, 2005).

wanted to eliminate the signs of her love passion. The result is a more rapid narrative structure, which, however, did not satisfy her, for she kept working on it with the hope of improving it. Laboring in a solitary and eccentric way, she continued to make additional changes and incorporated them into the 1597 version, her last effort at revising her poems, supposedly the end result, or perfection. The structure of this last version is the same as that of 1595, both in outline and design, but the proportions are better, edging closer to the longed-for equilibrium. It consists of 87 poems, 68 taken from the 77 compositions of the 1595 edition plus 12 new compositions and 7 salvaged from the 1555 edition, but with many textual retouches. The result is a new metamorphosis.

The prose writings, which form an integral part of the book, underwent a similar evolution, reflecting the author's aim to give an intentionally structured form to her collection. The two short prose items of the 1555 edition were only a first attempt, and neither the letter nor the oration found its way into the 1595 edition. The change is more drastic than that for the poems and seems to preclude a continuity, or even a relationship to the lyric compositions, but that is illusory. The 1555 edition openly reveals Matraini's years of passion, and the two prose selections expose her complex personality, unmasked by poetic artificiality. If her entire literary and sentimental output was mainly indirectly expressed in the form of a *canzoniere*, in relation to the catalyzing element "different from oneself" (the beloved, in the guise of the sun), in her prose Matraini's intellectual work, her ambitions, her personality, and her limits are openly laid bare. The letter addressed to M. L. has, in this sense, the value of a true manifesto. The theme of the letter is a defense of love as a moving force of all good sentiments and a defense of its study—a theme apparently reflecting a common Renaissance doctrine but in reality an excuse to write one of the most vibrant self-defenses. With ease the author passes from the generic and neutral tone of the first four sentences to a concise tirade:

But your very first effort has been to show me how unseemly it is for a woman born not of the noblest blood, nor raised in the most superb palaces in the midst of plenteous and most abundant riches, to spend her time constantly in the pursuit of studies and in writing, at complete odds with the customs of our city. And although one might have to grant even this, at least she ought to discourse of more praiseworthy affections than those of love (which you hold to be wicked). First, then, to reply to what you have said to me, I say to you that granted that I was not born of high and royal blood nor raised in grand and sumptuous palaces, in stately chambers or beds of gold, nevertheless I come not from an ignoble family nor poor and lowborn ancestors (as you have reason to know), but from famous blood, and I have benefited from the honest gifts of fortune, in a free city, and I was blessed with a great soul.[31]

These are ardent words that have a counterpart only in the private outburst of Chiara, as recorded in her letter to Coccapani already quoted, an outburst that was even more violent since it was not intended for print. Matraini never wrote anything else similar. Even in the letter to M. L. the emotional moment is only a brief one. She immediately returns to the subject matter, although the echo of that sentence vibrates for some time, so that her displayed use of the more diffused themes of the Neoplatonic tradition, or her naming of Pietro Bembo and Mario Equicola (arbiters of amorous subject matter), acquire the function of an erudite challenge. Her ambition to venture, like a male writer, into the terrain of humanistic culture and philosophy is also reflected in the second prose writing, the *Orazione dell'arte della guerra* (Oration on the Art of War), in which she elaborates on man's greatness through his intellect, one of the main themes of the Renaissance.

The letters in the 1595 version reveal the author's more subdued and vaster intention. The collection's sixteen new letters make up the entire first part of the volume, a counterbalance to the poems of the second part, indicating that the author meant to present an intentional symmetry. (In the 1597 edition Matraini put these letters in a somewhat different order and added two more, to reach a total of eighteen.) Yet even in this new form, the thread going back to 1555 has not broken off, for the old prose writings partially resurface. The "Letter to Maria Cardona,"[32] in which Matraini demonstrates the superiority of science over arms, derives its opening state-

---

31. This passage is taken from the 1555 letter to M. L. translated in the selections by Elaine Maclachlan. The Italian reads: "Ma perché vi siete primieramente sforzato di mostrarmi quanto disdicevole sia a donna non de' più alti sangui nata, né dentro i più superbi palagi fra copiose e abbondantissime ricchezze nodrita, andar continovamente il tempo consumando ne gli studi e nello scrivere, fuori in tutto dell'uso della nostra città, e che qualora pur questo da conceder s'avesse, almeno di più lodati affetti che quelli d'amore non sono (come che per malvagi gli tegnate), dover ragionare. Laonde primieramente a quello rispondendo che detto mi avete, vi dico che, quantunque io d'alto e real sangue nata non sia né dentro i grandi e sontuosi palagi, ne le pompose camere o ne' dorati letti nodrita, non però di ignobile famiglia né di poveri e bassi progenitori (come saper possiate), ma di chiaro sangue e di onesti beni di fortuna dotata, in città libera, e di grand'animo generata sono." Chiara Matraini, *Rime e prose* (Lucca: Busdraghi, 1555), 105–6, quoted in Rabitti, "Linee per il ritratto," 158.

32. Matraini uses Cardonia, the older form of the name for Maria Cardona, marchioness of Palude.

ment from the "Oration on the Art of War," where the same maxim of the Spartan sage Chilo is paraphrased, that is, that no one should attempt to undertake things beyond his strength. But the two letters differ, not only in subject matter, but also in form. The 1595 one is more concise, less scholastic, with better-expressed examples, even if the author is still anchored to the indisputable authorities of the classical tradition, such as Cicero, Sallust, Plato, and Aristotle. She is always faithful to Greco-Roman antiquity, the *forte* of her humanistic apprenticeship. The letter addressed to her son Federigo takes the form of her translation of Isocrates' *Letter to Demonicus*, as she openly declares. This is true not only for the concepts, as she would have it, but also for the rest: "it occurred to me, dear son, to give you and leave you after my death, a short and useful summary of the most worthy recollections (which also happen to be of the very sage philosopher Isocrates)."[33] This is, indeed, true recycling (not considered plagiarism in those days). The only difference between the two texts is that the second recasts the concepts of Isocrates as her own advice to her son, now expressed in a plainer language, with simpler sentence structure.

The links with the 1550s and 1560s, considered her most productive years, are more explicit in the letters than in the poems, for the simple reason that the names of the addressees of the letters permit us to date them more precisely than can be done with the poems. By looking at their names we realize that some of these people had died years ago: Lodovico Domenichi, Maria Cardona, as well as Chiara's son Federigo. A similar tie to that very same decade can be traced in some of the other letters, exemplary being the two addressed to Batina Centurione, wife of Agostino Centurione, who had been in the service of the Doria family of Genoa and had died in 1565. Therefore, the consolation letter addressed to Batina is of that year, while the other cannot be so precisely dated but pertains to Matraini's stay in Genoa. There is at least one more letter, the one addressed to Vincenzo Uva da Capua, whose composition cannot be dated beyond 1563, the year in which he became a monk under the name of Benedetto (and would have been addressed as such), and certainly not beyond 1575, the year in which Marc'Antonio Passero was arrested and put on trial as a heretic, for Matraini still refers to him as an active bookseller and as her contact with the Neapolitan literary circle. For all these texts, time stopped well before the year they were published. They, as well as others, must have been taken from

---

33. "egli m'è parso, carissimo figliuolo, di darti e di lasciarti in vita e doppo morte un salutevole e breve compendio de i più degni ricordi (che pur del molto saggio e gran filosofo Isocrate sono)." Chiara Matraini, *Lettere con la prima e seconda parte delle sue Rime* (Lucca: Busdraghi, 1595), 26; (Venice: Moretti, 1597), 18r.

Matraini's personal, dormant archives, which, of course, is not surprising—it was practically the norm for published collections of letters of that period. And yet the results that Matraini achieved do not reflect such an obviousness. All sixteen letters lack explicit indications of place and date, although the theme is always present, even if the addressee is often indicated by initials only. Thus we face a contradiction. If these letters cannot be considered a familiar correspondence, neither can they be considered a mere repertory of rhetorical exercises, for they are all crystallized in time even if the date cannot be established through their recipients or references to datable events. The variety of themes used by Matraini does not permit a listing by categories such as "humorous," "spiritual," "consoling," "amorous" that could be used as an interpretive key of all-encompassing validity.

The already discussed treatise-letter addressed to Maria Cardona and the "Letter to Cangenna Lipomeni," in which Matraini minutely explains the poem she wrote for her friend, are only two aspects of a collection that includes various themes. There are three types of consolations: for the death of a son (also addressed to Cangenna Lipomeni), for the death of a husband (Letter to Batina Centurione), and a generic one against ill fortune (to the anonymous M. C. M.). There is a spiritual letter addressed to Sister F., advising her to cultivate only the love of Jesus; a letter (in the 1597 version only) exhorting a young man (Cristoforo Degli Anselmi) to cultivate the study of philosophy; a narrative-pastoral letter (addressed to Centurione) on the leisure-time pleasures that can be enjoyed in a country house; a theological disquisition (only in the 1597 version), addressed to Theofilo Caldarini; letters of polite exchange between writers (addressed to Vincenzo Uva, and Francesco Musacchi); a discussion of the ability to create allegories (how to depict immortality is addressed to Tiberio Placidi and how to depict vice to Gianasio Ugoberti); and a letter (addressed to Lodovico Domenichi) on the old, *dolce stil novo* problem of the *cor gentile* (noble heart as opposed to aristocratic birth), in which she states that love cannot last between two lovers of unequal sentiments. Such a variety, which includes, in her letter addressed to her son Federigo, a typology of the popular letter written in Italian, concludes with a missive to a very exceptional addressee, the Virgin Mary. It was somewhat modified for the 1597 edition, its single sonnet linked to three new compositions—a madrigal, a sonnet, and another madrigal—which together form a chain, a continuity of the Virgin's glorification.

Almost all the letters include poems of various types, usually as a comment on the prose, given at the end with a recurring kind of formula asking the reader to please "read the sonnet that follows" (*leggete il sonetto che segue*), or they might simply be a display of her poetic creativity disguised as a tribute to the addressee—an amplification of the usual form used by other poets. The mixing of diverse genres is prominent and typical of Matraini. At the same time it is difficult to find another text constructed in such a planned way based on this kind of alternation, as is the case of the 1597 collection's first letter addressed to Cangenna Lipomeni, in which the author undertakes a doubling of the poetess Latona and herself, the writer: "Here is the sonnet, my dear friend, which you requested from your Latona with so much insistence" (see below, chap. 5).[34] In direct opposition to this particular case are the two sonnets in which Chiara assumes the voice of Florida Amaranti, who is addressing her husband. She begins: "Here, my kind madonna Florida, are the two sonnets that I composed in your name, as you requested, on the subject of the fine embroidery you made in order to send it to your dear and honored husband."[35]

Of the total of eighteen letters (1597 edition), nine are addressed to women, if we include the Virgin. This perfect proportion was not in the 1595 edition, where it was nine to seven in favor of the women.

The real problem is that Matraini's is a very particular kind of collection of letters. It includes almost all the themes of the many books published around the middle of the sixteenth century, with the exception of the true "love letter." She applied each known rhetorical expedient in one letter or another, making it very difficult to classify her work, as the literary critic Amedeo Quondam noted when he defined her letters as bearing the signs of a crisis of the genre of letter writing.[36] In fact, the impression the reader gets is that Matraini's letters obey only her own, finely stylized, interior laws. This is why the thread that originated in the 1555 edition holds the three versions together and is at the same time a key to their interpretation, which can come only from the knowledge of the book's inner story. The links between the various prose selections go beyond a mere textual form. The author's aim of self-promotion has not changed. Only the material and the structure are different, in order to better hide these intentions through a wise distribution of all the elements.

---

34. "Eccovi, cara compagna, il sonetto da voi alla vostra Latona con tanta instanza adimandato." Chiara Matraini, *Lettere con la prima e seconda parte delle sue Rime* (Venice: Moretti, 1597), 1r.

35. "Eccovi, madonna Florida mia gentile, i dui sonetti che ho fatti a vostro nome, sì come m'imponeste, sopra di i sottilissimi lavori ch'avete apprestati per mandare al vostro caro e onoratissimo consort." The sonnets state that Florida stitched for him, with her own hands, two shirts with embroidered collars and sleeves. Thus she is envious of them because they will embrace his neck and arms (letter 14 of the 1595 edition, or 13 of the 1597 edition).

36. Amedeo Quondam, "Dal 'formulario' al 'formulario': cento anni di libri di lettere," in *Le "carte messaggiere." Retorica e modelli di comunicazione epistolare: per un indice dei libri di lettere del Cinquecento*, ed. A. Quondam (Rome: Bulzoni, 1981), esp. 123.

SOURCES AND LYRICAL MODELS

Matraini is a Petrarchist poet of the traditional kind and fits well into the group of men and women who wrote in imitation of Italy's famous lyric poet. She can be compared to Vittoria Colonna, Isabella di Morra, or Laura Battiferra Ammannati. What should be focused on, however, is her relationship to the poetry of Pietro Bembo, given that most of the Petrarchists active around 1550 structured their collection on his posthumous *canzoniere*, published in 1548, which, in a simplified way, maintained, with its funereal ending, the Petrarchan separation into two parts—*in vita* and *in morte* (poems written while Laura was alive, and poems written after her death). The influence of Bembo on Matraini's compositions is massive and reaches its highest point when she faithfully imitates in her already mentioned poem, A 82 "Chiara, eterna, felice, e gentil alma," the complex, compositional structure of his *canzone* written for the death of his brother Carlo, "Alma cortese, che dal mondo errante."[37] She adopts his metric rhyming scheme of 20 lines (though twice she transgresses into 19 only) for her ten stanzas, but with a shorter *commiato* (concluding stanza) comes up with 205 lines (cut down to 114 in the 1597 edition, with corrections and a *commiato* just like his). Moreover, she adapts his expressions to her own situation, that is, to the death of her beloved and her own sorrow.

In spite of her faithfulness to the model of Bembo and Petrarch, the structure of Matraini's *canzoniere* of 1555 deviates somewhat from both. First of all there is no formal separation into two parts, *in vita* and *in morte*. The experience of falling in love (which, in Petrarch, is frequently a metaphor for man's existential journey) is described with the usual features of rhetorical models canonized by Bembo. Then the single relationship of lover-beloved is contaminated (or perhaps we might say "enriched") by a number of sonnets addressed to men of letters whose friendships she eagerly cultivated. In these, Matraini shows that she definitely belonged to her century, for her poetic experience reflects the social values of her time. Another "transgression" is noticeable in the way she gives an original twist to the lyric lexicon used by all Petrarchists by inserting elements taken from Dante, mainly his *Rime petrose*, as for example in her poem in the form of a *sestina* (A 70), "Felice sasso, ch'a sì bella pietra" (see below, chap. 1). Similarly she makes use of the fifteenth-century metric form of the eclogue, of the exaggerated metaphoric

---

37. It is very long, ten stanzas of 20 lines each, ending with a double *commiato*, or a total of 214 lines. Its metric scheme is unusual: ABC/BAC – CDEeDFGHHGFFII (with one *settenario* only) and a double *commiato* (without *settenari*): JKLLKJJLL – MNNOO.

language concerning light and flame, and of astrological symbols recalling Dante's *Divine Comedy*.

Another noteworthy element is Matraini's frequent insertion of direct and realistic autobiographical references (such as Graziani's assassination), as already pointed out for "Chiara, eterna, felice, e gentil alma"—an important text for various reasons, beyond the structural one.[38] Her *Rime e prose* (1555), a book which the printer (in his letter to the reader) wants us to believe was published without the author's consent, is written in the manner of Matraini, rather than in the manner of Bembo or Petrarch, because it reflects additional influences and personal peculiarities.

The other great model whom she would never renounce was Vittoria Colonna, active as a poet for twenty years, from 1525 to 1546. Colonna's poetry is different from the poetry of other women or men, because it is of a uniform, mature style. Her poems went through a wise and hidden period of incubation and were offered in print when already structured on set principles, which substantially remained the same, even if somewhat reshuffled to accommodate fixed themes. On the one hand they represent a perfect equilibrium between fine poetic language and content—rigorous Petrarchism based on the absolute integrity of a conjugal and widowed love. On the other hand, they reflect a perfect harmony between stylistic tension—always in search of an elevated tone of expression, both lexical and syntactic—and evolving sentiments, from mourning for her husband to divine love and contemplation of Christ. In other words, she made a precise choice in the arena of nascent Petrarchism, an alignment with those favoring Bembo's direction. Colonna's poetry, however, is more severe, made so through a substantial use of Dante's style and through a total elimination of mirth and amorous jocundity. In short, if there is a writer who appears immediately as mature, exemplary, rigorously "monolingual," and "monostylistic," it is Vittoria Colonna.

There is no doubt that these characteristics made Colonna a successful model for other women poets. If it was not possible to imitate the exceptionality of Colonna's quasi-mythical status (her rank and exemplary life were unreachable), her poetry, often impersonal, was easily adaptable and could serve as a source from which an imitator could draw material with the illusion of completing the same literary itinerary and making it her own. This was an attractive and irresistible challenge for Chiara, who, however, was hindered in her effort at imitation by her inability to renounce her own strong peculiarities. Testimony of this can be found in the death announcement "Ohimè l'alma beltade, ohimè il mio Sole" (see below, chap. 5), which marks, in the

---

38. See poem A 82 and in its rewritten form C 45.

final version of 1597 (C 41), the part *in morte*, poems written after the death of her beloved, and is at the same time a disarming confession of the need to follow established patterns. In fact, Matraini, who, biographically speaking, started out with a situation similar to Colonna's, chose not to make funerary lamentation her leitmotif, or perhaps she foresaw its claustrophobic limitations.

Yet Colonna's poetry remained the strongest influence on Matraini. It can be detected in her inventive imagination, in her way of perceiving love's physiology, in her description of the beloved, and even in her self-depiction. But above all, it became her constant guide in the progressive crystallization of real events and articulation of emotions, which, increasingly, were given a spiritual interpretation. Even her deeply felt love poems did not escape this influence. The unconditional acknowledgment of Colonna's supremacy on the part of Matraini is her opening sonnet, in which she declares that she composed her poems when young to glorify him who was an example of virtue, virtue that spurred her to seek glory. Therefore, her noble intention makes excusable such an attempt:

> If happy in my green age, I sang alone
> the dear passion of my inner flames,
> the virtue, the beauty, the sublime honors
> of that high Sun of mine whom I loved so much,
>
> indeed I had to conquer well all the others,
> showing that which the other women hid,
> because with his blessed divine splendors
> he conquered all, making me, Chiara, victorious.
>
> However, if beyond the common affection
> I found this a spur to the virtue of glory
> that encircled the soul with high thoughts only,
>
> may I be pardoned by all for such chaste feelings,
> the infinite victories and the crowns of Love
> which conquered the wise, the holy, and the strong.

> [Se lieta in verde età sola cantai
> dell'interne mie fiamme i cari ardori,
> la virtù, la beltà, gli eccelsi onori
> di quell'alto mio Sol che tanto amai,
>
> ben dovea tutte vincer l'altre assai,
> in mostrar quel, ch'altre celaron, fuori,
> poiché co' suoi divini, almi splendori
> vins' egli ogn'altro, ond'io sì chiara andai.

> Però, s'oltr'al comune affetto, sempre
> mi fu questo a virtù di gloria sprone,
> che sol d'alti pensier l'anima cinse,
> 　scusimi appo ciascun sì caste tempre,
> l'infinite vittorie e le corone
> d'Amor, che 'l saggio, il santo e 'l forte vinse.] (C 1, variant of A 1)

Although it was modeled on Colonna's opening sonnet, it does not reproduce the latter's mournful tone,[39] and it has a new, vibrating intonation all its own.

Extremely relevant is also Chiara's first description of her beloved in sonnet C 2 (originally A 6; see below, chaps. 1 and 5), in which he is depicted as the sun that never sets but always shines upon her—a concept that derives from Colonna and was also used by Veronica Gambara and Gaspara Stampa (1523?–54). But in Matraini it is cleverly intertwined with the arrival of the autumnal equinox, when the sun crosses the equator, making night and day of equal length, that fatal date when she saw "him" for the first time:

> With right intent the sun was poised around
> the second equinox . . .
> 　. . . . .

---

39. Colonna's sonnet (for variants see *Rime*, ed. Alan Bullock [Rome: Laterza, 1982], 423):

> Scrivo sol per sfogar l'interna doglia
> ch' al cor mandar le luci al mondo sole,
> e non per giunger lume al mio bel Sole,
> al chiaro spirito e a l'onorata spoglia.
> 　Giusta cagion a lamentar m'invoglia;
> ch' io scemi la sua gloria assai mi dole;
> per altra tromba e più sagge parole
> convien ch' a morte il gran nome si toglia.
> 　La pura fe', l'ardor, l'intensa pena
> mi scusi appo ciascun; ché 'l grave pianto
> è tal che tempo né ragion l'affrena.
> 　Amaro lagrimar, non dolce canto,
> foschi sospiri e non voce serena,
> di stil no ma di duol mi danno il vanto. (*Rime amorose*, 1)

Natalia Costa-Zalessow's translation reads: "I write only to unburden my inner sorrow / that his eyes, unique in this world, sent to my heart / and not to add glory to my beautiful Sun, / to his noble spirit and his honored mortal remains. / A just reason induces me to lament, / but I greatly fear to diminish his glory; / by another poet and by wiser words / should his great name be snatched from death. / Let my pure faith, my ardor, my intense pain / be my excuse to everyone; for my profound lamentation / is such that neither time nor reason can restrain it. / Bitter tears, not sweet songs, / deep sighs and not serene airs, / make my reputation, not of style, but of sorrow."

when Love, adorned with his immense graces,
showed me another Sun of beauty and of virtue,
honored by the world, which hour by hour
makes within my soul a perpetual sunny day.

[Con giusta meta il sol librava intorno
al secondo equinozio . . .

. . . .

quand'Amor, di sue grazie immense adorno,
altro Sol di beltà che 'l mondo onora
mostrommi, e di virtù ch'ad ora ad ora
fa dentro a l'alma un bel perpetuo giorno.] (lines 1, 5–8)

Similarly, Matraini reproduced, in poem A 88 (and C 44), the first four lines
of a sonnet by Colonna,[40] taken in turn from four different poems by Pe-
trarch,[41] which she recognized as such, as is evident from the fact that she
continued her version by adding additional verses of the great master in a
technique of rearrangement, not uncommon in her time:

My eyes, your Sun has been eclipsed,
Just as my great light has vanished from me

---

40. Colonna's sonnet (for variants see *Rime*, ed. Bullock, 425):

Occhi miei, oscurato è il nostro [vostro] sole:
così l'alta mia luce è a me sparita
e, per quel ch'io ne speri, al ciel salita;
ma miracol non è, da Tal si vuole.
  E se pietà ancor può quant' ella sole,
ch' indi per Lete esser non può sbandita,
e mia giornata ho con suo' pie' fornita,
forse, o che spero? il mio tardar li dole.
  Piagner l'aer, la terra e 'l mar dovrebbe
l'abito onesto, il ragionar cortese,
quando un cor tante in sé virtuti accolse!
  Quanto la nuova libertà m'increbbe,
poi che mort' è colui che tutto intese,
che sol ne 'l mostrò il Ciel, poi se 'l ritolse. (*Rime amorose*, 15)

Natalia Costa-Zalessow's translation reads: "My eyes, our [your] sun is obscured: / so that my light
has gone out for me / and, as I hope, he's gone to Heaven; / but it's not a miracle, it's God's will. /
And if pity by itself is still powerful enough / that it cannot afterward be banished by Lethe, / and
I have completed my earthly journey, / perhaps, oh, what am I hoping for, my tardiness pains
him. / Air, earth, and sea should weep for / his honest appearance, his courteous speech, / when
did a heart possess so many virtues! / How painful this new liberty was to me, / since he who
understood me is dead, / he whom Heaven showed to me only to take him away."

41. Francesco Petrarca, *Rime, Trionfi e Poesie latine*, ed. F. Negri, G. Martellotti, C. Bianchi, N.
Sapegno (Milan-Naples: Ricciardi, 1951), poem 275, line 1; poem 327, line 6; poem 91, line 3;
poem 207, line 42.

and, I may hope, has risen to Heaven;
but a miracle it is not: God wants it so.
    He passed by as a star flies through the skies,
in his most lovely and most flowering age.
Ah, merciless Death, ah, cruel life,
no other misfortune can be more grievous!
    So I, without the light I loved so much,
go on like a blind person, having no light:
I know not where I go and yet I move on;
    thus my singing is changed to weeping.
O my hard fortune, to this you lead me:
(A) Love is guilty, not a failure of my art.
(C) to see my high hopes strewn to the ground.

    (Occhi miei, oscurato è il vostro Sole
così l'alta mia luce è a me sparita
e, per quel che ne speri, è al Ciel salita;
ma miracol non è: da tal si vuole.
    Passò, com'una stella ch'in Ciel vole,
ne l'età sua più bella e più fiorita.
Ahi dispietata Morte, ahi crudel vita,
via men d'ogni sventura altra mi duole!
    Rimasa senza il lume ch'amai tanto,
vomene in guisa d'orbo, senza luce,
che non sa ove si vada e pur si parte;
    così è 'l mio cantar converso in pianto.
O mia forte ventura, a che m'adduce:
(A) colpa d'Amor, non già difetto d'arte.
(C) veder l'alte speranze a terra sparte.)

While this may strike the reader as being an appropriation, an assumption of Colonna's and Petrarch's identity, it must be recalled that Petrarchists frequently engaged in paraphrasing the master's verses or using his lines in their own poems to produce a new variant. What is significant in Matraini's case is that rather than directly starting out from Petrarch's *Rime*, she chose to compete with Colonna, the most important of the Renaissance women poets, in paraphrasing the great model's verses. Echoes of other Italian poets, male and female, can also be found in Chiara's *canzoniere*, but to a lesser degree. She shared with Isabella di Morra the pathos of a tragic destiny, as well as a densely expressive language that reflects her ambitions, a desire for recognition, and a strong, general passion, a passion radically different from that of

Gaspara Stampa, notable for her hyperfemininity. Matraini and Laura Battiferra Ammannati had a common interest in the penitential psalms, a common friendship with Benedetto Varchi, an inclination toward the moderate wing of Italian Protestant reformers, as well as the status of *gentildonna* or lady not of the nobility.

MATRAINI WITHIN THE FRAMEWORK OF
ITALIAN LITERATURE

Chiara Matraini's place within the history of Italian literature has been recognized by contemporary critics. Although she can be associated with other Renaissance women writers, she has a niche of her own. She distinguished herself as a poet capable of refined descriptions obtained through nuanced but rich lexical expressions that hide reality under a misty veil. Never monotonous, with leitmotifs always differently elaborated, her poems contain a sensitivity that is almost modern, quite appealing to the present-day reader, and perfectly reflected in this volume's faithful translations by Elaine Maclachlan.

The problem, not only for Matraini but for all Italian women writers, is that they have generally been considered as a group apart from male writers. Not many literary critics made an effort to look up old anthologies, reference works, or books written by women when they turned their attention to the various literary movements. So these "minor" writers were either left out or just mentioned, in spite of a continuity of interest in them as a special group throughout the centuries. It seems that during each period preference was given to contemporary writers.

Chiara Matraini, as we have seen, enjoyed a certain success after her *Rime e prose* came out in 1555. The fact that her poems were included in anthologies published in Venice was important, for these books had a relatively wide circulation. When she returned to the publishing scene, she succeeded in obtaining recognition from her contemporaries.[42] She was not completely forgotten; some of her spiritual writings were still read in the seventeenth century. Although left out of his anthology by Domenichi in 1559, her poems appeared in Luisa Bergalli's 1726 anthology, *Componimenti poetici delle più illustri rimatrici d'ogni secolo*, the first attempt at giving a historical overview of Italian women poets, a book which became the basis for later compilers. Matraini's name was mentioned in the major reference works of the past. But she was wrongly interpreted. Critics seemed more interested in the private lives

---

42. This was not the case with Gaspara Stampa, for example, whose posthumous book *Rime* (1554) went completely unnoticed until it was rediscovered by Apostolo Zeno and republished by Luisa Bergalli in the eighteenth century.

of women writers rather than in their works, and Matraini was no exception. In a remarkable book for its time, *Teatro delle donne letterate* (a sort of history of women writers, published in 1620), Father Francesco Agostino della Chiesa stressed her innate intelligence and piety:

> In the same city of Lucca . . . there lived a very noble lady named Chiara de' Matraini, who through her alert intelligence and mature judgment not only saw but could foresee things. There was no one who could equal her in eloquence; she wrote with an infinite invention of concepts and very copiously, as can marvelously be seen in her writings. She spoke, gifted only by nature without the help of art, full of distinct, orderly concepts, of flourishing and abundant words, so that she succeeded in persuading everyone to whatever she wanted. But most important is that to these noble talents she added religion and a love for the mother of God, which was great in her, as is attested by her fine sonnets written in praise of the great Mother, as well as her *Life* written in fine prose.[43]

If this is closer to myth than to reality, it is in part Matraini's fault, for she described herself as a prophetess and wanted to be remembered in the guise of a Sibyl.

The eighteenth-century commentators on Italian literature, Giovanni Mario Crescimbeni and Francesco Saverio Quadrio, did briefly mention her, while Girolamo Tiraboschi was only a little more eloquent. Such brief mention is common to many other writers—more details cannot be expected from these fathers of Italian literary history.

The nineteenth-century reference works, especially those dedicated to women writers, include Matraini.[44] But most of the information is imprecise or outright wrong, for little was known about her life and works. Selections of

43. "Nell'istessa città di Lucca . . . visse una nobilissima Signora chiamata Chiara de' Matraini la quale con prestezza d'ingegno e maturità di iudicio non solo vedeva, ma prevedeva le cose; in eloquenza non v'era chi l'uguagliasse; scriveva con infinita invenzione de'concetti e con tanta copia con quanta si vede a meraviglia ne'suoi scritti. Parlava per solo dono di natura e senza alcun aiuto d'arte, di concetti così piena, distinta, e ordinata; di parole così fiorita e copiosa, che persuadeva e faceva creder tutto ciò ch'ella voleva. Ma quel ch'è di maggior importanza, a sì nobili doti aggiungeva la religione e amor verso la madre d'Iddio, che in lei era grandissimo e di questo fanno fede i leggiadrissimi suoi sonetti, che in lode di sì gran madre scrisse, come anco la vita scritta in grandissima prosa." Francesco Agostino Della Chiesa, *Theatro delle donne letterate* (Mondovì: Gislandi & Rossi), 1620, 127; in Rabitti, "Linee per il ritratto," 148.

44. See Ambrogio Levati, *Dizionario biografico cronologico degli uomini illustri: Classe V: Donne illustri* (Milan: Bettoni, 1821), 2: 254; Pietro Leopoldo Ferri, *Biblioteca femminile italiana* (Padua: Crescini, 1842), 229–30; and the anonymous *Delle donne illustri italiane dal XIII al XIX secolo* (Rome: Pallotta, 1840), 126–27.

her poems, and some of the letters, were offered to the reading public in an-
thologies, as can be seen in the bibliography that follows this introduction.

The same is true of the twentieth century, but although Matraini's poems
and letters continued to find their way into anthologies (always aimed at the
general reading public), her *Rime* were not closely examined until Luigi Balda-
cci turned his attention to them in 1953 and included a number of her poems
in the collection *Lirici del Cinquecento* that he edited in 1957.[45] He defined her
as one of the most original women poets of her period, because her poems
are of a solemn and vibrating tone that fluctuates between the elegiac and the
tragic. Besides the traditional Petrarchism, he saw in her poems an unusual
sensibility and richness of poetic expressions that reveal the secret pathos of
her heartbroken anguish. He pointed out that her eloquence is steadily kept
in check and little by little becomes simpler, like a conversation with herself.
In comparing her to the poets of her time, he noticed a novelty of style and
of personal sentiment, accompanied by similes that are often original.

Giulio Ferroni, on the other hand, thought that Baldacci had overrated
Matraini. Yet he praised her fine style based on sixteenth-century models,
as well as the presentation of her ennobled love story, which she turned
into a model love tragedy suitable for an aristocratic taste.[46] But new stud-
ies followed. Alan Bullock and Gabriella Palange pointed out the need for a
critical edition of Matraini's works and called attention to Colonna's influ-
ence on her.[47] Then I myself reconstructed Chiara's life, using published and
manuscript material, and examined her poetry.[48] Finally, Matraini received
what women poets rarely have received—a critical edition of her *Rime e lettere*,
edited by me.[49] I subsequently also published a detailed study of her *Lettere*.[50]

45. Luigi Baldacci, "Chiara Matraini, poetessa lucchese del XVI secolo," *Paragone* 42 (1953):
53–67; Baldacci, ed., *Lirici del Cinquecento* (Florence: Salani, 1957), 497–530, reprint (Milan: Lon-
ganesi, 1975), 383–409.

46. Giulio Ferroni, ed., *Poesia italiana del Cinquecento* (Milan: Garzanti, 1978), 244.

47. Alan Bullock and Gabriella Palange, "Per un'edizione critica delle opere di Chiara Matraini,"
Studi in onore di Raffaele Spongano (Bologna: Boni, 1980), 235–62.

48. Giovanna Rabitti, "Linee per il ritratto di Chiara Matraini," *Studi e problemi di critica testuale*
22 (1981): 141–65; "La metafora e l'esistenza nella poesia di Chiara Matraini," *Studi e problemi di
critica testuale* 27 (1983): 109–45; "Inediti vaticani di Chiara Matraini," in *Studi di filologia e critica
offerti dagli allievi a Lanfranco Caretti* (Rome: Salerno, 1985), 1: 225–50; "Chiara Matraini," in *Italian
Women Writers: A Bio-bibliographical Sourcebook*, ed. Rinaldina Russell (Westport, CT: Greenwood,
1994), 243–52.

49. See Chiara Matraini, *Rime e lettere*, ed. Giovanna Rabitti, in *Scelta di curiosità letterarie inedite o rare
dal secolo XIII al XIX*, Dispensa 279 (Bologna: Commissione per i Testi di Lingua, 1989).

50. Giovanna Rabitti, "Le lettere di Chiara Matraini tra pubblico e privato," in *Per lettera: La
scrittura epistolare femminile tra archivio e tipografia secoli XV–XVII*, ed. Gabriella Zarri (Rome: Viella,
1999), 209–34.

Riccardo Scrivano, in one of the newest histories of Italian literature, mentions Baldacci's rediscovery of Matraini and Ferroni's skepticism but sides with the former when stating that in Chiara's poetry there is

> an extraordinary stylistic scansion, so that the Petrarchan instrumentation is lifted to a higher level, where everything appears to be imbued with acute feelings—the most lacerating sentiments, the most intense sensibility, the passions endured with a special composure and dignity. The depicted landscapes, too, attain a solemn sobriety . . . yet without excluding a kind of joyous serenity. . . . The theme of time's passing is semantically restructured, but with the usual sobriety. . . . And the same is true of the theme of her self-dedication to God, which, though taken from Petrarch, has a personal vibration.[51]

Chiara Matraini has received the deserved attention of Italian literary critics. But while some of her poems have appeared in English translations in anthologies and literary journals, this is the first time they are offered in a book entirely dedicated to her work, which, hopefully, will make her better known to readers beyond the borders of Italy.

Giovanna Rabitti
Translated by Natalia Costa-Zalessow

---

51. "una straordinaria misura stilistica, tale che tutta la strumentazione petrarchistica di cui si vale è promossa a una fascia più alta, dove tutto appare risentitamente partecipato, i sentimenti più strazianti, la sensibilità più acuta, le passioni vissute con speciale compostezza e dignità. Anche il paesaggismo raggiunge una sobrietà che è solennità . . . , senza che una sorta di gioiosa serenità sia esclusa. . . . Risemantizzato drammaticamente, ma con la solita sobrietà, il tema della fuga del tempo. . . . E lo stesso tema della resa a Dio, ripreso e ricalcato sul Petrarca, ha una vibrazione personale." Riccardo Scrivano, "La poesia del Cinquecento," in *Storia generale della letteratura italiana*, ed. Nino Borsellino and Walter Pedullà (Naples: Motta, 1999), 3: 523–24.

VOLUME EDITOR'S
BIBLIOGRAPHY

CHIARA MATRAINI'S PUBLISHED WORKS
(IN CHRONOLOGICAL ORDER)

Rime e prose. Lucca: Busdraghi, 1555.

Orazione d'Isocrate a Demonico figliuolo d'Ipponico, circa a l'essortazione de' costumi, che si convengono a tutti i nobilissimi giovani· di latino in volgare tradotta da madonna Chiara Matraini. Florence: Torrentino, 1556.

Meditazioni spirituali. Lucca: Busdraghi, 1581.

Considerazioni sopra i sette salmi penitenziali del gran re e profeta Davit. Lucca: Busdraghi, 1586.

Breve discorso sopra la vita e laude della Beatiss. Verg. e Madre del Figliuol di Dio. Lucca: Busdraghi, 1590.

Lettere con la prima e seconda parte delle sue Rime. Lucca: Busdraghi, 1595.

Lettere con la prima e seconda parte delle sue Rime. Venice: Moretti, 1597.

Dialoghi spirituali con una notabile narrazione alla grande Academia de' Curiosi e alcune sue Rime e Sermoni. Venice: Prati, 1602.

Vita della Beatissima Vergine Maria. Venice, Padua, and Basano: Remondini, n.d.

Rime e lettere. Ed. Giovanna Rabitti. In *Scelta di curiosità letterarie inedite o rare dal secolo XIII al XIX*, Dispensa 279. Bologna: Commissione per i testi di lingua, 1989.

ANTHOLOGIES CONTAINING WORKS BY CHIARA MATRAINI
(IN CHRONOLOGICAL ORDER)

Dolce, Lodovico, ed. *Rime di diversi signori napoletani e d'altri. Libro settimo*, 68–154. Venice: Giolito, 1556.

Domenichi, Lodovico, ed. *Delle nuove rime di diversi eccellentissimi autori*, 15v. Lucca: Busdraghi, 1556.

Scandianese, Tito Giovanni. *La fenice*, 104. Venice: Giolito, 1557.

Lettere volgari di diversi nobilissimi huomini et ecellentissimi ingeni: Libro terzo, 37r–38r. Venice: [Aldo Manuzio], 1564.

Ferentilli, Agostino, ed. *Primo volume della scielta di stanze di diversi autori toscani*, 412–21. Venice: Giunti, 1571.

Pino, Bernardino, ed. *Della nuova scelta di lettere di diversi*, 58–59. Venice: n.p., 1582.

Bergalli, Luisa, ed. *Componimenti poetici delle più illustri rimatrici d'ogni secolo*, part 1, 167–76. Venice: Mora, 1726.

Costanzo, Torquato, *Bernardo Tasso e poetesse del secolo XVI* (*Parnaso italiano ovvero raccolta de' poeti classici italiani, tomo XXX*), 241. Venice: Zatta, 1787.

Rime di pentimento spirituale tratte da' canzonieri de' più celebri autori antichi e moderni, 80. Milan: Silvestri, 1821.

Gamba, Bartolomeo, ed. *Lettere di donne italiane del secolo XVI*, 157–64. Venice: Alvisopoli, 1832.

Ronna, Antoine, ed. "Gemme o rime scelte di poetesse italiane antiche e moderne." In *Poeti italiani contemporanei maggiori e minori*, 2:1010–11. Paris: Baudry, 1843.

De Blasi, Jolanda, ed. *Antologia delle scrittrici italiane dalle origini al 1800*, 131–34. Florence: Nemi, 1930.

Baldacci, Luigi, ed. *Lirici del Cinquecento*. Florence: Salani, 1957. Reprint, Milan: Longanesi, 1975.

Muscetta, Carlo, and Daniele Ponchiroli, eds. *Poesia del Quattro e del Cinquecento* (*Parnasso Italiano*), 1297–1300. Turin: Einaudi, 1959.

Flora, Franceso, ed. *Gaspara Stampa e altre poetesse del Cinquecento*, 163–68. Milan: Nuova Accademia, 1962.

Costa-Zalessow, Natalia, ed. *Scrittrici italiane dal XIII al XX secolo: Testi e critica*, 93–98. Ravenna: Longo, 1982.

Allen, Beverly, Muriel Kittel, and Jane Jewell, eds. *The Defiant Muse*, 8–9. New York: Feminist Press at the City University of New York, 1986.

Forlani, Alma, and Marta Savini, eds. *Scrittrici d'Italia*, 53–56. Rome: Newton Compton, 1991.

Stortoni, Laura Anna, ed. *Women Poets of the Italian Renaissance: Courtly Ladies and Courtesans*, 93–103. New York: Italica Press, 1997.

Segre, Cesare, and Carlo Ossola, eds. *Antologia della poesia italiana*, 2:746–74. Turin: Einaudi-Gallimar, 1998.

Bianchi, Stefano, ed. *Poetesse italiane del Cinquecento*, 71–87. Milan: Mondadori (Oscar Classici), 2003.

RELATED PRIMARY AND SECONDARY SOURCES

Baldacci, Luigi. "Chiara Matraini, poetessa lucchese del XVI secolo." *Paragone* 42 (1953): 53–67.

———, ed. *Lirici del Cinquecento*. Florence: Salani, 1957.

Bandini Buti, ed. *Poetesse e scrittrici* (*Enciclopedia biografica e bibliografica italiana*), 1: 173. Series 6. Rome: Istituto Editoriale Italiano, 1941–42.

Bembo, Pietro. *Prose e Rime*. Ed. Carlo Dionisotti. Turin: UTET, 1960.

Berengo, Marino. *Nobili e mercanti nella Lucca del Cinquecento*. Turin: Einaudi, 1965.

Borsetto, Luciana. "Narciso ed Eco. Figura e scrittura nella lirica femminile del Cinquecento: esemplificazione ed appunti." In *Nel cerchio della luna: figura di donna in alcuni testi del XVI secolo*. Ed. Marina Zancan, 171–233. Venice: Marsilio, 1983.

Bullock, Alan, and Gabriella Palange. "Per un'edizione critica delle opere di Chiara Matraini." *Studi in onore di Raffaele Spongano*, 235–62. Bologna: Boni, 1980.

Colonna, Vittoria. *Rime*. Ed. Alan Bullock. Rome: Laterza, 1982.

Comba, Eugenio. *Donne illustri italiane, proposte ad esempio alle giovinette.* Turin: Paravia, 1901, 1920, and 1935.

Costa-Zalessow, Natalia. "Le *Fantasie poetiche* di Virginia Bazzani Cavazzoni." *Esperienze letterarie* 27, no. 2 (2002): 57–75.

Crescimbeni, Giovanni Mario. *L'istoria della volgar poesia.* Vol. 2, part 1, 402–3. Venice: Basegio, 1730.

De Blasi, Iolanda. *Le scrittrici italiane dalle origini al 1800.* Florence: Nemi, 1930.

Della Chiesa, Francesco Agostino. *Theatro delle donne letterate.* Mondovì: Gislandi & Rossi, 1620.

Delle donne illustri italiane dal XIII al XIX secolo, 126–27. Rome: Pallotta, [1840].

Dionisotti, Carlo. *Geografia e storia della letteratura italiana,* 183–204. Turin: Einaudi, 1967.

Ferri, Pietro Leopoldo. *Biblioteca femminile italiana,* 229–30. Padua: Crescini, 1842.

Ferroni, Giulio, ed. *Poesia italiana del Cinquecento,* 244–47. Milan: Garzanti, 1978.

Javion, Maurice. "Chiara Matraini: un "tombeau" pour Petrarque." In *Les femmes écrivains en Italie au Moyen Âge et à la Renaissance (Actes du colloque international Aix-en-Provence, 12, 13, 14 novembre 1992),* 247–58. Aix-en-Provence: Publications de l'Université de Provence, 1994.

Levati, Ambrogio. *Dizionario biografico cronologico degli uomini illustri: Classe V: Donne illustri,* 2: 254. Milan: Bettoni, 1821.

Lorenzi, Daniela. "Chiara Matraini: Mannerism under a Petrarchan Veil." *Romance Languages Annual* 9 (1998): 244–48.

Maclachlan, Elaine (Elena). "The Conversion of Chiara Matraini: The 1597 Rewriting of the *Rime* of 1555." *NEMLA Italian Studies* 16 (1992): 21–32.

———. "Poems by Chiara Matraini" (translations with a bio-bibliographical introduction). *Forum Italicum* 28, no. 1 (1994): 124–28.

———. "The Poetry of Chiara Matraini, Narrative Strategies in the *Rime.*" Ph.D. diss., University of Connecticut, 1992. Reproduction Photocopy: Ann Arbor, MI: UMI, 1993.

———. "*Quant' è fallace,* a *canzone* by Chiara Matraini." *Metamorphoses* 1 (1993): 2: 66–70.

Malpezzi Price, Paola. "Chiara Matraini: Petrarchist or Anti-Petrarchist? The Dilemma of a Woman Poet." In *Donna: Women in Italian Culture.* Ed. Ada Tagliaferri, 189–99. Toronto: Dovehouse, 1989.

Miscellanea lucchese. Biblioteca Governativa di Lucca. MS 1574.

Panizza, Letizia, ed. *Women in Italian Renaissance Culture and Society.* Oxford: University of Oxford European Humanities Research Centre, 2000.

———, and Sharon Wood, eds. *A History of Women Writings in Italy.* Cambridge: Cambridge University Press, 2000.

Paoli, Maria Pia. "Nell'Italia delle 'Vergini belle': A proposito di Chiara Matraini e di pietà mariana nella Lucca di fine Cinquecento." In *Religione, cultura e politica nell'Europa dell'età moderna: Studi offerti a Mario Rosa dagli amici.* Ed. Carlo Ossola, Marcello Verga, and Maria Antonietta Visceglia, 521–45. Florence: Olschki, 2003.

Pera, Pietro. *Miscellanea lucchese.* Biblioteca Governativa di Lucca. MS 1547, call number 397.

Petrarca, Francesco. *Rime, Trionfi e Poesie latine.* Ed. F. Negri, G. Martellotti, C. Bianchi, N. Sapegno. Milan and Naples: Ricciardi, 1951.

Quadrio, Francesco Saverio. *Della storia e della ragion d'ogni poesia*, 2: 251. Milan: Agnelli, 1741.

Quondam, Amedeo. "Dal 'formulario' al 'formulario': cento anni di libri di lettere." In *Le "carte messaggiere." Retorica e modelli di comunicazione epistolare: per un indice dei libri di lettere del Cinquecento*. Ed. Amedeo Quondam, 13–158. Rome: Bulzoni, 1981.

Rabitti, Giovanna. "Chiara Matraini." In *Italian Women Writers: A Bio-bibliographical Sourcebook*. Ed. Rinaldina Russell, 243–52. Westport, CT. Greenwood, 1994.

———. "Inediti vaticani di Chiara Matraini." In *Studi di filologia e critica offerti dagli allievi a Lanfranco Caretti*, 1: 225–50. Rome: Salerno, 1985.

———. "Le lettere di Chiara Matraini tra pubblico e privato." In *Per lettera: La scrittura epistolare femminile tra archivio e tipografia secoli XV–XVII*. Ed. Gabriella Zarri, 209–34. Rome: Viella, 1999.

———. "Linee per il ritratto di Chiara Matraini." *Studi e problemi di critica testuale* 22 (1981): 141–65.

———. "La metafora e l'esistenza nella poesia di Chiara Matraini." *Studi e problemi di critica testuale* 27 (1983): 109–45.

Russell, Rinaldina. "Chiara Matraini nella tradizione lirica femminile." *Forum Italicum* 34 (2000): 2: 415–25.

Scrivano, Riccardo. "La poesia del Cinquecento." In *Storia generale della letteratura italiana*. Ed. Nino Borsellino and Walter Pedullà, 3: 494–571. Naples: Motta, 1999.

Sergiusti, Gherardo. *Sommario de' Successi della Città di Lucca*. Ed. Riccardo Ambrosini and Albarosa Belegni. Pisa: Edizioni ETS, 1997.

Smarr, Janet L. *Joining the Conversation: Dialogues by Renaissance Women*. Ann Arbor: University of Michigan Press, 2005.

Tiraboschi, Girolamo. *Biblioteca modenese*, 2: 46–48 and 6: 87. Modena: Società Tipografica, 1782.

Villani, Carlo. *Stelle femminili: Dizionario bio-bibliografico*, 414–15. Naples, Rome, Milan: Società Editrice Dante Alighieri, 1915.

Figure 1. Frontispiece of the 1555 edition of Matraini's *Rime e Prose*, depicting the author when she was about forty years old. By permission of Houghton Library, Harvard University.

I

1555 / 56 VOLUME (BOOK A)

TRANSLATOR'S NOTE

Chiara Matraini's first book of poems was published by Busdraghi in Lucca in 1555. It was later republished in 1556 as part of the seventh volume of Giolito de' Ferrari's anthology of poets, a multivolume tribute to the creativity of the cinquecento lyricists and a powerful means of diffusion. The seventh volume was compiled by Lodovico Dolce and contains Matraini's poems. These poems are in the same order as, and in every other respect identical to, those published in 1555 at Lucca, except for minor differences in spelling and punctuation and occasional corrections or new errors.

At the end of the 1555 volume, Matraini has a *Letter* and an *Oration on the Art of War*. The letter was written to a person identified only as "M. L." It is not clear who that was. It contains her most personal, most direct apology for her writing in prose and in poetry. The letter refers to her life in Lucca and goes on with a paean about Love in all its forms which, at that time, she called our last desired end. These were quite naturally omitted from the anthology, being prose works.

The following pages contain my selection of her poems: forty-six out of a total of ninety-nine. Out of every five poems in order, I have chosen two or three which both respect her choice and portray her style of writing and the substance of her work. Together, they represent her tale of earthly love; it is described as beautiful and chaste but destined to end in failure. The stages of the unhappy story constitute a process of deterioration which is finalized in the physical death of the real man, a flesh-and-blood object of desire. His murder is the end of the narration, followed by a coda of consolatory poems.

In 1989, Giovanna Rabitti published Chiara Matraini's *Rime e Lettere*,[1] a critical edition. Until that time, Matraini was available only in scattered rare book libraries, mostly in Italy, and in a variety of anthologies. Rabitti's edition contains all of the 1555/56 and 1597 poems and letters, along with selected other writings and a long introduction. The Italian I have used for the most part follows hers, which differs from Matraini's original only in punctuation and spelling, bringing the text into a more contemporary Italian.

A 1 (B 1, C 1)

    Se lieta e verde, chiara, alta cantai[2]
d'amor sola, e de l'alma i santi ardori,
la virtù, la beltà, gli eterni onori
di quell'alto mio Sol che tanto amai,   4
    ben dovea vincer tutte l'altre assai
nel mostrar quel, ch'altre celaron, fuori,
poi che co' suoi beati, almi splendori
vins'egli ogn'altro, ond'io sì chiara andai.   8
    Però, s'oltra al comune affetto, sempre
mi fu questo a virtù di gloria sprone,
che sol d'alti pensier l'anima cinse,   11
    scusimi appo ciascun sì caste tempre,
l'infinite vittorie, e le corone
d'Amor, ch'in terra e 'n Ciel tutt'altri vinse.   14

A 5 (C 3)

    Mentre che 'l cor da gli amorosi nodi
pensava di tener sempre disciolto,
e d'ostinata voglia un gelo accolto
l'avea d'intorno con più saldi chiodi,   4
    dolce mio foco, con sì cari modi
ne l'amorose vostre reti involto
fu, ch'ogni schermo finalmente tolto
gli avete, e par che del suo mal si godi.   8
    Fur le reti amorose il dolce canto
di celeste armonia sempre mai pieno
e 'l parlar saggio, e la virtù divina,   11
    l'angelica beltà, ch'in sì bel manto
d'altr'anima nel mondo uom vide a pena:
così si segue quanto il Ciel destina.   14

A 6 (B 2, C 2)

    Con giusta meta il sol librava intorno
dal secondo equinozio, e 'l tempo e l'ora
già de l'ugual bilance uscivon fuora
per far al nuovo dì lieto ritorno,   4

A 1 (B 1, C 1)

If happy and green, I alone, bright and high,
sang of love, and the holy passion of the soul,
the virtue, the beauty, the eternal honors
of that high Sun of mine whom I loved so much,   4
    indeed I had to conquer all the others
showing that which the other women hid:
because with his blessed divine splendors
he conquered all, making me, Chiara, victorious.   8
    However, if beyond the common affection
I found this a spur to the virtue of glory
that encircled the soul with high thoughts only,   11
    may I be pardoned by all for such chaste feelings,
for the infinite victories and crowns of Love
which conquered all others on earth and in Heaven.   14

A 5 (C 3)

While my heart from amorous love knots
I thought of keeping always unattached,
and a chill of obstinate desire
had wrapped around it with more firm grip,   4
    my sweet fire, with such dear ways
it was caught up in your amorous nets,
that every defense you took away from it,
and it seems that of its evil it is glad.   8
    The amorous nets were the sweet song
of heavenly harmony always and ever full,
and the wise speech, and the divine virtue,   11
    the angelic beauty that, in such a beautiful cloak
of another soul in the world, we could hardly see:
thus there follows as much as Heaven intends.   14

A 6 (B 2, C 2)

With right intent the sun was poised around
the second equinox, and already the time and hour
of its equal balance shone on the face of the earth,
to make the new day a happy return,   4

quand'Amor diemmi assalto, e a bel soggiorno
destòmi a contemplar l'ardente aurora,
ch'in me gloria e virtute ad ora ad ora
crea dentro a l'alma ed un perpetuo giorno.   8

    Poscia, cantando col mio vivo Sole,
fu tanta l'armonia dolce e gli accenti
che si bearon l'alme e le parole.   11

    Sian benedetti i primi alti concenti,
che mi feron sentir quel che là suole
l'alma, su in Ciel, fra gli angeli contenti.   14

A 10. CANZONE

    Poiché tacer non posso
e 'l chiuso foco omai non pò celarsi,
convien ch'io torni a l'amorose note.
    Amor, là 've m'apparve,
scorga il mio stil d'ogn'ornamento scosso,
e le preghiere mie dolci e devote   6
    riponga in parte ove pietà le note,
donando a' desir miei parole eguali
di quel ch'occhio mortal già mai non vide:
luci serene e fide,
ond'io levo da terra al Ciel quell'ali
che dal vulgo lontana
giugner mi fanno al Sol che m'ard' e ancide,
e mi mantiene in vita altera e strana,
e quel che dir non potria lingua umana.   15

    Io penso: Se nel Cielo,
dov'il Motor de l'alte stelle ardenti
mostra l'opre sue altere e glorïose,
    son gli angeli contenti,
mirando fiso in Dio senz'alcun velo
sempre, quant'io mirando l'amorose   21
    luci dov'ogni bel Natura pose,
sia dal mortal lo spirto omai disgiunto
e 'l mio breve gioir si faccia eterno,
onde con state e 'l verno
sia sempre a tal diletto ivi congiunto,

when Love assaulted me and awakened me
to a lovely day to contemplate the burning dawn,
which creates in me and in my soul hour by hour
glory and virtue and a perpetual day.   8

 Then, singing with my living Sun,
there was so much sweet harmony and song
that the souls and words rejoiced.   11

 Let the first high harmonies be blessed
that made me feel what the soul feels there,
up in Heaven, among the contented angels.   14

A 10. SONG

 Since I cannot be silent
and the closed fire within me cannot be hidden,
it behooves me to return to the amorous notes.

 Let Love, there where it appeared to me,
notice my artistry free of every ornament,
and my prayers, sweet and devoted,   6

 and let him place them where pity may note them,
by giving words corresponding to my desires
for that which mortal desires had never beheld:
his eyes, both serene and faithful,
whereby I raise from the earth to Heaven
those wings which make me leave the crowd
and arrive far away at the Sun, which burns and kills me
and keeps me alive in a way both strange and proud,
which no human tongue could ever describe.   15

 I think that if in Heaven,
where the Prime Mover of the high burning stars
shows his proud and glorious works,

 the angels are contented,
gazing fixed at God without any veil,
as much as I, gazing at the amorous lights   21

 where Nature placed every beauty,
may my spirit be disjoined from its mortal state,
and may my short joy become eternal:
so that in summer and in winter
it may be joined there with such a delight,

e la tranquilla pace
goda quel che mi toglie in un sol punto
la luce che m'incende e mi disface,
com'a l'alta speranza si conface.   30

    Io, per me, quanto vede
di bello il mondo e di diletto insieme
cangerei solo a un ragionare, a un canto
    di lui, che ne l'estreme
parti in me vive in la più eccelsa sede,
né d'altrove venir puote mai tanto   36
    gioir, che dal bel foco onesto e santo;
a questo, com'al sol sparisce ogn'ombra
e per lui fassi allegro e bello il mondo,
così lieto e giocondo
si fa il core al suo lume che disgombra
ogni vil voglia e fella,
e s'empie d'un piacere alto e profondo,
tal che dovunque il sol splende né stella,
non vid'uom mai di lui cosa più bella.   45

    Quando primier' entrai
a ragionar di quel ch'in me sentia,
credetti in parte disfogare il core
    e trovar qualche via
ond'avessi rimedio alli miei guai,
e far pietoso a' miei pensieri Amore;   51
    or m'abandona ogni speranza e fuore
dell'alma fugge e sempre più s'accende
lo mio desir e 'l Tempo si dilegua.
Ma pur convien ch'io segua
l'alta mia impresa e 'l foco ove risplende
ogn'altro chiaro lume,
che da la notte e l'ombra si difende:
Amor la strada a' be' pensieri allume,
ond'a quanto conviensi alzi le piume.   60

    Dico che qual uom brama
saper quant'ha di belle ed onorate
virtù, degne d'etern' e immortal gloria

and the tranquil peace
may be enjoyed by the one who takes away from me
the light which burns me and destroys me,
as is appropriate to sublime hope.   30

What the world sees as beauty
and as delight, I myself
would exchange for only a speech, for a poem
        by him who lives there,
sublimely, in the most minute part of me;
from nowhere else can ever come such a delight,   36
        if not from that beautiful fire, honest and holy.
With this, as with the sun, every shadow disappears,
and because of him the world becomes merry and lovely;
so happy and joyful
the heart becomes at his light, which sends away
every base and treacherous wish
and fills itself with a high, profound pleasure,
such that wherever the sun or star shines,
never was seen a man more beautiful than he.   45

When I first began
to write of what I felt within,
I thought I would give vent to my heart
        and would find some way
where I should have a remedy to my woes,
and make Love full of pity for my thoughts;   51
        now all hope abandons me and flees
from my soul, but my desire is kindled
ever more, and Time melts away.
And yet I am pledged to follow
that high enterprise of mine, and that fire, where
every other bright light shines,
which defends itself from the night and shadow:
Let Love light the way to beautiful thoughts
so that I may spread my wings accordingly.   60

I say that whoever desires
to know how many beautiful and honored
virtues, worthy of eternal and immortal glory,

il mondo in questa etate,
miri il bell'angelo mio, che quanto s'ama
degno di vera ed immortal memoria,　　　　　　　　　66
  di tutte ei sol trionfa ed ha vittoria,
però che Dio, Natura, ed Amor volse
mostrar de le sue grazie un vero essempio
in lui, com'in suo tempio,
dov'ogni bene, ogni bellezza accolse,
ond'a lui sempre chieggio
quello ond'io solo i be' pensieri adempio;
e qualor del mio error meco vaneggio,
più fida scorta al mio sentier non veggio.　　　　　　　75

  Come nocchier già stanco
da la tempesta e da' contrarî venti,
ch'a' due lumi ch'ha sempre il nostro polo
  si gira, a' suoi lucenti
lumi mi volgo e 'l travagliato e manco
vigor rinforzo al suo conforto solo,　　　　　　　　81
  fuggendo al suo apparir angoscia e duolo;
né potrei imaginar, non che dir mai,
gli effetti de' be' lumi alti e soavi,
qualor par che m'aggravi
penoso giogo; ond' ho per meno assai
tutti gli altri diletti,
che volgon di Fortuna ambe le chiavi;
né più credo di gioia e gloria aspetti
uom mai nel mondo, de' suoi grandi effetti.　　　　　90

  Canzon, io temo di stancare altrui
col lungo dire, ond'ognor più m'accendo,
però mi taccio e 'l troppo ardir riprendo.　　　　　　93

A 13 (B 7, C 6)

  Alto mio Sol, se l'anima beata
che vi rivolge, a la mia stella desse
tanto del suo splendor, che pur vedesse
farsi un giorno da lei chiara e lodata,　　　　　　　4

the world has at this time,
shall look at my beautiful angel,
because he alone triumphs and is victorious   66
      over everything loved, worthy of true, immortal memory,
since God, Nature, and Love wanted
to show of their graces a true example
in him, as in their temple,
where every good, every beauty he received,
wherefore I always ask of him
that I may accomplish only beauteous thoughts,
and whenever I am raving in my error,
I do not see a more faithful escort to my pathway.   75

      Like a helmsman, now so weary
of the storm and contrary winds,
who steers to the two lights which our pole always has,
      I turn to his shining eyes,
and the troubled, fainting
vigor is strengthened by only his support,   81
      fleeing anguish and grief at his appearance.
Nor could I imagine, or yet ever tell
the effects of the lovely eyes, high and gentle,
whenever it seems that a painful yoke
oppresses me; whence I do not ever care
for all the other delights
that both the keys of Fortune turn;
nor do I believe that one can obtain more joy and glory
in this world than can be had from their grand effect.   90

      Song, I fear that I am tiring to others,
with too much discourse, with which I am ever more burning,
so I will be silent, and find fault with too much daring.   93

A 13 (B 7, C 6)

      My Sun on high, if the blessed soul
which turns to you would give enough of its splendor
to my star that it would even see itself
become one day greatly bright and praised,   4

credo che con la mente innamorata
ne' raggi vostri (l'altre luci oppresse)
arderìa sì, che delle fiamme stesse
vedreste nuova luce al mondo nata.   8
    O felice suo corso, se le vostre
rote il guidasse ove l'eterna fronte
volgete voi dalla mia mente stanca!   11
        Ma vedo in giro andar le sfere nostre
contrarie sì, che mentre a l'orizzonte
v'alzate voi, ella in ponente manca.   14

A 14. MADRIGALE

    Ne' primi incontri della bella vista,
Signor, m'accende una gelata fiamma
che m'arde e strugge dentro a dramma a dramma,
e sì soave è 'l foco
che 'l cor gioisce e l'alma si disface,   5
e se l'un gli dà loco
a l'altra il suon ben spiace;
così, s'io vivo o muoio i' non comprendo,
mentre che col piacer me stessa offendo.   9

A 17

    Se l'aver per altrui se stesso a vile,
e far d'una bell'alma e d'un bel volto
idolo al suo, nè mai da lor rivolto
star col pensier devotamente umile;   4
        s'arder dì e notte a un foco almo e gentile
fra mille cari e forti lacci avvolto,
e voler poco desïando molto,
nè per pioggia o per sol cangiar mai stile;   8
        se languir dolce, e gioia ogni tormento,
e provar com'in un crudele e pio
spesso si mostra a' suoi seguaci Amore,   11
        fede pò far d'un saldo, acceso cor,
fede insieme ed amor s'acquisiti il mio,
ch'ardendo in voi, s'è in me di vita spento.   14

I believe that with my mind enamored
of your rays (the other lights overshadowed),
I would burn so much that in those same flames
you would see a new light born to the world.   8
  Oh, happy its course, if your wheels
would only guide it where you bend
your eternal brow from my tired mind!   11
  But I see the movement of our spheres
in contrary directions, so while on the horizon
yours is rising, mine descends in the west.   14

A 14. MADRIGAL

  When first encountering this beautiful sight,
my lord, I am engulfed by an icy flame
that little by little burns and destroys me from within.
Yet so sweet is that fire
that my heart rejoices even as my soul shatters,   5
and if the one gives it place
the other truly detests the sound.
So I do not understand if I live or die,
while I go on offending myself with pleasure.   9

A 17

  If to place all one's value in someone else
and to make a lovely soul and face
one's idol, without ever turning from them,
to stay with one's thought devotedly humble,   4
  if to burn day and night in a divine, gentle fire,
wrapped up in a thousand dear and strong ties,
and to want little, desiring much,
nor for rain or for sun ever changing ways,   8
  if to pine sweetly, and in every torment find joy,
and to feel at the same time both cruel and merciful,
as Love often shows itself to its followers,   11
  if these can bear witness to a firm, burning heart:
let mine then acquire both faith and love,
which burning in you, has died in me.   14

A 22 (B 5, C 5)

Quant dolci pensieri, alti e felici,
son esca oggi al bel foco che nel seno
nutrisce il cor, d'alta speranza pieno
di trar frutto immortal da su radici!   4
    Oggi i campi apparir lieti ed aprici
veggio, ed al mio sperar chiaro e sereno
renders'il cielo oltra l'usato ameno
per far del viver mio l'ore beatrici.   8
    O immenso Sol, che co' be' raggi puoi
alma scura mortal far bella e diva
e trarl'in Cielo a più beata parte,   11
    se prego odi mortal giusto tra noi,
fa' che il caro desir mio giunga a riva,
anzi che le sia trônco arbore o sarte.   14

A 21

    Mentre di voi con Amor parlo o scrivo,
s'erge l'alma e la mente in tant'altezza,
colm'ambe di ineffabile dolcezza,
che ratta al terzo Ciel beata arrivo;   4
    ivi scorgo nel ver, quantunque a schivo
tener si deve quel che il vulgo apprezza,
che la virtute ornar con la grandezza
m'insegnate pur voi, spirito divo.   8
    Ma poi ch'io torno al mio misero stato,
dove superba l'orgogliosa fronte
Fortuna scopre ne' miei certi danni,   11
    vedo al fin senza voi, mio lume amato,
di Fetonte l'ardir, d'Icaro i vanni
avere, secco lauro in vivo fonte.   14

A 25

    Com'elitropio al sol, sempre mi giro
a voi, luce gentil de gli occhi miei,
nè d'altra vista l'alma o 'l cor potrei
pascer già mai, dovunque i' vado o miro.   4

A 20 (B 5, C 5)

How many sweet thoughts, high and happy,
are kindling now in the beautiful fire which
gives nourishment to the heart, full of high hope
of drawing immortal fruit from its roots!   4
        Today I see the fields appear
glad and sunny, and to my hopes the sky
becomes clear and serene beyond the usual way,
to make blessed the hours of my life.   8
        O immense Sun, which with your lovely rays
can make a dark and mortal soul beautiful and divine,
and draw it to a more blessed part in Heaven,   11
        if you hear a just prayer among us mortals,
let my dear desire come to shore
before the mast or ropes are broken off.   14

A 21

        While I speak or write of you with great Love,
my soul and mind rise to so great a height,
both filled with indescribable sweetness,
that I swiftly arrive at the third Heaven.   4
        There I perceive in truth how one should scorn
what the common people dare to prize,
for you, divine spirit, indeed teach me
to adorn virtue with greatness.   8
        But then as I return to my misery,
where haughty Fortune manifests
her proud brow to my certain harm,   11
        I see finally that without you, my beloved light,
I have the daring of Phaeton,[3] the wings of Icarus,[4]
and dry laurels in a living fountain.   14

A 25

        As a sunflower to the sun, forever do I turn
to you, kindly light of my eyes:
on no other sight could my soul or heart
ever feed, wherever I go or gaze.   4

Per voi m'accendo, in voi sola respiro,
nè se volessi ben, fuggir vorrei
gli ardenti lampi a me sì dolci e rei,
che la strada a ben far sempre m'aprîro.   8
 Così l'alta Cagion, che prima diede
a le cose create ordine e stato,
dispose a voi il mio core e la mia fede;   11
  così poteste voi, lume beato,
mirar quel che mortal occhio non vede,
in quell'alto pensier ch'al cor m'è nato.   14

A 28 (B 38, C 49). MADRIGALE

 Era il mio Sol venuto al mio languire,
più che mai bello in sonno a consolarme,
che, vinto da pietà del mio martire,
mi dicea con parole
rare nel mondo o sole: 5
—Perché sì mesta fra' sospiri e 'l pianto
tutta la verde etade,
senz'aver mai di voi stessa pietade,
vi consumate tanto?
Deh prendete, mia vita, omai conforto;   10
volgete il pianto in amoroso riso!—
E appressandomi il viso
mi porse infra rubin due fresche rose,
non mai ne l'odorifero orïente
viste più belle o lassù in Paradiso;   15
in cui soavità tanta il Ciel pose,
che altra maggior fra noi qui non si sente;
la cui sì bella vista
e 'l disusato odore
tornò subito al core   20
la smarrit'alma sconsolata e trista:
cose ch'a pena in Ciel veder si ponno.
Deh, perché non fu eterno un sì bel sonno?

A 29

 Se l'alto essempio sol del valor vostro
ha tal forza, mio Sol, che l'alma tira

For you I blaze, in you only do I breathe;
great though the want, I would not wish to flee
your ardent beams, to me so sweet and cruel,
forever showing me the path to virtue.   8
    Thus the high Cause, which first gave
to things created order and estate,
disposed to you my heart and my fidelity.   11
    Thus would that you, O blessed Light,
could so behold what mortal eye sees not:
within my heart, the birth of lofty thoughts.   14

A 28 (B 38, C 49). MADRIGAL

    My Sun had come to my languishing,
more beautiful than ever, to comfort me in my sleep,
and he, vanquished by pity for my martyrdom,
said to me with words
rare or unparalleled in the world: 5
"Why do you consume yourself so much,
so sorrowfully, among sighs and tears
all your green years,
without ever taking pity on yourself?
Here, my life, take comfort at last;   10
turn your tears into loving laughter!"
And drawing his face near me
he placed between my ruby lips two fresh roses,
never in the sweet smelling East,
nor high above in Paradise, were seen more lovely.   15
Heaven put there so fine a softness,
that no greater is felt among us;
whose so beautiful sight
and the extraordinary scent
brought my lost soul,   20
disconsolate and sad, immediately back to my heart.
These are things that hardly can be seen in Heaven.
Alas, why was such a lovely dream not eternal?

A 29

    If the lofty example of your worth
has such power, my Sun, that it draws the soul

al divin lume suo, mentre ella il mira,
tal che sprezzar gli fa le gemme e l'ostro,   4
    che fòra il santo aiuto, se dal nostro
aere quest'alma al Ciel ond'ella aspira
alzerà col bel raggio ch'in voi spira,
su dal divino e sempiterno choistro?   8
    Alma reale, in cui si vede quanta
virtù risplende dal mar Indo al Mauro,
guid'il Sol nostro il piè, du' l'alma accese,   11
    qual sotto l'ombra glorïosa e santa
di voi cerca trovar quel bel tesauro
ch'è lunge a quel che sempre il vulgo intese.   14

A 33

    Voi, mia fidata e rilucente stella,
tra le più care Idee l'alma Natura
scegliendo, per mill'anni ogn'altra oscura
lasciò per non formar cosa più bella.   4
    Dentr'al vostro splendor si vede quella
vera virtù ch'a Morte il nome fura,
dinanzi al cui santo apparir non dura
vil nebbia o lume di minor facella.   8
    In voi mostrâro, il Ciel, Natura, e Dio
tutta lor possa, onde nel primo assalto
mi transformai, da quel ch'esser solio.   11
    Ma ne ringrazio Amore e 'l desir mio,
poiché mi strinse a sospirar tant'alto,
ch'ogni basso pensier posi in oblio.   14

A 34 (B 16, C 21). MADRIGALE

    Smarrissi il cor, ghiacciossi il sangue quando,
dipinto di pietà, l'almo mio Sole
udii, con un sospiro:—O mio sostegno—,
dirmi con dolci ed umili parole:
—mesto men vo, ma 'l cor ti lascio in pegno—.   5
In questo, l'aspro suo dolore accolto
sfogò per gli occhi, e 'mpallidì il bel volto.
Quel ch'io divenni allor, sasselo Amore,

to her divine light while she gazes at it,
and so she becomes scornful of gems and Tyrian purple;   4
     what will our salvation be, if from the earth
it will raise this soul to heaven to which she aspires,
with the lovely ray which springs forth from you
there, from the divine and everlasting cloister?   8
     Majestic soul, in which we see as much virtue
as glitters from the Indus to the Mauritanian Sea,[5]
may our Sun guide us where he inflamed the soul,   11
     as under your glorious and holy shade
he seeks to find that lovely treasure
so distant from the hopes of the common people.   14

A 33

     You, my trustworthy and glittering star,
that noble Nature chose among the dearest Ideas,
for a thousand years leaving every other one
in darknesss so as not to form a more beautiful thing,   4
     within your splendor can be seen
that true virtue which steals the name from Death,
before whose sacred appearance there does not last
ignoble haze or light of a lesser torch.   8
     In you, Heaven, Nature, and God showed
all their might: thus at the first assault
I was transformed from what I once was.   11
     But I give thanks to Love and my desire,
since they forced me to yearn so high that
every low thought I placed in forgetfulness.   14

A 34 (B 16, C 21). MADRIGAL

     My heart went astray, my blood turned to ice, when
painted with pity, I heard my beloved Sun
with sweet and humble words
tell me, and with a sigh, "O my support,
sadly I go, but I leave you my heart as a pledge."   5
His eyes then wept, and he surrendered
to the bitter grief, and became pale.
What I became then, Love only knows,

e sallo ancora ogn'invescato core,
che quasi morta, in voce rotta e frale,
a gran pena formai:—Signor mio, vale!—   11
E più non potei dire,
ché mi senti' morire.

A 35 (B 18, C 23)

    Fera son io di quest'ombroso loco,
che vo con la saetta in mezzo il core,
fuggendo, lassa, il fin del mio dolore,
e cerco chi mi strugge a poco a poco;   4
    e, com'augel che fra le penne il foco
si sent'appresso, ond'ei volando fore
del dolce nido suo, mentre l'ardore
fugge, con l'ali più raccende il foco,   8
    tal io, fra queste frondi a l'aura estiva,
con l'ali del desio volando in alto,
cerco il foco fuggir, che meco porto.   11
    Ma, quanto vado più di riva in riva
per fuggir il mio mal, con fiero assalto
lunga morte procaccio al viver corto.   14

A 37 (B 36, C 52)

    L'aura gentil, che mormorando torna,
ornando i prati di novelli fiori,
spargendo da lontan soavi odori,
le rive e' colli di be' rami adorna.   4
    Né 'l bel lume del ciel oltra soggiorna
a far noti di sé gli antichi onori;
cantan gli augelli i lor felici amori
ed ogni cosa allegra omai ritorna.   8
    Ma da me, lassa, un lagrimoso verno
non parte mai, ché, lunge al mio bel Sole,
lo provo ognor ne l'amoroso inferno;   11
    né trovo scampo a le mie doglie sole,
ché sì fero è 'l martir nel core interno,
che Tempo né Ragion frenar lo puole.   14

and every entangled heart knows it well:
that nearly dead, with a voice broken and frail,
with great sorrow I formed, "My lord, farewell!"   11
And more I could not say
for I felt myself die.

A 35 (B 18, C 23)

A wild beast am I of this shady place,
and I go with an arrow in the center of my heart,
fleeing, alas, the end of my grief and pain,
yet I seek him who bit by bit destroys me;   4
    and, as a bird who among his feathers
feels the fire, and flying out of his sweet nest,
while he flees the fierce, impetuous heat,
he fans, with his wings, the hot fire more;   8
    so I, among these branches in the summer breeze,
with wings of desire flying up high,
seek to flee the fire, which I bear in me.   11
    But, as much as I go from here to there,
to flee my evil curse with fierce assault,
a long death do I gain for my short life.   14

A 37 (B 36, C 52)

The gentle breeze which murmuring returns,
adorning the meadows with spring flowers
sprinkling from afar those sweet smells,
brightens the banks and hills with colorful boughs.   4
    Nor does the light of heaven linger
to make the ancient glory apparent;
the birds sing their happy, serene loves
and everything by now returns to joy.   8
    But for me, alas, a tear-filled winter
never departs, because far from my beautiful Sun,
I feel it always in the lovelorn hell;   11
    nor do I find escape from my lonely sorrows
because so wild is the martyrdom in my heart
that neither Time nor Reason can suppress it.   14

A 38 (B 17, C 22). CANZONE

Quant'è fallace e vario il nostro corso
e come a' be' desir volgon le stelle
contrario il tempo, ch'al pensier si cela.
    Ahi, quanto il mio disegno oggi trascorso
vedo da quel, che l'alte voglie e belle
aveano ordito alla mia nobil tela!   6
    Libera credev'io poter la vela
ferma tener de la mia ricca nave,
ed aver l'aure a' miei pensier seconde;
lassa, che sotto l'onde
la speme è gita, ed a giogo aspro e grave
l'alma mia quiete libera e soave.   12

    Ma non può nocchier saggio o guerrier forte,
senza fidata guida o le fort'armi,
contrastare al nemico od a gli scogli;
    così non poss'io gir contra ria sorte
cieca, e senza il mio Sol dritta guidarme,
e col nudo voler frenar suo' orgogli;   18
    né posso far ancor ch'io non mi dogli
de l'empia e vïolenta mia Fortuna,
che mi diede e ritolse in un sol giorno
quel Sol, che d'ogni intorno
fe' l'aër lieto, or fa mia mente bruna;
ch'or foss'io spenta al latte ed alla cuna!   24

    Ma di me stessa ho da dolermi,
ché per troppo mirar perdei la luce
per cui veder potea gli eterni campi;
    or piango e grido, e co' pie' lassi e 'nfermi
cerco guidarla ancor là 've riluce,
né sentier trovo che dal duol mi scampi.   30
    Ma s'avvien pur che quei beati lampi
riveda, e le divine alte promesse
sian stabilite in Ciel per mio destino,
per lungo, alto camino
seguirò l'orme sue ne l'alme impresse,
perché più chiara ad alto fin m'appresse.   36

A 38 (B 17, C 22). SONG

How greatly deceptive and various is the course of our life,
and how the stars turn time, which is hidden
from our planning, against our fond desires!
    And, oh, how greatly do I see my own design,
that I had mounted in great faith, and fine,
upon my noble loom ruined today and in shreds.   6
    I had believed that I could hold
firm and steady the free sail of my rich ship
and have the winds propitious to my plans.
But no, for under the waves
my hopes have gone; and my blessed peace of mind,
once sweet and free, under a rough and heavy yoke.   12

    But neither wise helmsman, nor strong warrior,
without a trustworthy guide or powerful weapons,
can compete against the enemy or the rocks of the sea:
    so I cannot move against my evil fate,
blind as I am, and without my Sun cannot steer straight,
and with my naked will alone rein in fate's pride;   18
    nor yet can I keep from lamenting
about that wicked, violent destiny of mine,
which gave and in a single day took back
that Sun, which everywhere he turned
made the air bright but now makes my mind dark;
oh, that I were dead now in my cradle, a milk-fed babe!   24

    But of myself alone I must complain:
I stared too long, that is how I lost the light
which helped me see the eternal fields.
    Now weeping and wailing, on weary feet and weak
I attempt to follow it still to where it shines,
yet find no path that will deliver me from pain.   30
    But if ever I should see those blessed lights
again, and if divine and fair decrees
are pledged in Heaven for my good fate,
on the long high road
I will follow his footsteps sealed upon my soul,
so that more clearly I may approach my lofty goal.   36

Lassa, che parlo? Or se l'eterne rote
ferme non stanno, ma in contrario giro
volgon le stelle, e spesso a' nostri danni,
        quai promesse mortal, stabili, immote
trovar potransi, e lunge ogni martiro
aver nel lungo trapassar de gli anni?   42
        Pur si deono schivare i certi danni,
e volger sempre a chiaro e divin segno,
con verissimi essempî, ogni consiglio.
Cade, qual rosa o giglio,
ogni nostro diletto e gran disegno,
se da salda virtù non ha sostegno.   48

        Dunque per l'orme di virtude intendo
seguir mia stella, ch'a bel fin mi scorge,
ogni basso pensier posto in oblio;
        né d'invidia o minacce il cor temendo,
lasserò il bel, che da lontan mi scorge,
per gli scogli contrarî al desir mio.   54
        Tornin dunque i be' lumi, e 'l tempo rio
scaccin da l'onde, e con dolce aura e lieta
drizzin le vele al desïato porto,
anzi che sia risorto
il nuovo tempo, o 'l lucido pianeta
torni alla libra con sua giusta meta.   60

        Canzon, chi tua ragion facesse oscura,
dille che non n'hai cura,
perché tosto averai chi dal bel velo
ti disciorrà, dov'io ti chiudo e celo.   64

A 40

        Viva mia bella e dolce calamita,
che partendo con sì mirabil modo
stringeste l'alma in quel tenace nodo
ch'a voi sol la terrà più sempre unita,   4
        non è la mente mia da voi smarrita,
se ben lontana a voi, di voi non godo
l'amata vista; anzi via più sempr'odo

Alas, what am I saying? Now if the eternal wheels
will not stand still, and if against their proper way
the stars turn them, and often to our pain:
 what pledge of permanence stable and unmoved
can we find on earth, or how can we keep torment
distant from us in the long passing of the years?   42
 Yet certain pain is much to be avoided,
and we must always turn our every counsel
to bright and heavenly goals, based on true example.
Gone, like the rose or the lily,
are all our pleasures and our great plans at last,
unless with good and steady strength we hold them fast. 48

 Thus I intend along the path of strength and virtue
to follow my star that guides me to a lovely goal,
with all lowly thoughts consigned to oblivion;
 nor shall my heart fear envy or threat,
nor will I give up the beauty that guides me from afar
past the rocks that are contrary to my desire.   54
 So let the lovely lights return, let them drive the storms
out of the waves, and with sweet breeze and fair
set the sails straight for the port I seek,
before the new age
can arise, or the bright shining planet
can return to Libra[6] and its just destination.   60

 Song, if anyone should find your meaning obscure,
tell them that you do not mind;
for soon someone will come and free you
from the lovely veil in which I conceal and enclose you. 64

A 40

 My dear, beautiful, and sweet magnet,
you who, leaving in such a marvelous way,
drew my soul into that firm knot which to you
alone will keep it ever more united,   4
 my mind has not strayed from you,
although far from you; of you I do not enjoy
the beloved sight: nay, I hear ever more

da voi chiamarmi ove il desio m'invita.   8

    Per voi sì ricco laccio Amor m'avinse
di salda e pura fede al collo intorno,
ch'ogn'altra umil catena sdegna il core.   11

    Sciols'ogni nodo quando questo strinse,
e ruppe l'arco con vittoria il giorno
ch'in me fe' eterno l'ultimo suo ardore.   14

A 41

    Quel lume di virtù ch'oggi m'ha tolto
il Cielo, e 'l ragionar cortese e santo
ond'appagar soleva il grave pianto,
lunge ora stassi in bei pensieri accolto;   4

    ben vede da lontan dentro il mio volto
il cor che ne portò nel suo bel manto,
e dice:—Or fossi col desir mio a canto
a chi ne l'alma dolcemente ascolto!—   8

    Io, ch'odo le dolcissime parole,
dico:—Deh, foss'io pur, lume beato,
con voi, dove tant'alto il pensier ergo!—   11

    Così soavemente par che invole
l'alma ciascun da sè, chè ne l'Amato
cerca di star, cangiando il proprio albergo.   14

A 43

    Quando fia 'l dì ch'io vi riveggia ed oda,
dolce del cor mio nudrimento ed esca,
e, col foco gentil che m'arde e 'nvesca,
la viva luce de' begli occhi goda?   4

    Lassa, ch'io temo che nel cor si roda
prima lo spirto, che di me v'incresca,
tanto martir ne l'anima rinfresca
quel forte laccio che mi stringe e annoda.   8

    Ma se pur ritornar vedessi apparo
co' miei dolci desiri i pensier vostri,
misurata allegrezza i' non avrei.   11

    Deh perchè tanto, empio Destino avaro,
lunghe mi fai con gli amorosi inchiostri
quello che n'ha portati i pensier miei?   14

your calling me where desire invites me. 8
    For you Love bound me with such rich rope
of firm and pure faith around my neck
that every other lowly chain the heart disdains. 11
    It undid every knot when it tightened this one,
and broke the bow with victory, the day
that it made his final passion eternal in me. 14

A 41

    That light of virtue which today the Heavens
have taken from me, and the kindly, soulful speech
that used to quiet my mournful weeping,
are gathered in memory now as lovely thoughts; 4
    for he sees, from a distance, within my face
the heart he carried in his beautiful breast,
and he says, "If only I were now with my desire,
near the one whose voice I sweetly hear in my soul!" 8
    I who hear these sweetest words
say, "O my blessed light, would I were also
with you, where I raise so high my thoughts!" 11
    Thus, it seems that the soul gently steals
each of us from ourselves, and changes over
its dwelling place and tries to lodge in the Beloved. 14

A 43

    When will it be that I may see and hear you again,
sweet sustenance and bait of my heart,
and, with the gentle fire that burns and entices my love,
shall I enjoy the bright light of your beautiful eyes? 4
    Alas, for I fear that my spirit will
wear away before you will have pity on me,
so great is the martyrdom which that strong knot
which tightens and binds me restores in my soul. 8
    But even if I should see your thoughts
returning again, together with my sweet desires,
my joy would not be measured as complete. 11
    Alas, why do you, cruel and pitiless Destiny,
keep so far from me the one who with my lovesome
letters carried away my thoughts of him? 14

A 44. SESTINA

Freschi, ombrosi, fioriti e verdi colli,
dov'or si siede dolcemente a l'ombra
quello ch'ovunque va riporta il giorno,
e movendo i be' pie' fra la fresch'erba
fa, dove tocca, il terren lieto e verde;
deh foss'io pianta in voi di lauro o mirto!   6

Io mi torrei di star dentro ad un mirto
o 'n verde lauro in cima a gli alti colli,
sol per vederlo quando entro il bel verde
sen viene a diportar soletto a l'ombra,
ov'alcun fior non è sì bello in erba,
che non s'inchini a lui la notte e 'l giorno.   12

Lassa, quando sperar debb'io quel giorno,
ch'a la dolce ombra d'un bel verde mirto
cogliendo seco fiori, or frondi, or erba,
mi senta dir da lui, fra lieti colli
in un bel prato assisa alla dolce ombra:
—Meco sempre starai fin ch'io sia verde—.   18

Non sentii fiamma ne l'età più verde,
e lieta andava più di giorno in giorno
fuggendo Amor per l'alte selve a l'ombra,
cercando intorno a' fonti, edera e mirto,
quando voce udii dir da gli alti colli;
—Ferma i be' passi qui tra' fiori e l'erba—.   24

Qual si fe' Glauco nel gustar de l'erba,
sentii mutarmi allor tra l'erba verde,
e trarmi da un desio che per i colli
mi fe' seguir il mio bel Sol quel giorno,
che m'arde or sì, che non di lauro o mirto
potrà giovarmi o de la notte l'ombra.   30

Nulla mi può da lui far scudo od ombra,
nè per forza d'incanto o virtù d'erba;
sannolo i campi, i poggi, ogn'antro e mirto.
Ma una speranza sol mi mantien verde
dicendo:—Tosto ancor vedrai quel giorno
che tornerà il tuo Sol da' lieti colli—.   36

Deh qual giorno sarà ch'a la dolce ombra
de' colli seco qui fra la fresch'erba
corona tesserò di lauro o mirto?   39

A 44. SESTINA

Fresh, shady, flowering and green hills,
where now he sweetly sits in the shade:
he who wherever he goes brings back the day,
and moving his lovely feet in the fresh grass,
where he touches, makes the land happy and green:
oh, would that were I a plant in you, a laurel or myrtle!   6

    I would accept to dwell within a myrtle
or in a green laurel on top of the high hills,
just to see him when, in the beautiful green,
he comes all alone to play in the shade,
where the flowers are not so lovely in the grass
that they do not bow to him night and day.   12

    Alas, when must I hope for that day,
when to the sweet shade of a lovely green myrtle
gathering to himself flowers, now leaves, now grass,
I will hear him say to me, in the happy hills,
in a lovely meadow, seated in the sweet shade,
"You will always stay with me, as long as I am green."   18

    I did not feel the flame in my years more green,
and, content, I used to go day by day
fleeing Love through the high forests in the shade,
seeking around the springs, both ivy and myrtle,
until I heard a voice saying from the high hills,
"Stop your lovely steps here, among the flowers and grass."   24

    Just as Glaucus[7] did, in his tasting of the herbs,
I felt myself change then, in the grass so green,
and was drawn by a desire that along the hills
made me follow my beautiful Sun that day,
which now burns me so, that neither laurel nor myrtle
can be of use to me, nor of the night, the shade.   30

    Against him, nothing can offer me shield or shade,
neither by power of enchantment or healing herbs;
even the fields know this, the hills, every cave and myrtle.
But one hope only keeps me green,
saying, "Soon now you will see that day
when your Sun will return from the happy hills."   36

    Ah, what day will it be, when in the sweet shade
of the hills, with him among the fresh grass,
I will weave a crown of laurel or myrtle?[8]   39

A 46

Sì chiara è la mia fé, sì chiaro il foco
dell'acceso cor mio, viva mia luce,
e di tanta bellezza a l'alma luce,
ch'oscurar nol pò mai più chiaro foco.   4
    Questo a l'alta cagion dov'io m'infoco,
guida il pensier ognor con la sua luce,
a mirar la beltà di quella luce,
che m'arde e nutre del celeste foco.   8
    Così l'alma in voi stassi, e nel mio petto
l'imagin vostra ancor sì bella siede,
ch'indi non la pò trar forza né ingegno: 11
    ed ha già dodici anni che nel petto
onesta e bella sopr'ogn'altra siede,
e di farvela eterna ancor m'ingegno.   14

A 48

    Quant'ho più da lontan l'aspetto vostro,
più lo sento ne l'alma a parte a parte
scolpito e vivo, e 'n ciascheduna parte
insignorirsi del mortal suo chiostro;   4
    né poggio, sasso, o valle Amor m'ha môstro
fin dove il Serchio arriva e donde parte,
ch'io non vi veda con mirabil arte
scritto il nome ch'adorna il secol nostro.   8
    Così potesse del mio amor far fede
il cor che nel partir vi lassai in pegno,
ond'ugual fosse amor sempre tra noi,   11
    ché sì nel petto il bel nodo mi sede,
ch'unqua nol cangerà tempo né sdegno,
ma sempre v'amerò viva e dapoi.   14

A 53

    L'intensa vostra pena e 'l mio dolore,
il tardar lungo e mia fallace speme,
e quel ch'a dire il cor più m'ange e preme,
maligne stelle mi mostraron fore,   4

A 46

So bright is my faith, so bright the fire
of my burning heart, my living light,
that it illuminates my soul with such a beauty
that a brighter fire can never obscure it.   4
This, to the high cause where I am set on fire,
still leads my thought with its light
to admire the beauty of that light
that burns and feeds me with the heavenly fire.   8
Thus my soul resides in you, and in my breast
your image is ever so beautifully seated,
that it cannot be dislodged by either wits or force: 11
and already it is twelve years that in my breast
your gracious image is, above all others, seated,
and to make it eternal is still my only desire.   14

A 48

The more distant your image is from me,
the more I feel it in my soul, thoroughly
engraved and alive, and in every part
it takes possession of its mortal cloister.   4
Love has shown me neither hill, rock, nor valley,
where the Serchio River⁹ ends or where it begins,
that I do not see, written with amazing art,
the name which adorns our century.   8
If only my heart, which I left you in pledge
of my affection, could bear witness to my love,
so that love would always be equal between us;   11
because in my breast the tight knot is so lodged
that neither time nor scorn will ever change it,
for I will always love you, living and beyond.   14

A 53

Your intense suffering and my sorrow,
the long delay and my false hope, and what
my heart needs to say afflict and trouble me;
malicious stars displayed this to me,   4

pria che quell'infelici ed ultim'ore,
in ch'io sperai d'ogni mia gloria il seme,
fosser giunte, e 'l piacer con l'alma insieme
togliessero al desir ch'avea nel core;   8
    né molto andò ch'io vidi il ver più espresso
ne' vostri inchiostri, e 'l duol che meco porto
e sempre avrò fin ch'io vi veda appresso.   11
    Facci omai, Delia, il termine sia corto
del mio vano sperar, sì che con esso
la vostra luce i' mi ritragga in porto.   14

A 55

    Qual gioia in Ciel, su, l'anime beate
dinanzi a Dio nel bel perpetuo giorno
sentono, stando al divin foco intorno,
quasi ardenti faville innamorate,   4
    tal io sentiva in quelle luci amate
che fêro al sol più volte invidia e scorno,
mentre facevan meco alto soggiorno
piene di grazia tutte e di pietate;   8
    quali, ognor più di lumi ardenti accese,
parean dirmi:—Cor mio perchè partito
ti sei da me, s'io senza te non vivo?—   11
    Ond'io rispondo allora:—Altro vi rese
di me l'affetto, onde da voi gradito
dev'esser più l'amato in ch'io m'avvivo.—   14

A 57 (C 30)

    Lassa, non so qual ombra il mio bel Sole
m'asconda e vieti il suo dolce ritorno,
per cui sì chiaro e lieto ogni mio giorno
solea mostrarsi più ch'altro non suole.   4
    Io pur ascolto e non odo parole
che mi facciano noto il suo soggiorno,
e temo, e spero: ognor dentro e d'intorno
lo chiama l'alma che per lui si duole.   8
    Lassa, dove son or que' chiari lumi,
che mi mostrâr con be' vestigi santi

before those unhappy and last hours, in which
I hoped the seed of every glory of mine had arrived,
took away instead both pleasure and soul
from the desire that I had in my heart;   8
    nor was it long after that I saw the truth expressed
in your letters, and the sorrow that I bear with me
and will always have, until I see you near me.   11
    Now, Delia,[10] my Moon, shorten the time
of my vain hope, so that with the time shortened,
I may carry your light back into my harbor.   14

A 55

    Such joy in Heaven as the blessed souls feel
before God in the glorious everlasting day,
as they arc around the divine fire
like blazing sparks that have fallen in love,   4
    the same joy I felt in those beloved eyes
that often brought envy and scorn to the sun,
while they were living with me on high
all full of mercifulness and of grace,   8
    which, more and more lit up by burning lights,
appeared to tell me: "My heart, why did you
leave me, since I cannot live without you?"   11
    So now I answer, "Your affection for me
changed you so much; therefore you should appreciate
the more the loved one in whom I live."   14

A 57 (C 30)

    Alas, I know not what shade hides my lovely Sun
from me and forbids his sweet return,
whereby every day of mine once appeared
so clear and happy that the other days were shamed.   4
    I listen carefully and do not hear the words
that make known to me his place of lodging,
and I fear, and I hope: always within and around,
the soul that grieves for him calls to him.   8
    Alas, where are they now, those clear eyes
that showed me in that lovely holy path

di gir al Ciel con glorïosi passi?   11
     Dove son or gli altissimi costumi?
Lassa, non so: so ben ch'in doglie e pianti
gli occhi e l'alma a tutt'ore ardendo stassi.   14

A 60 (B 15, C 20). MADRIGALE

     Da la più bella mano
ch'occhio dritto mortal vedesse mai
soavemente il cor senti' legarme,
e dalla pura neve
stringer le sparse fiamme in spazio breve.   5
O benedette l'ore
ch'al cor mandaron tant'alta dolcezza!
O fortunato ardore,
cui l'alma più ch'ogn'altro bene apprezza!
Quando sarà quel giorno,
ch'io faccia a tanto ben già mai ritorno?   11

A 64

     Beata l'alma che beando altrui,
fuggendo del suo albergo giunse a riva,
e de l'aura vital d'altrui nodriva
se stessa tal, che si fea viva in dui.   4
     Lo spirito d'Amor, vagando, a cui
porgea l'ardire, a cui la mente schiva
per soverchio timor, talor gli univa
in un stesso voler, caro per lui.   8
     O felice ora, o fortunato giorno,
che in sì bella unïon l'alto concento
s'udì, che fa parer dolce la Morte.   11
     Quanto n'avrebbe avuto invidia e scorno
chi fosse stato a rimirare intento
de' due cari fedel sì lieta sorte!   14

A 65

     Alma donna real, pompa e ricchezza
di tutto il mondo, in cui l'alma Natura

the way to Heaven with radiant steps?   11
    Where are they now, his noble ways of being?
Alas, I do not know, but I know that in pain and tears,
my eyes and soul will be forever burning.   14

A 60 (B 15, C 20). MADRIGAL

    By the most beautiful hand
that a fair mortal eye ever might see,
softly I felt my heart being bound,
and by the purest snow
I felt the widespread flames being contained rapidly.   5
Oh, blessed be the hours
which sent so fine a sweetness to my heart!
Oh, happy the burning passion
that the soul values more than any other good!
When will that day ever come
that I may ever return to so much good?   11

A 64

    Blessed be the soul which, glorifying another
and fleeing its shelter, arrived on shore,
and with the living breath of another it nourished
itself, so that it was made alive in two souls.   4
    The spirit of Love, wandering afar
accompanied by courage, Love whom the mind
avoids from too much fear, would join them
at times, in one common will, dear to him.   8
    Oh, happy hour, oh, lucky day,
when in such a fine union the high harmony
was heard, making even Death seem sweet.   11
    Whoever could have gazed intently
would have had such envy and shame
at seeing such a glad fate for those dear faithful ones.   14

A 65

    Noble, regal woman, the pomp and richness
of the whole world, in whom noble Nature

pose tant'altamente ogni sua cura,
per non formar dipoi maggior bellezza,   4
   quella vostra ineffabile dolcezza,
ch'a discioglier la lingua or m'assecura,
scusi il desio, se de l'ardente e pura
vostra virtù cerca veder l'altezza;   8
   ché se norma celeste a chi più intende
sete, ché solo in voi si vede quanta
virtù risplende dal mar Indo al Mauro,   11
   ben poss'io creder che quant'alta ascende
la debbol vista mia fra tanta e tanta
nebbia, a me sia scorta lodata e vera.   14

A 66. CANZONE

   In un verde boschetto
a la dolce aura estiva
vidi due innamorati almi pastori
   soli andar con diletto
sopr'una verde riva,
cantando lieti i lor felici amori;   6
   indi fra l'erbe e' fiori
un di lor, ch'avea nome
Androgeo, prese a dire,
pieno d'alto desire:
—Deh, foss'or qui fra noi con l'auree chiome
la bella amata Ninfa,
discinta e scalza in questa chiara linfa!—   13

   A cui rispose Infido,
che così si chiamava
l'altro pastor, che di lei seco ardea:
   —Di te, folle, mi rido,
ch'un tal desio t'aggrava
d'ella, che sola in terra è la mia dea!—   19
   Ond'egli allor dicea:
—Sacrato Pan, che vedi
lo mio sincero affetto,
mostra qual abbia eletto
di noi a lei il Cielo, ond'a l'un l'altro cedi;

placed so highly every concern of hers,
so that she would not fashion any greater beauty;   4
     that indescribable sweetness of yours
that loosens my tongue now assures me
that I will be excused if I try to see the heights
of your so ardent and pure virtue: 8
     for you are a heavenly ideal for those
who understand, because only in you one sees
how much virtue shines from the Indus Sea to the Mauritanian,[11]   11
     so I believe indeed that insofar as my weak sight
can rise clear from such a deep, dark fog,
you are the guide to me, praised and true.   14

A 66. SONG

     In a green woodland
in the sweet summer breezes
I saw two noble shepherds, in love,
     walking alone with pleasure
by a green riverbank,
singing joyously of their happy loves.   6
     Whereupon among the grass and flowers
one of them, whose name was
Androgeo,[12] began to say,
full of lofty desire,
"Oh, would that the beautiful and beloved Nymph
were now with us, barefoot and lovely,
with golden hair, among these clear waters."   13

     And to him there answered Unfaithful,
as the other shepherd was named,
who was set ablaze and burned for her,
     "I laugh at you, foolish man,
that such a desire for her wounds you,
for she alone on the earth is my goddess!"   19
     Whereupon then Androgeo said,
"Sacred Pan,[13] you who see
my true sincere affection,
show us which one the Heavens
have chosen for her, so that one may withdraw;

e, se fra queste frondi
spirto amoroso è di pietà, rispondi—.   26

    Allor da un arbuscello
nel bel fiorito Aprile
a l'Infido pastor sovra il suo grembo,
    vago, amoroso augello
con voce alma e gentile,
volando, scese in parte del suo lembo;   32
    quando da un caro nembo
subito fu coverto
il pastor Androgeo,
de la rete che feo
Vulcano allor che la sua donna certo
vid'al suo amante in braccio,
onde gli strinse intorno il forte laccio.   39

    Quanto di gaudio pieno
in quel felice giorno
fosse il ben nato, aventuroso amante
    del bel Lappato il seno
sallo, che d'ogn'intorno
grazie render sentio devote e sante.   45
    Ei dicea:—Sacre piante,
da le cui verdi fronde
tanto annunzio felice
de l'alma mia Fenice,
oggi è disceso in quest'ombrose sponde,
sempre vi doni il Cielo
grazie, nè mai v'offenda il caldo o 'l gelo—.   52

    Indi vicino a sera,
al caro albergo i passi
volgendo, lieto poi si dipartio;
    così la Ninfa altera
che nel suo core stassi,
venne sola a incontrar lungo il bel rio,   58
    che da un dolce desio
di lui portata, in dono
veniva a darli il core.
O che felice Amore,

and if among these green boughs
there is a loving spirit full of pity, let it respond."   26

    Then from a slender green tree
in the fine flowering April,
a beautiful love-smitten bird,
    flying over the bosom of Unfaithful,
with soft and gladsome song,
landed at his feet.   32
    Suddenly Androgeo the shepherd
was covered by a lovely misty cloud
of the net made by Vulcan
when he saw the lady of his heart
in the arms of her lover,
whereupon he bound him with the strong snare.   39

    How full of mirth
in that happy day
was the well-born, adventurous lover:
    the source of the brook Lappato[14] knows this,
who heard from all around
thanks given devoutly and piously.   45
    He said, "O sacred plants
from whose green leaves
today has come such happy news
of my noble Phoenix,
in these shady banks:
may the Heavens always give you
thanks; may neither heat nor cold ever offend you."   52

    When it was near to evening,
turning his steps to the cherished lodging,
Androgeo went happily on his way;
    then the proud Nymph,
who was in his heart,
came alone to meet him along the lovely riverbank;   58
    by a sweet desire she was
drawn to him, and as a gift
she came to give him her heart.
Oh, what a happy Love:

ond'io mi trasformai da quel ch'io sono,
facendomi di chiara
fonte, una fiamma al mondo eterna e rara.   65

    Canzon, il lor felice, alto destino,
prega devotamente
che faccia le lor voglie ognor contente.   68

A 67 (B 57, C 67)

    Donna gentil, che be' pensier tenete
sempre da queste basse cure sciolti,
come gli occhi de l'alma a Dio rivolti
nel vostro saggio e santo oprare avete,   4
    renda il Ciel largo a voi benigne e liete
le stelle ognor, nè mai da voi sian tolti
quei veri onor ch'avete in seno accolti,
per cui norma celeste al mondo sete;   8
    nè di vera amistà quel santo nodo,
ch'ambe l'anime nostre insieme cinse,
sia per lunga stagion sciolto da voi,   11
    ma sempre forte e con più caro modo
costà vi leghi, quanto qui vi strinse,
ch'io son vostra e sarò, viva e dapoi.   14

A 69 (B 25, C 36). STANZA

    Sempre sperar si deve anzi la morte
che possa tornar lieto ogni suo giorno,
però ch'un valoroso animo e forte
rend'al Tempo e Fortuna oltraggio e scorno,
nè teme il grave duol che la sua sorte
gli fa sentir per lungo, atro soggiorno;
ond'avvien poi, quando lo spera meno,
che vede il sol più chiaro e 'l ciel sereno.   8

A 70. SESTINA

    Felice sasso, ch'a sì bella pietra
sarà congiunto in ciascheduna notte,
né per forza già mai di vento o pioggia

it made me change from what I was,
transforming me from a clear fountain
into an eternal and rare flame of the world.   65

    Song of mine, pray devoutly
that their happy, high destiny
always makes their wishes come true.   68

A 67 (B 57, C 67)

    Noble lady, you who keep your lovely thoughts
forever away from these evil cares,
for you have turned the eyes of the soul
toward God in your wise and saintly work,   4
    may Heaven be kind to you and make the stars
gracious to you, and may those true honors
that you have welcomed in your heart always be yours,
for you are a divine example to the world.   8
    Nor let that saintly knot of true friendship,
which tied both our souls tightly together,
be untied by you for ages to come;   11
    but ever strong and in a more cherished way
may it tie you there, as here it did:
for I am and will be yours, now and forever.   14

A 69 (B 25, C 36). STANZA

    One always has to hope until death
that every day may become joyful,
seeing that a worthy and strong spirit
repays Time and Fortune with outrage and scorn,
nor should we fear the heavy grief that our fortune
makes us feel for a long, bitter time;
for it happens then, when we hope for it least,
that we see the sun more clear and the sky serene.   8

A 70. SESTINA

    Happy rock, that to such a beautiful stone
will be joined each and every night,
nor ever by the force of wind or rain

da radice fia svelto, in fin che il sole
meni a l'occaso il suo ultimo giorno
e sia coperto in fredda terra a l'ombra.   6

    Ma io, fuggendo il caldo giorno, a l'ombra
a mezzo il tempo andai di questa pietra,
dove fui chiusa e mai non vidi il giorno,
ma spesse nubi dentro a la sua notte,
fin che m'apparve un raggio poi di Sole
che scoperse d'intorno ogni ombra e pioggia.   12

    Sparsi per gli occhi allor più larga pioggia,
e comincia' a pregar quella chius'ombra
ch'a sé lasciasse alquanto entrare il sole,
ch'io starei fissa in lei qual taglio in pietra;
ma quella, dura più di notte in notte,
non volle mai veder sua luce un giorno.   18

    Onde turbato il mio tranquillo giorno,
dissi:—Se molle mai non fia per pioggia
la tua durezza, almen da la tua notte
fammi uscir fuora, o fammi terra od ombra—.
Ma ella, che fu sempre dur pietra,
giù da l'altezza sua mi trasse al Sole.   24

    Non così incende le campagne il sole,
com'io d'ira e d'orrore arsi quel giorno,
e per gran doglia al fin diventai pietra;
che non curo del Ciel più vento o pioggia,
né della lunga notte la fredd'ombra,
anzi cerco star sempre ove sia notte.   30

    Ma vedrò prima il fin d'ogni mia notte
e sorger fuor de l'occidente il sole,
ch'io non ritenga ancor quella fredd'ombra
nel cor di pietra, ove il fatal suo giorno
la circunscrisse contra a vento e pioggia
e a sé mi trasse come ferro pietra.   36

    Pietra fredd'aspra e dura, ogni tua notte
allumi il giorno, fin ch'arrivi il sole
che ti copra di terra, e pioggia, a l'ombra.   39

A 72 (C 73)

    Quando formò di voi la bella figlia,
Cangenna mia gentil, l'alma Natura

from its root will be uprooted, until the sun
sets in the west on its last day,
and the earth is covered in cold in the shade.　　　　　　　　　　　6

　　But, fleeing the hot day, to the shade
I went, in the noontime, of this stone,
where I was enclosed and never saw the day,
but dense clouds were within its night,
until finally there appeared to me a ray of the Sun
that all around uncovered every shade and rain.　　　　　　　　　12

　　There flowed from my eyes then greater rain,
and I began to pray to that enclosed shade,
that it would permit the entrance of the sun,
that I would be fixed in shade as a cut in the stone,
but that shade which was harder night by night,
never wished to see her light by day.　　　　　　　　　　　　18

　　Whereupon disturbing my tranquil day,
"If your hardness is never softened by rain,"
I said, "at least from your night
let me come out, or let me be soil and shade."
But she, who was always a hard stone,
down from her height drew me to the Sun.　　　　　　　　　24

　　The countryside is not burned by the sun
as I burned with rage and horror that day.
and with sharp pain in the end I turned into stone;
nor do I mind the Heaven's wind or rain
or the long night's cold shade;
I even try to stay where it is always night.　　　　　　　　　30

　　But I will see the end of all my nights,
and will see, coming out of the west, the sun,
before I stop holding that cold shade
in my heart of rock, where its fated day
circumscribed it against the wind and rain
and drew me to it as iron draws rock.　　　　　　　　　　36

　　Cold, bitter, and hard rock, every night
may you enlighten the day, until the Sun arrives
that covers you with earth and rain, in the shade.　　　　　　39

A 72 (C 73)

　　When blessed Nature fashioned from you,
my gentle Cangenna,[15] your lovely daughter,

tutt'arte, ingegno, ed ogni estrema cura
pose ne' be' sembianti e ne le ciglia.   4
  Ogni maravigliosa maraviglia
restò ammirata allor fuor di misura,
quando il parto gentil, ch'ogn'altro oscura,
vide, e quel bel ch'a null'altro simiglia.   8
  Venere e Giove con benigni aspetti
si miravano in Ciel, cantando a prova
le Grazie in terra e' più felici Amori.   11
  Così a lei sempre più benigni affetti
mostrin le stelle, e 'n lei tal virtù piova,
che merti aver al mondo eterni onori.   14

A 73

  Felice lui, che gli fu dato in sorte
d'accôrre in sé quel gran valore interno
che nol potrà cangiar la state o 'l verno,
correndo il sol le sue vie lunghe e torte.   4
  Ed a bella e gentil fida consorte
compagno è fatto in saldo nodo eterno,
di cui frutto gentil, s'io ben discerno,
vedrà del suo bel seme anzi la morte.   8
  Rare volte dal Ciel congiunte insieme
vengon grazie sì rare a tant'altezza,
com'a' suoi gran pensier son giunte a paro.   11
  Sia lunga, e lieta, e colma di dolcezza
la vita loro infino a l'ore estreme,
ed ogni giorno più soave e chiaro.   14

A 77

  Or che mia dolce pace e desiata,
lieta godea ne le speranze prime
di coglier frutti e fior da l'alte cime
de' rami santi, in quei ria serpe è entrata.   4
  Ah Fortuna crudel, Fortuna ingrata,
tu mi levasti in quel pensier sublime
perché, cadendo, il cor mi roda e lime
il duol, ch'ha l'alta piaga avelenata.   8

she placed all art, every talent and care
in her beautiful appearance and form.   4
    Every marvelous marvel stood
then in admiration beyond measure
when it saw the newborn babe, which eclipses all,
and that beauty which resembles nothing else.   8
    Venus and Jove with kind faces looked at
each other in Heaven, while on earth the Graces,
along with the joyous Loves, were singing together.   11
    Thus may the stars show her their kind affection,
and in her may be poured such virtue
that she will deserve eternal honors in this world.   14

A 73

    Happy is he who was destined
to receive that great inner worth
which neither summer nor winter can change
as the sun races along its long, twisted ways.   4
    And to a lovely, gentle, faithful wife
he is made companion in a firm eternal bond,
whose delightful offspring from his beautiful seed,
if I am right, he will see before death.   8
    Rarely do so rare and so high graces
come from Heaven, bound together,
equaling the greatness of his thoughts.   11
    May their life be long and happy,
and filled with sweetness until the last hours,
and every day more pleasant and clear.   14

A 77

    Now that I may happily enjoy
my sweet and desired peace in the first hopes
of harvesting fruits and flowers from the highest
of the branches, alas, a wicked snake has entered.   4
    O cruel Fortune, O ungrateful Fortune,
you raised me in that sublime thought
so that, falling, my heart tortures me, and grief
wears me out, having embittered the deep wound.   8

Or hai fatto l'estremo di tua possa,
maligna Invidia, or la mia dolce e cara
gioia hai temprata del più amaro tòsco;   11
    or d'ogni bene hai la mia vita scossa,
or non più luce avrò serena e chiara
fin che chiaro il mio Sol non riconosco.   14

A 78 (C 17)

Empia Invidia crudel, che ne' miei danni
per cieco error così tacita entrasti,
come vilmente a' be' pensier contrasti
mentre fingi la voce, il volto, e' panni!   4
    Come pòi far che 'l tuo livor condanni
quel chiar'oprare, o lo nascondi e guasti
dinanzi al mio bel Sol, dove mandasti
lo tuo fosco venen, sì che l'appanni?   8
    Ma scoprin d'ira pur l'inique fronti
Fortuna e 'l Cielo, e con rabbiosi denti
Saturno i figli suoi sempre divori,   11
    che sempre fian più manifesti e conti
a gli occhi miei que' divin raggi ardenti,
perch'io gli renda sempre eterni onori.   14

A 81

Ohimè, dov'è or quel vago viso
e l'angelico riso, che solea
far chiara e dolce l'aura fosca e rea,
e me gustar del ben ch'è in paradiso?   4
    Ove sono i be' lumi, dove assiso
si stava Amore e' duri cuor rompea?
Ove il senno, il valore alto ch'avea,
con parlar dolce, me da me diviso?   8
    U' la virtute, il portamento altero,
l'andar celeste, i be' costumi santi,
ch'eran mia scorta in questo camin cieco?   11
    Poscia che 'l mio Destin crudele e fero
la dolce vista m'ha tolta dinanti,
lume de gli occhi miei non è più meco.   14

Now you have done the worst in your power,
malicious Envy, now that my dear, sweet joy
you have tempered with the bitterest poison.   11
    Now you have shaken off all good from my life,
now I will have no more light serene and clear
until I recognize my clear Sun.   14

A 78 (C 17)

    Cruel, wicked Envy, by blind mistake
and to my harm you entered so silently;
how basely have you clashed with my lovely thoughts
while you feign his voice, his face, and his form!   4
    How can it be that your spite should condemn
that clear life, or hide and shatter it
before my beautiful Sun, where you sent
your wicked poison, to darken it wholly?   8
    But let Fortune and Heaven uncover
their vile face of wrath, and Saturn[16] keep devouring
his sons with his mad, rabid teeth,   11
    still ever more manifest and important
to my eyes will be those divine, burning rays,
so that I may render to him eternal honor.   14

A 81

    Alas, where is that fond face now
and his angelic laughter, which used
to make clear and sweet the gloomy wicked air
and make me enjoy the good that is in Paradise?   4
    Where are the handsome eyes, where was seated
Love, who reigned and softened the hard hearts?
Where the wisdom, the high courage, which
with sweet talk had sundered me from myself?   8
    Where the virtue, the noble behavior,
the celestial gait, the handsome holy customs,
which were my escort on this blind journey?   11
    Because my cruel fierce Destiny
has taken from me the sweet sight of him,
the light of my eyes is no longer with me.   14

A 82 (B 32, C 45). CANZONE

Chiara, eterna, felice, e gentil alma,
che, fornito il tuo corso a mezzo gli anni,
volata sei fra l'anime beate,
    volgi la vista or da' superni scanni,
che mostrar mi solei sì chiara ed alma,
e mira in quanto duol l'alta pietate   6
    di te m'ha posto, e quelle luci amate
da te, colme vedrai di pianto amaro
bagnare il fido mio dolente petto,
    però ch'ogni diletto,
ogni mia gioia e viver dolce e caro
tolto mi fu quando da me partita
facesti, fida mia celeste scorta.
Da indi in qua non passo un'ora sola
mai senza pianto, né altro mi consola
se non la speme sol che mi conforta,
    diva mia bella, ardente calamita,
di rivedersi in Cielo a miglior vita;
però che senza te rinchiusa e spenta,
esser non posso qui mai più contenta.   20

    Più grave doglia o fiero, orribil caso
(misera) non poteva il Ciel mostrarme
di questo, ohimè, che tanto il cor previde.
    Tu 'l sai s'io 'l dissi; e quel che di negarme
cercasti un tempo, un punto in ver' l'occaso
lontan sentisti alle tue luci fide.   26
    Questo solo dal cor l'alma divide,
nè quanto di rimedio il sol circonda
potria bastare a consolarmi mai;
    tu solo indi lo sai,
dove scorgi la piaga alta e profonda,
nè si vide giá mai per la foresta,
di notte, afflitto e stanco pellegrino,
tra crude fiere e boschi, in ogni via
chiamar la sua perduta compagnia,
così dolente com'io in quella e 'n questa
parte ti chiamo ognor, sera e mattino,

A 82 (B 32, C 45). SONG

    Pure, eternal, joyous, and noble soul,
you who, ending your life in your mid years,
have flown among the blessed spirits,
    now turn your sight from the heavenly abode
that you once showed me, so bright and noble,
and observe in what grief the deep pity   6
    for you has placed me, and those beloved eyes
that you loved you will see full of bitter tears,
drenching my faithful mournful breast:
because every delight
every joy of mine and my sweet dear life
was taken away from me when you departed,
O my faithful, heavenly guide.
Since then, I never pass a single hour
without weeping, nor does anything console me,
except the single hope that comforts me—
my beautiful, burning, magnetic power—
to see each other in Heaven in a better life,
because without you, lost and lifeless,
I cannot be content here any longer.   20

    A deeper pain or a more fierce, horrible fate
(miserable me) Heaven could not show to me
than this, alas, which the heart foresaw so deeply.
    You know that I said so; and what you once tried
to deny to me, you felt one moment near death,
distant to your faithful eyes.   26
    This alone divides the soul from the heart,
and not even all the help the sun encircles
would ever be enough to console me;
you alone know what happened,
where you see the wide, deep wound.
Nor was a distressed and weary pilgrim
ever seen in the forest at night,
among cruel, wild beasts and thickets,
forever calling his lost companion,
as mournful as I, everywhere
and always calling you, evening and morning,

per questo periglioso, atro camino,
ov'io fui sol per te cara a me stessa,
ed or m'ho in odio e vo cieca e depressa.   40

    Dinanzi al tuo apparir, doglia e tormento
spariva, come al sol sparisce ogn'ombra,
e rallegravi il cor, sì com'ei suole
    far doppo pioggia; or fosca nebbia ingombra
de' più foschi pensieri ogni momento
l'alma, che senza te null'altro vuole;   46
    e quell'ond'or via più m'afflige e duole,
è ch'io non posso o debbo ancor morire,
dubitando da te farmi più lunge.
Così mi frena e punge
or la ragione, ed ora il mio desire
pur ti richiama: e tu di me non curi,
come sia spento il puro, ardente affetto
ver' me, cui sol non vide mai nè stella,
per questa tempestosa e ria procella.
Ne' tuoi saggi consigli ogni perfetto
discorso intesi, e vidi esser securi
tutti i miei passi, e per monti aspri e duri
rendermi lieve, e 'n mar da' fieri venti
tôrmi, e dalle Sirene e lor concenti.   60

    Tutti ne la tua fronte i miei pensieri
veder soleva, e nel mio seno scòlte
tu le tue voglie ancor vedevi espresse,
    quai gigli e rose in bel cristallo accolte,
piene di casti affetti, alti e sinceri;
cosa che raro il Ciel largo concesse,   66
    di far sempre mai in due le voglie stesse.
Così, senza saperlo, anco il tuo duolo
quanto più forte teme
l'accorta Aragne il suo nemico, solo
toccato un fil della sua tela senta;
perch'io, sentendo il tuo mortale affanno,
in orribil visione, atra e funesta,
vidi farti lasciar la mortal vesta
a cruda serpe irata e nel tuo danno

in this dangerous, dark journey,
where I was dear to myself only for you,
and now I hate myself and I go blinded and crushed.   40

    When you first appeared, grief and torment
disappeared, as the sun makes every shadow vanish,
and you made my heart rejoice, as the sun
        makes everything glad after a rain; now
a dark fog of troublesome thoughts burdens
my soul, which wants nothing but you;   46
        and what now still torments and grieves me most
is that I cannot and must not yet die,
fearing that I would make myself more distant from you.[17]
Thus my reason restrains me
and wounds me, and now my desire
still calls you: but you care for me not at all,
as if the pure burning affection for me were extinguished,
which the sun never saw nor the star,
in this strong, evil tempest.
In your wise opinions I understood
each perfect discourse, and saw all my steps
secure, and through rough and hard mountains
I was made light, and in the seas I was saved
from the wild winds and from the Sirens[18] and their songs.   60

    All my thoughts I once could see
in your forehead, and sculptured in my breast
you saw your wishes, still expressed
        as lilies and roses gathered in a beautiful crystal,
full of chaste affections, high and sincere;
a thing that Heaven rarely concedes fully   66
        to make the same wishes in two lovers.
So, without knowing it, I felt also your grief
coming from far away,
as the cautious Arachne[19] can strongly feel
her enemy coming, if he touches
only one thread of her web.
So, feeling your deadly pain
in a horrible vision black and deadly,
I saw you leave your mortal body

intenta solo, ond'il cor morse, e spenta
fu la tua vita il dì poscia, e contenta
si rimase ella. O cruda, acerba sorte!
O dispietata, inesorabil Morte!   80

    Tu m'hai lasciato senza l'alma in vita,
la notte senza stelle e sole i giorni,
la terra scossa e 'l Ciel turbato e negro,
    e pien di mill'oltraggi e mille scorni
veggio ov'io miri, e la virtù sbandita,
e quanto scorsi già bello ed allegro   86
    or veggio al tuo partir languido ed egro.
Valore e cortesia per terra giacque
quel dì che ne lasciasti in doglia e pianto,
né mai più riso o canto
s'udio, ma ciascun tristo e mesto tacque,
con pianti che potean rompere i sassi
della pietade, e gravi alti sospiri;
né più sereno giorno il Cielo aperse:
Parnaso un nembo eterno ricoverse,
e' fiumi e fonti da' lor proprî giri
voltârsi indietro addolorati e lassi,
per non veder quel ch'or celato fassi
dell'empia micidial, ch'a Dio s'aspetta
di farne tarda e poi maggior vendetta.   100

    Or, quanto a me, non ha più bene il mondo
senza te, la mia stella e il mio conforto
che fosti a l'alma travagliata e stanca.
    Tu il sai, ch'essendo a me celato e morto,
nulla ved'io più bello o più giocondo
in questa vita lagrimosa e manca,   106
    né vedrò fin che questa chioma bianca
non sia ancor tutta, e 'l vital nodo sciolto,
che mi ritiene in questo basso incarco.
O Cielo invido e parco,
Cielo oggi a impoverirmi in tutto vòlto,
perché non festi in un medesmo punto
ch'un medesmo sepolcro ambi chiudesse,

to a merciless serpent, intent only
on your destruction, wherefore it stung your heart,
and your life was ended the very next day,
and the serpent was contented. Oh, merciless, bitter fate!
Oh, pitiless, unrelenting Death!   80

　　　You have left me living without my soul,
in nights without stars and days without sun,
the earth shaking and the sky gloomy and black,
　　　and full of a thousand abuses and contempt
I see wherever I glance, and virtue abandoned;
and all that I perceived glad and joyous   86
　　　now I see languishing and faint at your departure.
Worth and courtesy were destroyed on the earth
that day when you left it in grief and weeping.
No more laughter and song were heard,
but everyone was hushed, wounded, and heavy of heart,
with weeping that could move stones
to compassion, and deep mournful sighs.
No more did Heaven open a serene day:
an eternal storm cloud covered Parnassus,[20]
and the rivers and springs turned back
from their headlong course, sorrowful and weary,
to avoid seeing what is now hidden
of the murderous cruelty, which is waiting
for God to wreak a late and still greater revenge.   100

　　　Now, as for me, the world has no more worth
without you, O my star and my comfort
that you were to my troubled, tired soul.
　　　This you know, that with you buried and dead to me,
I see nothing more beautiful and more joyous
in this tearful and wanting life,   106
　　　nor will I see it until these locks of hair
are all white, and this knot of life is untied
which keeps me in this low mortal state.
O Heaven, envious and miserly,
today aiming in every way to impoverish me,
Heaven, why did you not arrange that in the same moment
the same tomb should embrace both of us;

dovendo a tanto duol rimaner viva,
e del morto mio ben spogliata e priva?
Forse per far ch'a' suoi gran merti avesse
uguale il pianto, e le mie doglie impresse;
perch'io tregua non vo' col pianto mai,
e tanto il piangerò quanto l'amai.   119

    Chi mi darà le voci, o chiaro spirto,
ch'a sì gran merto, al miserabil canto
convenghin, lassa, e al mio mortal dolore?
    O come potrò mai lagrimar tanto?
O quai corone dar di lauro o mirto,
ch'ornar possan la tomba entro e di fuore?   125
    Venner l'alme sorelle a farti onore
con le Ninfe del Serchio (ahi duro scempio)
lacere tutte e pien di morte il volto,
gridando:—Ohimè, che tolto
n'è stato oggi di gloria il nostro Tempio,
e secchi i nostri lauri e 'l nostro fonte!—
Così s'udîr per l'alte selve ombrose
voci di pianto, e' boscarecci dei
d'olmi e cipressi poi mille trofei
far per l'opre tue altere e glorïose;
e gir con mesta e lagrimosa fronte
si vider sopra il bel sagrato monte:
—Androgeo! Androgeo!—gridando—come
n'hai qui lasciati soli, e 'l tuo bel nome?—   139

    Venner poi le tue caste e pie sorelle
colme di pianto e con le treccie sparse,
    e' cari figli, e' frati, e 'l padre antico
gridando:—Ahi sordo Ciel, nemiche Stelle,
Destino ingiusto e di pietà nemico,   144
    solo al gran traditor crudele amico,
perché a tanto valor, tanta bontade,
per man sì vili il fido seno apristi?
O giorni oscuri e tristi!
O maligna, inaudita crudeltade!
Chi potrà mai soffrir sì ingiustamente
sì grave torto? E lui che il nostro cuore

why do I remain alive to such sorrow,
so truly deprived and bereft of my dear dead one?
Perhaps so that his great merits would have
tears to equal them and my engraved pains,
for I will never ask for a truce for my tears,
and my tears for him will equal my love.   119

    Who will give me the words, O clear spirit,
that may be suited to such great merit,
    to the pitiful song, alas, and to my mortal grief?
      Or how can I ever weep so much?
Or what crowns of laurel or myrtle
can I give to adorn his tomb in every way?   125
      The kind sisters came to give you honor
with the Nymphs of the Serchio River[21] (ah, hard ruin),
all disheveled and their faces full of death,
shouting, "Alas, how our Temple
has been deprived today of glory,
and our laurels and our springs, dry now!"
Thus were heard through the deep shady forest
voices of weeping, and the sylvan gods
of elms and cypresses then made
a thousand trophies for your noble and glorious works;
and they were seen on the holy mountains
going with sad and tearsome faces:
"Androgeo! Androgeo!"[22] shouting, "How
you have left us alone, and your beautiful name?"   139

    Then your chaste and pious sisters came
full of tears and with their hair all unkempt,
    and your beloved sons and brothers and your ancient father,
shouting, "Ah, deafened Heaven, hostile Stars,
unjust Destiny, and enemy of compassion,   144
      you alone, cruel friend to the awful traitor,
why in the face of such worth, such excellence,
by hands so vile did you open the faithful breast?
Oh, days dark and gloomy!
Oh, malignant, unprecedented cruelty!
Who can ever suffer such a grave wrong
so unjustly? And he that to our heart

Né fiera é in selva, o pesce in acqua, o 'n ramo
augello, o 'n arbor fronda, ovvero in terra
erba, o pietra si giace entro la rena,
che testimon non sia della mia pena.
Tu, Re del Ciel, cui null'asconde o serra,
prego che mandi l'alma che tant'amo
pietosa a ricondurmi al fin ch'io bramo,
dove m'aspetti e dond'io fei partita,
omai lasciando questa mortal vita.   198

    Canzon, tu te n'andrai
dov'é spento il mio lume, ingegno, ed arte;
ivi chiusa starai
con lui, che tien di me la miglior parte,
e sopra il lembo e 'l suo bel viso santo
versa mai sempre doloroso pianto,
fin che di questa spoglia i' mi disarme,
e dolce l'oda e lieto a sé chiamarme.   206

A 84 (C 51)

    Vago augelletto puro, almo e gentile,
che dolcemente canti e sfoghi il core
mercé sperando aver del tuo dolore,
non longe assai dal bel fiorito Aprile,   4
    ma io già mai col mio dolente stile,
in ch'io piango e mi doglio, a più liet'ore
giugner non spero, o 'ntepidir l'ardore
ch'io sento, o m'oda la bell'alma umile.   8
    Tu la tua dolce, amata compagnia
troverai forsi in aere, in ramo, o in terra;
io la mia dove o quando, i' non saprei.   11
    Te la tua sente; ma chi dolce apria
mio cuore e speme, è spento oggi sotterra,
né le mie voci ascolta o' pianti miei.   14

A 86

    S'uguale avessi al gran dolore il pianto,
o stil conforme a quel ch'in me si serra,

No beast in the woods, nor fish in water, nor bird
on a branch, leaf on a tree, nor even blade in the earth,
nor stone lying in the sand
that does not witness my pain.
O King of the Heavens, from whom nothing is hidden or shut away,
I pray you to send the soul that I love so well,
full of pity, to lead me to the end I yearn for,
where you wait for me and whence I departed,
leaving now this mortal life.   198

    Song, you will go now
where my light, my talent, and art are dead;
there you will be together
with him who has the better part of me,
and on his body and on his beautiful holy face
you will pour forever tearful weeping,
until I am freed of my mortal remains
and I hear him sweetly and joyfully calling me.   206

A 84 (C 51)

    Wandering little bird, lovely and gentle,
you who sweetly sing and open your heart,
have hope of finding pity for your sorrow,
so close to the fine flowering April,   4
    but I, with my sorrowful ways,
in which I weep and grieve, never hope
to arrive at happier hours, nor quell the passion
I feel, nor hope that his humble soul hears me.   8
    You will find your sweet beloved
companion in the air, on a branch, or on the ground;
I do not know where or when I will find mine.   11
    Your own love hears you, but the one who sweetly
opened my hopes and my heart is dead and buried today,
and he does not hear my words or my cries.   14

A 86

    If I had weeping equal to my great grief,
or poetry true to what is locked inside

fida Cangenna mia, fra tanta guerra,
movre' a pietade Aletto e Radamanto.   4
    Ahi del mondo ingiustizia ardita, quanto
le degne imprese altrui subito atterra!
Oggi Fortuna a noi tutto diserra
quanto d'amaro ha mai portato a canto.   8
    Or dell'ardente suo fuore il nostro
nemico traditor trïonfa e gode,
qual fea Neron ne l'alta arsion di Roma.   11
    Ma se di così ardente e crudel Mostro
la giust'ira di Dio l'ardir non doma,
che direm noi? Ch'ei pur lo vede ed ode.   14

A 88 (C 44)

    Occhi miei, oscurato è il vostro Sole,
così l'alta mia luce è a me sparita
e, per quel che ne speri, è al Ciel salita;
ma miracol non è: da tal si vuole.   4
    Passò, com'una stella ch'in Ciel vole,
ne l'età sua più bella e più fiorita.
Ahi dispietata Morte, ahi crudel vita,
via men d'ogni sventura altra mi duole!   8
    Rimasa senza il lume ch'amai tanto,
vomene in guisa d'orbo, senza luce,
che non sa ove si vada e pur si parte;   11
    così è 'l mio cantar converso in pianto.
O mia forte ventura, a che m'adduce:
colpa d'Amor, non già difetto d'arte.   14

A 93

    Vergine, in cui l'eterno Sol si pose
con la sua gran divinitade intera,
come talor contiensi in poca spera
la grand'imagin de le vere cose;   4
    senza macula, intégro in Te s'ascose,
quasi raggio di sol ch'in vetro fera,
e col suo puro ardor, casta e sincera,
umil al gran disegno ti dispose;   8

of me, my faithful Cangenna, in this war
I would move Alecto[24] and Rhadamanthus[25] to pity.   4
 Ah, fierceful injustice of the world,
how quickly you destroy the worthy deeds of others!
Today Fortune unveils to us every
bitterness that it has ever created.   8
 Now for his inflamed fury, our traitor
and enemy triumphs and rejoices
as Nero[26] did, in the high burning of Rome.   11
 But if the just anger of God cannot
control the burning and cruel Monster, what shall
we say? For surely God sees and hears it.   14

A 88 (C 44)

 My eyes, your Sun has been eclipsed
just as my great light has vanished from me,
and, I may hope, has risen to Heaven,
but a miracle it is not: God wants it so.   4
 He passed by as a star flies through the skies,
in his most lovely and most flowering age.
Ah, merciless Death, ah, cruel life,
no other misfortune can be more grievous!   8
 So I, without the light I loved so much,
go on like a blind person, having no light:
I know not where I go and yet I move on;   11
 thus my singing is changed to weeping.
O my hard fortune, to this you lead me:
Love is guilty, not a failure of my art.   14

A 93

 O Virgin, in whom lodged the eternal Sun
with his manifold, complete divinity,
just as, at times, the great image of what
is true is contained in a small space;   4
 O spotless Virgin, he was wholly in You—
like a ray of sun that lies hidden in glass—
and he prepared you, with his pure devotion,
chaste and sincere, meek according to the grand design;   8

A 99

    Lassa, mente infelice, ogn'altra cura,
e risguarda l'eterno, alto Motore
star sopra il duro legno affisso, e 'l core
offrir e 'l sangue suo con l'alma pura.   4
    Pianga il mondo, il Ciel pianga, e la Natura
debole e 'nferma per l'antico errore.
Piangi alma, con interno, aspro dolore,
l'ingrata voglia tua proterva e dura.   8
    Vedi le man che feron gli elementi,
e' piedi che solean premer le stelle,
per liberarti, star co' chiodi affissi.   11
    O inaudita pietà, con quai tormenti
offristi a noi sì precïose e belle
piaghe, per trarci de gli eterni abissi!   14

A 99

    Leave off, unhappy mind, all other cares,
and behold the Eternal High Mover
fastened onto the hard wood, and his heart
proffered, and his blood with his pure soul.   4
    Let the world weep; let Heaven weep, and Nature
weak and ailing for the ancient wrong.
Weep, my soul, with bitter grief inside,
over your stubborn, hard, ungrateful will.   8
    See the hands, creators of the elements,
and the feet, that used to press upon the stars
to make you free, fastened now with nails.   11
    O unprecedented Passion, with what pains
you tendered us your beautiful, most precious
wounds to draw us up from the eternal depths.   14

LETTER

Not of inferior spirit, nor of less high talent, worthy and most virtuous M. L.,[28] have I always judged you in your desire and expertise in defending, even if false, every opinion of ours; for you have always been thoroughly recognized by all in every respect as an expert in arms. And although nothing was lacking to make me fully aware of this, whatever was needed has been abundantly furnished, for I have perceived from your last letter the generosity of your spirit, in its attachment to the defense of even the most vile and weak part of our discussion of the two alternatives we have proposed: that is, whether one ought to praise or condemn Love. Namely, you decree that one ought to condemn it altogether, and this position you have adorned with such fine lies that it appears to have the very face of truth. It now remains for me to remove this mask and lift the veil of your false calumnies.

But your very first effort has been to show me how unseemly it is for a woman born not of the noblest blood, nor raised in the most superb palaces in the midst of plenteous and most abundant riches, to spend her time constantly in the pursuit of studies and in writing, at complete odds with the customs of our city. And although one might have to grant even this, at least she ought to discourse of more praiseworthy affections than those of love (which you hold to be wicked). First, then, to reply to what you have said to me, I say to you that granted that I was not born of high and royal blood nor raised in grand and sumptuous palaces, in stately chambers or beds of gold, nevertheless I come not from an ignoble family nor poor and lowborn ancestors (as you have reason to know), but from famous blood, and I have benefited from the honest gifts of fortune, in a free city, and I was blessed with a great soul. For should we regard matters straight on (if any faith whatsoever is to be granted the learned pages of the most famous and worthy writers), we shall surely see that it is not the blood of ancient lineage, not the power over peoples, not gold nor crimson, but a soul shining with virtue that makes a person truly noble.

But who draws us to this virtue? and who makes us become more perfect in it? Certainly no one, let there be no doubt of this, but Love. But since all our debate must be this, whether to praise or condemn this Love, it appears to be a reasonable thing (although you have proceeded in the opposite direction) in the first place to show what Love is, whether good or evil, so that having this attribute well understood, we may then reason more readily, and with greater insight, concerning it and its effects. I state then, most noble M. L., that Love (if my judgment is not mistaken) is none other than desire for a thing which is beautiful and good, to achieve its happiness and ultimate perfection, rather than its delight. Thus all things that approach those toward which they feel most inclined become more and more perfect, and only in recognizing their perfection do they come to rest.

As we see by experience, if we begin with inanimate things, heavy things descend to the center and lighter things, such as fire, rise to the heights, and they never come to rest until they arrive at the origin and the last limit of their perfection. We can say the same of plants and the irrational animals, and finally of ourselves and our souls. Since the eternal and greatest Wisdom is the first cause and the last end, our soul feels more inclined and steadfast always to investigate and understand the most occult things. This soul will never be content until it arrives at the highest Wisdom, where its best principle consists finally of its happiness and ultimate perfection.

Love is the mean between human things and divine things: although they are discordant among themselves, love unites them and makes them more perfect. Love was first born in God, who created and maintains all things, which know themselves content and most perfect for Him. Love is therefore a good thing, insofar as it is produced by an excellent cause. It has been ingrained in our minds by God for a perfect and happy end: to make us participate in His blessedness not only in Heaven but also on earth. For with our desire we try to enjoy that beauty which by the shadows of these fallen and earthly bodies we sometimes see and to which we are always drawn and impelled (without our knowing what we follow, and unable to find it again with our fragile senses), by divine law with eternal order.

If we should wish to say that Love has often been the cause of the death of men, and of changes in conditions and other similar things, and of our every danger (we are thus more apt to exhibit the ill fortunes and ugliness of others than their works worthy of memory), we must say this does not really come from Love. There are people who, while their weak breasts receive Love, and while they let it quickly occupy their best part, banish the most beautiful gift given by God, violently, with great fury. They could do nothing either just or reasonable or human, therefore, except to enjoy only unseemly and illicit acts, as if they were brutal animals.

Nor can we say with reason that Love has forced us to any unseemly act, for Nature, which in truth can never err, would not have given our free will the power to lead us astray following our feelings if she had not also given us the power—by sending us reason—to make us rise. For Nature would have operated with malice, unjustly to us more than to all the other creatures of which she made us masters and possessors, if she had taken back the most beautiful gift that she had ever given us; hence she alone would have been the cause of greater damage.

But as we see that water and fire are very useful elements, but damaging and harmful when they are used wrongly by evil men, in the same way Love was created by God tranquil and pure, distant from every ugliness, full of peace and repose, in order to be the cause of uniting all things with the same agreement and harmony in their final and most perfect end (no matter how conflicting they may be among themselves). But if we let ourselves be conquered and overcome by our bodily senses, the defect is truly ours, and we come by it ourselves; Love does not give it to us—Love from whom there cannot come anything but good and our entire happiness.

Therefore, Love is not, my virtuous M. L., as you have declared it, a secret passion in our souls caused by evil and wicked destiny and sent by the gods continually to torment us, because they wanted to punish harshly the excessive boldness of Prometheus (our first parent) when he took the flame of the heavenly carriage, or rather when he, with his marvelous power, united the holy and divine spirits with the untiring heavens and made the shining stars spread their lights in the elements. Love causes the purest fire to move the air, and the solid Earth to pull all waters to itself, and the plants, trees, and the brute animals are also produced by Love, and man by this same Love and desire is drawn to search for eternity and its perfection, without which nothing is peaceful or in repose forevermore. That is why heaven itself turns and moves continuously, seeing as how the soul of that Heaven is found in every point, and Heaven, desirous of enjoying this soul, swirls around so fast that every part of it, everywhere, can enjoy the beautiful universal soul, so that it may be, as much as possible, in every place where the soul is, wholly together.

Just like the heavens, so we too are moved by this divine flame. We begin with the senses to delight our mind with that spiritual and divine beauty which sometimes we perceive in the appearance of the human form, like the rays of the sun in a lucid and transparent crystal vase. We begin to work them with ample and spacious turns of our best reason, by developing all those fine sciences and most noble virtues by which, adorned with similar spiritual beauties, we can please the person loved and by them be worthy of uniting with the loved person. And thus, many people have been seen, because of Love, to have been excellent and remarkable, and to have had the prize among valorous people, having learned through Love in a short space of time that which many other people without Love have tried to find with long and solicitous study. This makes us prudent, shrewd, and wise. Love, with useful reins and helpful spurs, turns and pushes us on to the way of honor and health, making us always audacious in honorable undertakings, steadfast in following them, and prudent in maintaining them.

Love makes dear to us all those works which belong to a most noble soul; and is there anything else which invites us to virtue more than Love? Love makes us skillful in the arts, in ingenious, modest, and pleasurable conversations, in harmonies, songs, and rhymes, in graceful manners, and in every praiseworthy usage. It gives us grace in everything, making us inventors of fine entertainments, of pointed witticisms, of sensible inventions, and of unusual, commendable undertakings.

Finally Love is the one who, enlightening our minds, shows us not only the true road of honor but that of Heaven, our final, desired aim, so that, stealing away from us these fleeting and earthly beauties that are always changing, little by little, sweetly, with the wings of the mind, we are raised to Heaven. There we consider the greatness and power of God in having formed a work of such exceeding beauty as great as it is, or as we appraise it to be, and which we love. So from this lovely ray of light we begin to glimpse, in this dark prison, the high beauties of Heaven, the riches of earth, and, finally, to contemplate what the beauty of the Angels might be and their blessedness in enjoying the divine essence. So that, as if made drunk by the divine fire, purging our highest thoughts of all vices and reviving the strength of the intellect, we begin to hear the celestial harmony, so in accord with the soul that discordance no longer has any place in it.

Therefore who would ever want to condemn Love, which is, in sum, far from all evil and the cause of all good? But what insanity is mine, to try to get you to drink from this tiny stream? Go to the source, run to the sea. The entire Academy of the Philosophers speaks of nothing else, poets labor on this, Bembo[29] discourses of it fully, Mario Equicola[30] dedicates all his study to it. Read their pages, for every book is full of it. But this is no undertaking for my limited strength, hence I will do as Apelles[31] did: having painted Juno and Minerva with such marvelous beauty that he could not surpass them, he still had to craft the most shapely Venus, who had to surpass both the others, so he painted her with her face hidden, to make up for his shortcoming.

So too I will leave off now from celebrating Love any longer, so as not to diminish further his praises, and to avoid entering the deep waters, where I might be submerged by the waves. And making here my conclusion, lest I bore you any longer, humbly I express my devotion to you.

Figure 2. Engraving of Chiara Matraini praying before the crucifix. This depiction of her appears in both her *Spiritual Meditations* and *Seven Penitential Psalms.* By permission of Houghton Library, Harvard University.

II

SPIRITUAL MEDITATIONS

TRANSLATOR'S NOTE

Spiritual Meditations is the first of four books in which Matraini deals with the spiritual life. It was published in 1581 by Vincenzo Busdraghi, in Lucca. There are only two original copies of the book: one at the Biblioteca Nazionale di San Marco in Venice, the other one at the Biblioteca Capitolare Feliniana at Lucca. Of these, the superior one is at Lucca, having fewer errors and being much better preserved. The Venice copy is in microfilm at the Widener Library of Harvard University.

The book is divided into twelve meditations or chapters. It begins with a first chapter that recounts how the book was created: a dream in which the author was submerged by a tempest, after which the Supreme Power came to her to show her the virtuous way to a good life. This done, she recounts a meditation for each day of her narrative, beginning with a thought of her own, illustrating it by a sonnet, and then turning to the Supreme Power for illumination of the matter. The themes of the narration are the laws of Christ and God, with horrifying accounts of disobedience, followed by reforming obedience to the church and to the just way of salvation. The book ends with a *canzone*, "Padre del Ciel," which also appears as the next-to-last poem in the 1597 volume.

FROM SPIRITUAL MEDITATIONS

In the deeper silence of the darkest night, which is rest and calm for the labors of mortals, I was oppressed by the most profound sleepiness.[1] It seemed to me (I do not know whether it was because I had previously thought about my deep and long travails, or perhaps because of some other divine disposition) as if I were walking alone, through a shady and dark forest, near a great, roil-

---

1. Chiara Matraini, *Meditazioni spirituali* (Lucca: Busdraghi, 1581), chap. 1, 4r–9v.

ing, muddy river, with my mind completely occupied by diverse and grievous thoughts. And while I was thinking of these things, and as step by step I went along, I saw before me, in a very small boat within the roiling water, three beautiful Maidens, of pleasing aspect, who were gently singing with such agreeable accents that I was intent on listening to their sweetest voices.

I do not know how, but in a moment I felt myself drawn to their boat. And there, led by them by a deceitful route, I found myself in an open and tempestuous sea, full of monsters and of infinite storms, among many contrary winds, which forced the weak little boat to strike a tall rock. The boat then broke into many pieces, with great harm to me.

Whereupon falling into the horrible waters of the sea, I turned from the shipwreck to beseech some help. And in the rushing waves I instantly felt myself thrown against the same rock, with a great fury. On this rock I was stranded by the fleeting and receding maidens. And in the greatest darkness of the night, finding myself alone and almost dead, without any hope of human assistance and in the marvelous fury of this most cruel storm, with horrible thunder rolling over me, I seem to form, dismayed by so great and such diverse and miserable events, these or similar words of unspeakable grief.

"Oh, wretched me, above all the other human and unhappy creatures, how will I be able now, in any way, to flee my imminent and most cruel death? And alas, here I am, separated from the land and driven by the fluctuating waves of the sea and by contrary winds upon this rock; and now even the heavens, so strongly enraged with me, threaten me with most horrible death. But since no hope of living any longer is left in me, I want at least, with this last suffering, to end quickly all my other most bitter passions, and my miserable life, at one and the same time."

And this said, it seems that I suddenly threw myself into the sea, and in so doing I felt myself sink and drown. So great was the breathlessness which in drowning I seemed to feel that the deep sleep was broken, and I awoke with my face full of tears and with the painful impression of the past dream. This impression reminding me of all the impetuous winds which had already blown through my unhappy and tormented life—that is, the stormy winds of tribulations, worldly misfortunes, the betrayals of its false sirens, the blows of the crashing waves of sea, and the hard rocks of my bitter and inexplicable pains—I began to moan (although it was inappropriate) of my great disgrace and cruelest fate.

And while fully awake from my sleep I was grievously speaking thus to myself, there arose within me that most excellent and Greater Power of the soul, which is eternally seated in the manner of its own queen, in its highest and most sublime part. I say that Greater Power which alone has the strength to bring out the truth from difficult and doubtful things, by which we perfectly arrive at divine and high contemplation. At times, the learned call this the mind, and at other times the active intellect, and sometimes superior portion.

This Greater Power, moved by many serious and righteous causes, appeared before me, and with the following words, in this way began to reprove me severely: "How can this be, that a person of reasonable discourse, trained in the sacred study of the divine scriptures, has let herself be overwhelmed by such excessive grief for lost worldly things, to such an extent that she now dares to complain so loudly of the troubles and travails that she suffers in this miserable world, thus unjustly blaming the Maker of all things? Are you not the one of wise counsels and true and powerful thoughts who used to arm others against the battles of adverse fortune?"

"Yes," I said, my face turning completely red for shame, being stabbed by the strong stimulation of my conscience, and as if I were talking with another person and not to myself.

"And why now," she said, "in defending yourself, have you thrown your worthy and potent weapons on the ground? And in the greatest need, do you not use that virtue which you tried diligently to learn with so much study?" But as I was silent to this, she added: "Now, I see you are forgetful of yourself, having become the miserable prey of your bitter and blind passion. Dry, dry then those tears and those eyes, obscured by the shadows of your blind and most base affections; and do not turn away from your more worthy and precious treasures, which are those of the soul, rather than those most vile and earthbound riches you have lost. But you must know by now that all those who possess true wisdom need very few things of the world, and that fortune rules completely only those who are devoid of wisdom. But alas, how blind is the mind of mortals and how buried they are in the sheer depths of earthly things, for they weep and grieve deeply at having lost vile things. They do not content themselves with the precious, the true, and the most honorable things, because they do not know that they have these within.

"Then remove, remove from your sight the veil of the greatness and pleasures of this untrustworthy, miserable world; and do not keep recalling the great and cherished joy of your past happiness. For in the guise of enchanters they entice your desire, and like infernal furies they torment you with a thousand irritating punishments. And rest assured that one must not judge a treasure as precious or worthy unless it is firm and eternal. Otherwise, since you have to lose that treasure, as it is certain to be lost, it cannot bring anything other than the gravest and sharpest pain and bitter damage, for it is not in the power of man to make forsaken and transitory things of the world stable, and losing them one becomes very depressed and unhappy.

"Therefore, it is not enough to see the present things that the world brings, but it is still necessary to measure their end with prudence, which is the ability to change from one disposition to another; that is from prosperous to adverse, and from sweet to bitter. If you have not done that, though you should have, and if you placed yourself into the ship of your dreams and into its government, then you should not have been sure of going where you wanted, without any opposition, but rather wherever the blowing winds drove you, and where miserable and sorrowful they finally left you. Alas, foolish are you, O mortals, who do not realize that those things which are composed of many opposite elements that are all changing and corruptible cannot be but corruptible and mortal things themselves.

"Now, finally you see that in this life there is nothing if not inconstancy, instability, and deception. Infinite are the examples of this that you may be shown, both of valorous men and of most singular women who, falling from a dizzying height, have arrived at a wretched depth and horrid misery. Therefore, with your soul founded in the hope of eternal and stable things, like a rock against the waves of the stormy sea, you must be constant and intrepid against the blows of all adversities without ever being disturbed, laughing at those who try to offend you.

"You must, however, recognize that as mud or other wretched things cannot befoul the bright and most lucid rays of the Sun, similarly there cannot be any human offense that can befoul a temperate soul and corrupt a thoroughly strong mind in any way. For just as a high column placed in the bottom of a well is still just as tall, and a little Dwarf on a huge tower is small, so the strong and brave spirit, being placed in a humble and low state, shows, with the help of divine grace, its constancy, nobility, and greatness; and the weak one, raised to the heights, demonstrates all the more its lowliness and vileness. Thus, be of brave spirit and be constant, if ultimately you wish to trample, with divine aid and with the foot of the intellect, the heights of all the world, and to say with the wise Bias,[2] 'I always carry with me every good and every treasure of mine in myself.'

"But, I wish that you would tell me briefly why you complained so much of your numerous misfortunes."

I responded then: "For no reason other than, having many times seen bad things happening to good men and good things to bad ones, I believed this was unjust. Good should always happen to good men and evil to the others."

"Well," she answered then, with extremely furrowed brows, "are men perhaps of such sane and complete judgment that those men whom they judge to be either good or evil are necessarily so?"

---

2. Bias of Priene (mid-sixth century BCE) was one of the Seven Sages, famous for a certain practical wisdom, the fruit of experience.

"Certainly not," I responded then, "if one rather looks rightly to the truth. For many times, those whom we judge worthy of honor and of very great reward are often rightly worthy of censure and correction, and those who should be praised for virtue and richly rewarded are held in base worth, and evil is always said of them."

"Well then," she said, "from these examples you can very well recognize and clearly understand how the vision of your low intellect is unable to penetrate the hidden secrets of the divine mind in any way. But that is not a wonder, for many are the causes which, because of their effects, may easily be learned through the discourse of reason and the light of the sciences, and nevertheless you do not know them well: neither those causes, nor yourselves, nor your own errors. Then how are you truly to understand the incomprehensible things of the divine mind and its high and secret judgments? . . ."

". . . [I]n order[3] to save your life you must hide in the most secret room of your own home where no one sees you: I say in the most internal and profound part of your heart, and having locked the door against your troubles (so you do not feel the fury of your strong passions), you must invoke your heavenly and beloved Father. He is the only one who can help and console you. However, if you have recourse to external consolations, and if you go wandering after the deceitful and treacherous sirens of worldly and flattering sweetness, and if, through the sea of your troubles, you delay finding the harbor of your true and secure peace, then the impetuous winds of the world's conflicts and its labors and afflictions will come utterly to submerge and drown you in the headlong depths of your final desperation. . . ."

[The Author speaks:][4]
. . . And having said these things she fell silent, and then I, realizing that Dawn was already appearing above our horizon, left my sluggish bed, and with the following verses (dictated to me, according to the spirit of God) I began thus to say:

SONNET

Heavenly Father, after many, many years
that without your light I have wandered
enclosed in this mortal shadow, and been lost,
I pray that you turn my soul to a good path.

---

3. Chiara Matraini, *Meditazioni spirituali* (Lucca: Busdraghi, 1581), chap. 1, 11v–12r.

4. Ibid., chap. 1, 14v–15r.

And make my misleading and foolish thoughts,
which brought about my leaving your path,
always be turned to a more prized enterprise,
to a better life, with your gracious help.

Save from the rocks, to a safer place,
Lord, the sail of my tired and weary boat,
that I may be far from Charybdis and Scylla.[5]

Gather in yourself my high hopes strewn away
and turn these studies and this talent of mine
to a safer port, a more tranquil life.

[Padre del Ciel, doppo molt'anni, e molti
Che senz'al lume tuo da te son gita
Per quest'ombra mortal chiusa, e smarrita
Prego, ch'a buon sentier l'anima volti.

E fa, sì, che i pensier fallaci, e stolti,
Ond'io mi son dal tuo sentier partita,
A più lodate imprese, a meglior vita,
Stian sempre, col tuo aiuto, ogn'or rivolti.

Trahe da gli scogli, a più secura parte,
Signor, la vela del mio stanco legno,
Sì ch'io stia lunge da Cariddi, e Scilla.

Raccogli in te l'alte speranze sparte,
E volgi questi studi, e quest'ingegno,
A più secura vita, e più tranquilla.]

[The Author speaks:][6]
. . . I pray you, then, my God, that you do not wish to accuse me in your fury
according to my merits and damn me, but that you wish to save me according
to the merits of your very kindly Son. I confess by my many and great sins to
have called your wrath and your fury down on me, and I confess myself to be
worthy of your contempt and infinite punishments.

Nevertheless I am still certain that you are most admirable (you are, of
course, admirable in all your works) in those works of your great mercy: and
so the sinner who repents is pardoned, and if he comes to you, you will receive
him cheerfully; and if he knocks on your door, you will open it to him. Open
to me, therefore, most benign Lord, knowing that you have moved the hand

5. Charybdis and Scylla in Greek mythology are monsters who lived on rocks on opposite sides
of the Straits of Messina.

6. Matraini, *Meditazioni spirituali*, chap. 2, 27r–27v.

of my will to knock on the door of your great mercy so that I may beseech from you alms of your divine grace. Open the door, O my celestial and most clement Father, so that you may not have moved me in vain to ask for your divine aid. However, you know that you said: "Knock and it will be opened to you, look if you want to find, ask and it will be given to you,"[7] and so, my eternal Father, I knock and seek and ask for this your grace.

[The Greater Power speaks:][8]
". . . This [wisdom] leads to the excellent gradations of the supernatural reasons, where you can understand the profound and secret mysteries that are hidden under them, which the highest God reveals to his most humble and faithful servants, and turning to the sublime cause of his high, spacious, and huge circles, with that sight that penetrates the abyss of waters and the depths of the earth, he makes you recognize the First Cause and the Prime Mover of those high intelligences that move these heavens of ours, and the dimensions and the dispositions of the moving stars and the fixed stars. Here, one finally hears, with the ear of the soul, from the opposition of motions, the changing positions of planets, the variety of their natures and powers, a very harmonious agreement and correspondence, so that the soul is astonished and admires the infinite and admirable wisdom of its highest and most perfect Maker. So this divine knowledge, my soul, is enough to make you rise to the great heights of the supreme and everlasting glory. Therefore, now seek with reason and with examples and humble and most devoted prayers, that God will give you this knowledge, so that for his glory you may know what is your true and happiest goal, how the world deceives you, and that life and the glory of men and all their hopes are fleeting and short and above all deceptive; and that in God alone are found all your perfections, the immortal life, the highest and true pleasure, and the infinite glory." And here she was silent. . . .

[The Greater Power speaks:][9]
". . . The Poets have sung, the Philosophers have written, the Sibyls have spoken, the Prophets have foretold, and the Apostles have proclaimed Jesus Christ to the whole world. Christ is that only and most perfect friend, in whom the souls that are faithful must place their love and faith and all their hopes, not in deceiving, inconstant, and mortal man. Man does not love, except to receive pleasure, usefulness, or honor. And even when he loves a

---

7. Matt. 7:7, Luke 11:9.
8. Matraini, *Meditazioni spirituali*, chap. 4, 42r–43r.
9. Ibid., chap. 5, 47r–48r.

person because he knows her as good and virtuous, his love in any case is neither true nor stable. Because if it happens to him, as it can happen with human fragility, that in some unusual error not expected by him, she commits or he receives from her some injury, then he not only no longer loves her, or appreciates her, or offers her any honor, but she becomes so distasteful and so hateful that he avoids her, flees her, and speaks evil of her.

"Just when she would have greater need and greater necessity of his help, of his counsel, and of being lifted by him when she has fallen, instead she remains despised, derided, and abandoned. Therefore, my soul, you will love Jesus Christ, a friend who is stable and most perfect, who, not for any need he has of man, in every time, everywhere, and in everything always shows you his real and most stable love, not only in prosperous fortune but in adversity, and not only in life but in death, and not only when the soul is just but when it is indeed guilty. This is because he is always sweet, always kindly, and full of every salvation." . . .

[The Greater Power speaks:][10]
". . . O Adam, what did you do to defy the divine commandment of your good and just Lord? Oh, how great, truly, was your ingratitude toward Him, for He did not create you for anything else but for you to enjoy His eternal delights. Therefore, He gave you for your own beautiful dwelling the Earthly Paradise, all full of the choicest plants, of green grasses, of sweet-smelling flowers, and of fruits that were savory and sweet. Here were spacious meadows, thriving gardens, and many lovely and delightful woodlands made (as it was well shown) by the divine paintbrush. Here above the green branches were heard the sweet birds singing softly, and the air was so pure and temperate that above it (more than above us) the clear and dazzling stars were shining. Here the Sun and Moon had quieted their influences, and the winds gently breathed sweetly, so that there was always a joyful, happy, and glad springtime. The fields delighted in it, the hills rejoiced in it, and all the grasses and flowers made themselves beautiful. Here the balsam, the salvia, and the cinnamon and all the virtuous and sweet fragrances were abundant, but this was not enough, because the magnificent and great King of the universe even gave you, through no merit of yours, a gracious, beautiful, and sweet companion; with great affection you loved her and held her dear.

"Oh, how cheerful and happy were those hours that you lived in the earthly paradise, and how clear was that day which the divine presence illuminated and which the serenity of protection purified and the measureless joy

10. Ibid., chap. 7, 56v–57v.

adorned. Oh day, full of peace, overflowing with every virtue, abundant with all the pleasures, day of every clearness and gentleness! It was not disturbed by any mist of error, no anguish plagued it, nor did any shadow of infirmity cover it. This was that day, my soul, that Adam enjoyed among the delights of paradise, before he fell from the state of justice, because he was guilty of disobedience and ingratitude.

"But you know how brief all that good was for him, how immediate was his departure, and how swift his flight: for barely six hours had passed before he let himself be deceived by the ancient and evil serpent, and believing that deceptive and lying creature rather than trusting his true and perfect Creator—oh, alas—forgetful of the duty of obedience, he let the weapons of justice fall from his hand; and raising himself above his being, he became ungrateful for the immense gifts and treasures received from God."

[The Author speaks:][11]
Give me, O Lord, your holy and divine spirit, symbolized by those waters that you already promised to all the souls in thirst, waters that nourish the hearts of your elect and make them germinate herbs and sweet-smelling flowers of gentle and divine reasoning, and the blessed fruits of holy works. To you I come, deepest fountain of living water, because you alone are powerful enough to cleanse me of all the stains of my unrighteousness. To you I shout, heavenly helmsman, in the tempestuous sea of this miserable world, where I am agitated by the surrounding storms of the multitude of temptations. To you I appeal for weapons, invincible captain, against the great army of my wicked and mortal enemies, who with me and outside me provoke me to battle, and leave me no peace and security in any place.

In your presence, most perfect and most kindly doctor, I display all my mortal wounds, and I narrate, weeping, all my passions and infirmities, and I beg for medicine to cure me. To you I come, my heavenly host, for I am tired by the troublesome journey of this suffering and most unhappy life, full of the thorns of many sharp affections from which I have brought away nothing but hunger and thirst and the most grave weight of miseries and sins. Therefore you, O heavenly King, rich in all goods, and the magnificent giver of all substantial and supreme nourishments and true contentment, I pray you, give me, weary and weak, some of your sweet food, and accept this soul in your lodging, who knocks at the door of your highest and infinite mercy, shouting with the love and the grief of her heart, that you will want to open to her . . . so that happy, she can say with you, my God, I will always rest in eternity.

11. Ibid., chap. 10, 73v–74v.

SONG

Heavenly Father, if my heavy, bitter weeping,[12]
from your immense supreme goodness
can still beseech pardon for my sins,
do not be (I pray) miserly with your grace,
for I weep, and the tears that fall from my eyes
are still a true gift from you.
Father, you know that I am
your daughter, and only created of you; and that
if I am banished from your grace
in this mortal life,
my harsh adversary, wicked and evil,
will be victorious over your work
in this war, where he lies hidden.[13]
. . .

O Lord, you said once that whoever has faith
in you will always have eternal life,
full of holy and desired peace.
Thus, since my hope has placed its foundation
in you, may you alone teach and govern me,
for I want only what delights and pleases you.
O high and truthful Father,
how could it ever be that my great offense
against your divine and holy love
would make you so harsh
against this humble soul which has returned to you,[14]
if the clear and burning flames show something different,
which you cannot conceal from others in your body.
Therefore in you I wish
to believe always, and place all my hopes in you,
that you are able and want to help me in my great need
and to take up arms for me

12. Ibid., chap. 12, 89r–91v. This concludes the book of *Spiritual Meditations*. In her 1595 volume of poems it appears as poem number 73, out of 77 selections. It is the concluding song in her 1597 volume, where it is followed only by a short madrigal. It has been adapted for the republication.

13. Stanzas 2–10 have been omitted.

14. This line is not present in *Spiritual Meditations* but is included in her 1597 volume of poetry. I have added it here because she undoubtedly wanted the poems to be almost identical.

in your divine supreme power
against my enemy, whence I may gain
victory, and you triumph and glory.

[Padre del Ciel, se'l mio gran pianto, amaro
Può dall'immensa tua somma bontade
Impetrar di mie colpe ancor perdono,
Non m'esser (prego) di tua gratia avaro,
Ch'io piango, e 'l pianto, che da gl'occhi cade
È proprio, ancor, di te verace dono.
Padre tu sai, ch'io sono
Tua figlia, e sol da te creata; e ch'io
Se sarò della tua gratia sbandita
In questa mortal vita,
Il mio duro avversario iniquo, e rio
Sarà dell'opra tua, fra tanta guerra
Vittorioso, ov'ei s'include, e serra.

. . .

Già dicesti, Signor, chiunche ha fede
In te, che sempre ha teco vita etterna,
Piena di santa, e desiata pace,
Dunque, poi, che mia spene ha in te sua sede
Posta; tu sol m'insegna, e mi governa;
Ch'io vo' sol quel, ch'a te diletta, e piace.
Ah, Padre alto, e verace,
Com'esser potria mai, che tanta offesa
Facessi a l'amor tuo divino, e santo
Nel'indurarti tanto
Contra ad anima umil ch'a Te sia resa,
S'altro mostran le faci ardenti, e chiare,
Che nel tuo corpo, altrui non puoi celare.
Dunque in te creder sempre
Voglio, e por tutta in te la mia speranza
Che possi, e vogli al gran bisogno aitarme,
E per me prender l'armi,
Della divina tua somma possanza,
Contra 'l nemico mio, donde vittoria
Io ne riporti, e tu, trionfo, e gloria.]

Figure 3. Engraving of David that appears on the frontispiece and again several times as an illustration of *Seven Penitential Psalms*. By permission of Houghton Library, Harvard University.

III

CONSIDERATIONS ON THE SEVEN
PENITENTIAL PSALMS OF THE
GREAT KING AND PROPHET DAVID

TRANSLATOR'S NOTE

The seven penitential psalms are 6, 32, 38, 51, 102, 130, and 143. They were used liturgically from early Christian times, and later in the Middle Ages they were ordered to be recited on Fridays during Lent.[1] Matraini's *Considerations on the Seven Penitential Psalms of the Great King and Prophet David* (1586) is the second of three books of prose which she elaborated from 1580 to 1590. She was approximately seventy-one years old at this point. It has a dedication and prayer, and then the prayer to the Lord and the prologue which appears here. It then takes the psalms line by line, in Latin, and explains them thoroughly. Some of these explanations I have translated here. All of the psalms are followed by a sonnet of praise, in which she generally asks for deliverance for her soul. It is her longest book: two hundred pages.

The book can be found at various libraries, including the British Library, from which my copy was obtained, and in microfilm at the Widener Library of Harvard University.

PRAYER TO THE LORD

To you I have recourse, O high, immortal Creator and infinite abyss of mercy, and with my knees bent to the ground, with my heart most fervently affectionate, I beg you to illuminate my intellect, which (as you see) is blinded by the darkness of ignorance.[2] Loosen, I pray you, O Lord, and untie my tongue; and move my pen so that I may write your worthy and most holy praises and

1. See F. L. Cross, ed., *The Oxford Dictionary of the Christian Church*, 3rd ed., ed. E. A. Livingstone (Oxford: Oxford University Press, 1997), 1489.

2. Chiara Matraini, *Considerationi sopra i Sette Salmi Penitentiali del Gran Re e Profeta Davit* (Lucca: Busdraghi, 1586), B.

recount the redeeming penitence of your faithful servant, David.[3] O my most merciful Lord, if those who had to build your Tabernacle by the order of your servant Moses did not venture to begin their work until they felt themselves full of your holy and divine Spirit, how will I, miserable sinner, without your grace, dare to write the holy fruits of true penitence and the greatness of your mercy toward repentant sinners?

Surely if you do not fill my heart with that upright spirit, and if you do not give me your grace in that abundance with which you once gave it to our penitent David, I shall write nothing, certainly nothing good. And who is that man who does not know that such a marvelous contrition, a humility so deep, was not able to lodge in his heart because of his wicked sins, nor even find in his mouth a true and loyal confession and final resolution, if you first did not awaken him with your divine spirit? Surely it is grace and not less than that which you granted him when you gave him the spirit of prophecy, by which he foresaw the profound and high mysteries of your birth and death, with the deliverance of the human race.

Then, O high and most gracious Lord of mine, create in me an upright and sincere heart, and renew within me your holy spirit. For if you give me a sufficient abundance of your grace, that I am able to awaken from the profound sleep of ignorance, my pen will surely write your divine praises and will manifest your infinite mercy, which is always shown toward the penitent. And who knows if these writings of mine will not inspire even the souls of sinners to look for their salvation? To that end they may turn aside from their evil works and ceaselessly praise your high and divine Majesty.

PROLOGUE

Many are the examples and infinite are the causes which ought to inspire us, out of love, or at least out of fear, to reach toward that true and holy penitence which so adorned the great king and prophet David, and many other sinners, both male and female.[4] But above all, that sweet and holy recollection of the profound benefit given by the great and immortal God, when (without any merit of ours) he gave us a being so worthy and so excellent, would be enough. For he made us heirs to the supreme kingdom of Heaven, bought with his most precious blood.

But if these precious graces did not produce those results in us, we should

3. The story of David is also the story of the conversion of David to penance. Uriah the Hittite was killed by David indirectly when he was sent to the frontlines of the battle. See 2 Samuel 11:2–17. For the entire story of David's life and rule, see 1 Samuel 16–25 and 2 Samuel 6–24.

4. Matraini, *Considerationi sopra i Sette Salmi Penitentiali*, A2.

at least think that when we show ourselves ungrateful to him for such rich and magnificent gifts, we ought to expect grave and bitter punishment. And allured and inspired by so many and such powerful incentives, as are those of love and of fear, we shall begin to drive out the sin from our hearts, which (as everyone knows) is the only offender and the mortal enemy of God and of ourselves. It is true that having to go against this merciless monster, we must not rely upon our own weak strengths. Rather, we must turn for help to our most pious heavenly Father, and with every act of humility we must ask him for his just, saintly favor, which we surely shall obtain, because he is prepared continuously to give it to everyone who asks for it with their best thoughts.

There remains only this: that with a brave and strong mind, we are determined to drive from our hearts (the true temples of God) all sin, his opposite and our mortal enemy. And truly if we are so cautious and precise in our actions on which depend the honor and dignity of an earthly prince, how much should we be cautious and precise in the actions on which depends the honor of the highest God? And if a man, however reckless and bold, refuses to give shelter to a public enemy of his earthly lord, but drives him away and persecutes him, how much more do we have to drive away and persecute sin, which is the enemy of our God? And even if a man were so completely rash that he would instead shelter the enemy, what bitter punishment and severe justice would this miserable man expect from his earthly lord?

Therefore, if a man, for offending another with such unspeakable injury, deserves to be gravely punished and severely reprimanded, what punishment do we anticipate receiving from our eternal Father and divine Creator, every time that we, in his own house and before his eyes, receive his own mortal enemy? Certainly we ought to fear greatly that, in revenge for such great offenses, he will condemn us to infernal punishments. And yet he does not wish to do this immediately after we have sinned, because he waits for us to be repentant, directing his infinite mercy toward us, by which he unceasingly calls and invites us to penitence.

Certainly, when he has endured our sins and wickedness for a long time, and when he has with so many affectionate invitations enticed us to the enjoyment of his holy virtues, seeing us remain obstinate in our evil doing, he punishes us with rough floggings in revenge for our injuries to him. However, those who wish to escape so grave a danger have to abandon and flee sin as a thing harmful to themselves and an enemy of their Lord. May the people, therefore, take the sword of penitence, the shield of firmness, and the fire of the holy confession with its true satisfaction; and thence may they come to this fierce dragon in order to slay him completely, never to rise again.

And may they hasten to this holy task without wasting any time; all the more so since the most holy blood of Jesus Christ our Redeemer continuously inspires us to such beautiful work, shouting with a loud voice, "Come to me, O sinners, while you have time: because I am the true fountain in which all the sins of the world can be washed, and those who scornfully refuse my sweet and saving waters and my blood will always remain unclean and tortured with eternal punishment." These are words truly loving, which ought to coax man from those works which are sinful and harmful to him, and to inflame him to those works which are holy and deserving.

And why did the greatest God give us intelligence, if not in order to think continuously of the things of heaven, rather than immerse ourselves in the mire of earthly and transitory things? Oh, how ugly and unseemly it is for a man to waste all his time with earthly things and forget those heavenly things for which he was created. And what greater madness can he do than to devote all his thoughts to the sciences of the world, to know how to reason about them, and never try to know, miserable man, where he came from, nor where he must go, or where to find his happiest goal.

But in order that simple, devout men have a living example of these celestial virtues, I have thought to show them the true penitence of King David, a man truly rare and divine, a man, if I am not deceived, who will show them their goal and how they should govern themselves to obtain it. But because our weakness does not let us walk directly toward it, he will demonstrate how, with humble prayers and hot tears, we must seek this from our God, who, all beneficent and courteous, never fails to help us in our wandering and leads us to Heaven to enjoy that blessed life endlessly. And since I have to expound the seven penitential Psalms (before anything else), I think I should advise the reader not to expect from me the high, subtle reasoning which has already been done by many excellent, divine minds. Since I have not taken such pains except to help those who either were not easily able to read the fine theologians who have elucidated those Psalms, or perhaps did not truly understand their reading of them, I have wished to write an easy and brief interpretation for them, so that it may be useful and consoling to their souls.

But before I come to interpret the words of the Prophet, I should explain why these Psalms are seven in number, and also why they begin in tears and end in joy. I say, therefore, that the aforesaid Psalms are seven in number in order to beseech mercy from God for the seven mortal sins, each time that we have grief and enough repentance for them. They are also seven to demonstrate to us that in all the seven stages of man until the seventh, which is the final stage of the world, we must always weep and greatly grieve—owing to the penance to which we are obliged, on account of the sin by which we have been banished from the Paradise of delights and placed in this vale of tears and miseries, where we live under the hard servitude of our enemies. And the prophet, when he wrote, thought of this exile of ours, if I am not deceived.

How shall we sing the praises of the Lord in a land far away from our heavenly homeland? That is to say, while we live in this miserable and unhappy life we do not have just cause to rejoice, but instead to weep and grieve constantly over our calamities and sins. Thus, the Psalms begin in bitterness and weeping but end in bliss and joy: to show us that from tears, which come from true penance, people recover the lost grace and then eternal life.

But, as to why these Psalms were composed by King David, it is clear that the Prophet sinned gravely; and the sin that he committed against Uriah the Hittite was very grave: because beyond the adultery, he committed even murder. This displeased God so much that to correct him, God sent Nathan the Prophet, who recounted to him the parable of the rich man who, not wishing to reduce his own herd, took a lamb, to make a feast for his traveler guest, from a poor neighbor who had only that one lamb.

With this example, King David came to realize his sin as it is clearly said in the second book of Samuel, chapter 12.[5] Then Nathan said to him, "Since you have recognized your sin, hold this firm, O King, that God will not withdraw the sword from your house in eternity, because of your serious errors. And as you have tried to keep your fault hidden, so he will manifest it and make it evident to the eyes, not only of Israel, but of the entire world."

Then David responded, "I have sinned against the Lord," and Nathan answered him, "Because of your confession, the Lord has taken away your sin, so that you shall not die. Instead, the boy that is born to you from Bathsheba shall truly die." And having said these things, Nathan left him. At this time the child fell gravely ill, and David began to realize that the disasters threatened by God were already beginning to happen. Whereupon repenting of his faults, he entered into a dark place far from his house, and all full of bitterness, throwing himself before God, he burst out with these words.

THE FIRST PSALM

Domine ne in furore tuo arguas me, neque in ira tua corripias me.[6]

Meaning to say, O omnipotent Lord, I know very well that on account of the grave wickedness I have committed against you, I must fear your severe

---

5. Matraini attributes this to 2 Kings, chap. 12, but in contemporary Bibles it is actually in 2 Samuel, chap. 12.

6. Psalm 6:2 (Douay Rheims): "O Lord, rebuke me not in thy indignation, nor chastise me in thy wrath."

punishment greatly.[7] But because I also know that for all of time, you have ordered that your great power must give way to your infinite mercy, so I have ventured to appear before your high Majesty, humbly, and with the greatest possible affection of my heart, to beg that you do not wish to condemn me to those piercing punishments to which I should be condemned, justly, on account of my solemn errors. But I beseech you, with all the affection of my soul, that you pardon me according to your fatherly benevolence and infinite mercifulness.

And although David the Prophet uses this word "fury" when he says, "Lord, do not rebuke me in your fury," nevertheless, it must be known that in God there is found in neither anger nor fury, nor any other agitation or emotion, so to speak, because the being and the nature of God are totally different from ours. But as we cannot speak of the things of God except by using human concepts and in conformity with our way of understanding, therefore we say, but incorrectly, that in God there are such passions, or flaws. . . .

THE SEVENTH PSALM

Et perdes omnes qui tribulant animam meam, quoniam ego servus tuus sum.[8]

We said elsewhere that the Sacred Scriptures use "the soul" for "the life" of man, as is said in the verse cited earlier, "Educes de tribulatione animam meam," meaning: "You will free my soul from adversity," that is, my life and my being.[9] The same thing is understood here when he says: "And you will eliminate all those that afflict my soul, and bring constant danger to my soul and to my life," meaning his enemies, Saul and the others, who sought to murder him day and night. However, we can still say that for his enemies that afflicted his soul, he means the common enemies of man, which are the world, the flesh, and the demons, who, without fail, continuously assault us to kill and bury us in the depths of hell.

Therefore, he begs the Lord to destroy these enemies of his, so that they cannot dissuade him from his holy service, which is to say, "Lord, give them no power over me and I will not consent to their lies, but give me the power to defeat them, so that victorious in this battle, I may be able to triumph in Heaven, with so many blessed spirits that continually praise your Divine

7. Matraini, *Considerationi sopra i Sette Salmi Penitentiali*, 10r.

8. Psalm 142:12 (Douay Rheims): "And thou wilt cut off all them that afflict my soul: for I am thy servant." In other versions of the Bible, this is Psalm 143.

9. Matraini, *Considerationi sopra i Sette Salmi Penitentiali*, 99r.

Majesty." And so that the Lord may be led more easily to give him that grace, he gives an explanation, and says, "You ought to grant me this, because I am your servant." And what can the Lord ever deny to his faithful servant? Why should he not want to help him, if it is his servant who requires help?

Through this Psalm, the true penitents will understand that they must give thanks to God for their liberation from, or remission of, their sins. Together they will see the rules and form of praying: because, having to ask God for grace, it is reasonable that they also ask for high and divine things, such as to be freed from the continuous troubles that plague them and that prevent them from serving God with all their hearts. And if our enemies are merely men, we should pray and beg the Lord to illuminate them to act justly, not to do evil to them but, on the contrary, to pardon them for their sins. Even though we wish them to be punished, we ought to desire it in the way that the prophet desires, who said that in his mercy he scattered his enemies. Beyond that we see how David's petition is always directed to the glory of his Lord's majesty and to the praise of his most holy name, adding almost always that he is the faithful servant and worshiper of his God. Thus we learn to serve God with purity of life and sincerity of heart, to love him as we are beholden, because then without fail we shall obtain the desired grace for the salvation of our souls.

Figure 4. Engraving of Chiara Matraini at about seventy years old, made for inclusion in *Seven Penitential Psalms*. By permission of Houghton Library, Harvard University.

IV

A BRIEF DISCOURSE ON THE LIFE AND
PRAISE OF THE MOST BLESSED VIRGIN
AND MOTHER OF THE SON OF GOD

TRANSLATOR'S NOTE

The year 1590 is the date of Matraini's third book of prose, *A Brief Discourse on the Life and Praise of the Most Blessed Virgin and Mother of the Son of God*. The entire book appears in this series along with the writings on Mary by Vittoria Colonna and Lucrezia Marinella, translated by Susan Haskins. So I have included here only her dedication, her prologue, her poem "This, women . . . ," and a few of her thoughts on Mary, to serve as witness to her ideas. The book concludes with fourteen annotations by Giuseppe Mozzagrugno, which are noted in the Italian text.

The book can be found in various libraries, especially in Italy, and in microfilm at the Widener Library of Harvard University.

DEDICATION

To the venerable Lady Juditta Matraini, the Most Worthy Abbess of the Monastery of Saint Bernard of Pisa.

Most dear venerable Cousin, you have very often requested of me and prayed with affectionate words, that I should wish to send you a writing of mine on some devout subject. So I had thought to reason with you (as a Virgin dedicated to Jesus Christ) of that Virgin who is the Queen of Virgins, Empress of the Angels, and Mother of the Most High God. But considering, then, how base is my rough and weak intelligence, and how much it differs from that so very high and sublime subject, I do not dare to open my mouth to proffer the most sacred praises to her, nor to try my hand at so lofty and difficult an undertaking. However, I realize, indeed, that every mortal creature and even the celestial creatures would never be enough to praise her sufficiently. Besides, I am frightened by those words that say praise is not beautiful in the mouth of the sinner. On the other hand, considering the profound humility of this most singular Virgin, for which she became the Mother of the Supreme and Immortal God, and how she is always benevolent and favorable toward those who faithfully appeal to her for help, a firm hope arises in my mind that she will not scorn this good desire of mine, nor ascribe it to me as a vice of presumption.

Nay, I have become very certain that she will accept it as a sign of gratitude for the many good things I have received from her and that we all receive continually, our City in particular, which today, for her, not only is called Lucca, but Light. Our city is magnificent for the many stupendous miracles it demonstrates, for all the Christian people who are drawn by most devout affection from near and distant countries, and who come with splendid gifts to render the Virgin due honors and to ask for her grace. Whence I also have resolved to offer this most gracious Queen of the Heavens a certain small gift of my affectionate praise, if not according to her infinite worth, at least according to my small, insufficient means. With that favor, however, she will dictate to me. But first, with my heart humble and my knees on the ground, I want to pray to her that she will give me her holy favor, as I speak of things to her praise, honor, and glory, and to the glory of all the Christian people.

Your most affectionate cousin,
Chiara Matraini

PROLOGUE

Just as the beautiful, bright stars within the dark night precede Aurora,[1] messenger of the clear and already approaching sun, so a multitude of stars preceded the birth of Mary the Virgin, bright and spotless Aurora of the supreme and eternal Sun of justice and mercy; that is, many prefigurations of her most pure light, which came from that clear and everlasting Sun, who was to emerge from her chaste and virginal womb. Of these, one was the Ark made by Noah,[2] in the time of the great deluge. Although only eight people were saved by the Ark, because of the holy burden[3] of Mary the Virgin, the whole human race was freed from eternal death. She, that most blessed Virgin, also was symbolized by the rod that blossomed for Aaron,[4] because from her was born the fragrant flower which scattered its supreme and sweetest-smelling perfume.

Similarly, the prefiguration of her unique conception was given by that

---

1. Aurora is the goddess of the dawn.

2. The Ark bore to safety Noah, his wife, and their three sons, each of whom had a wife. See Genesis 6–9.

3. She means Christ, who was a burden to Mary in her womb.

4. Aaron was the elder brother of Moses. He was chosen to lead the Israelites by his staff, or rod, which blossomed. See Exodus 4.

chosen fountain which was enclosed within the garden;[5] since it was within the womb of her mother that she was thus sanctified, and completely identified with the sign of the most blessed Trinity, no baseness or stain ever entered into her. She is that most splendid star of Jacob, foretold by Balaam,[6] who was to be the special guide of all those who found themselves in the tempestuous sea of the tribulations of this world, leading them to the gate of the celestial homeland.

She was prefigured then by the closed gate that the Lord showed to Ezekiel, through which only the Lord was to pass, even though it was locked and never opened.[7]

She was also prefigured by that most excellent temple that Solomon had built to the glory of the highest God: the facade was fabricated of the whitest marble and within all adorned with the purest gold; so Mary the Virgin was always the most immaculate temple of God for chastity, and within she was all adorned with the purest gold of charity.

Similarly, the birth of this most blessed Virgin (as Landolfo the Carthusian[8] says) was signified by the case of the daughter of King Astyages, who saw in a vision, coming out of the womb of his daughter, a beautiful vine all filled with leaves and flowers and fruits, spreading and covering all his kingdom; of which the interpreters said that a most powerful King would be born of her (as he was indeed), for she bore Cyrus, who liberated the Israelites from the servitude of the Babylonians.[9] And so it was prefigured through her how the Virgin would give birth to that most potent celestial King, who was to liberate us from the wretched and cruel tyranny of the great enemy of human nature. Many other things, indeed, prefigured this heavenly Virgin, such as the ark of the covenant, the urn which contained the manna, and infinite other things, of which all the sacred and holy Scriptures are full, which I will omit for brevity.

Let us then place before ourselves her beautiful and holy example, distinguished in every virtue, and looking at it as if in a bright mirror, let us consider with what rich and very precious adornments of rare virtues she was adorned to please her dearly beloved husband, and let us seek to imitate her

5. The fountain which was enclosed in a garden was the prefiguration of Mary as conceived without concupiscence in the Immaculate Conception.

6. See Numbers 22:1–35. Balaam was converted to Judaism by an angel, who appeared to him on the road to the Jordan valley.

7. See Ezekiel 44:2 (Douay-Rheims): "And the Lord said to me: This gate shall be kept shut; it shall not be opened, and no man shall pass through it: because the Lord the God of Israel hath entered in by it, and it shall be shut." This became a well-known metaphor of Mary's virginity.

8. Landolfo the Carthusian is still unidentified. The Carthusians were a monastic order of the church, possessing a chapter at Galuzzo (1342–1957) and others at Farneto (near Lucca) and Calci (near Pisa).

9. King Astyages was the last king of the Medes, who reigned in the sixth century BCE. His daughter Amytis married Cyrus. See Daniel 1 and 14.

with every desire of ours (insofar as it is possible), to please our eternal and most benign God.

> This, women, is the mirror in which you must gaze
> intently and fixedly, with the beautiful eyes of the soul;
> and if you wish
> to see our face ever more beautiful;
> and if to Him, from time to time, you will turn
> the clear gaze within,
> always, in summer and in winter,
> you will be more beautiful and pleasant for our true lover,
> and in earth and heaven you will be praised, and holy.

> [Questo donne è lo speglio in cui dovete
> Cò begl'occhi dell'alma, intento, e fiso,
> mirar; se voi volete
> veder sempre più bello il nostro viso;
> E s'a lui, d'hora in hor, rivolgerete
> Il Chiaro sguardo interno,
> Sempre, l'estate, e 'l verno,
> Più belle, e grate, al nosto vero amante
> Sarete, e'n terra, e'n ciel, lodate, e sante.]

THE SUPREME, AND MOST SINGULAR GRACES OF THE VIRGIN MARY, MOTHER OF THE HIGHEST OMNIPOTENT GOD THE CREATOR AND RECTOR OF THE UNIVERSE

The divine and supreme excellence, the insuperable love, the beginning without beginning and the end without end of all things, wishing to share with others his inestimable and infinite goods, first of all created the Angels, perfect by nature, adorned with every beauty and full of wisdom.[10] Among these was foremost the great Lucifer, who was named for the light which shone from him. By divine will, recognizing that the son of God was to take on a human nature and, united with it, the eternal word, and that he was to be exalted above all the choirs of the Angels, and that many men would make themselves equal to the Angels, and perhaps greater, in glory, Lucifer was blinded by excessive pride of his excellency and refused to have anyone superior to him. . . .

When the most pure Virgin had returned from visiting Elizabeth, she was in her parents' house, distant from all the cares of this world.[11] She was

10. Matraini, *Breve discorso . . . della Beatissima Vergine* (Lucca: Busdraghi, 1590), 4.
11. Ibid., 32.

so inflamed by the divine love that she did not want anything, except to be happy in thinking of her Creator, who had created her and adorned her with so many singular graces and had made her the mother of God. She demonstrated and manifested signs of her great virtue and singular perfection more clearly from day to day. And while she remained in such a worthy and happy state, her chaste spouse, Joseph, arrived in Nazareth to celebrate their wedding and then to lead her to live in his house. He saw that she was with child, and still not knowing the secret of the divine mystery, he was greatly unsettled in his thoughts. He became most astonished and amazed at such a new and unexpected event, and knew not what to do with this fact, not because he suspected her of being less than honest, but because he believed more in the honesty and the chastity of Mary than in her pregnancy, and more in grace than in nature. He would rather believe that a virgin, without a man, could conceive than that Mary the Virgin could sin. But he feared that if he confided to others that she had conceived, it would bring blame and punishment on her, since the law required that adulteresses be stoned to death. But he also feared that if he were silent about it and she were seen big with child, he would be blamed and ridiculed by all the people.

> TO THOSE WHO ARE VERY DESIROUS OF TRUE WISDOM.[12]
> Whoever wants, from the great eternal Master
> who is shown as a little child to us today,
> to receive high and true intelligence,
> with the internal Clear light,
> should follow the steps
> of our guide, Mary, the mighty Virgin:
> He will be found in the Temple, among the doctors,[13]
> debating and winning, with men of greater
> age, and every human experience.
>
> [Chi dal gran mastro eterno
> Ch'oggi picciol fanciullo a noi si mostra
> Vuol'haver alta, e vera intelligenza
> Col chiaro lume interno
> Seguiti della nostra
> Scorta i passi, Maria, Vergine immensa:
> Ch'l troverà nel Tempio in fra dottori
> A disputare, e vincere, i maggiori
> D'etade, e d'ogni humana esperienza.]

---

12. Ibid., 58–59.
13. "Doctors" refers to the learned men in charge of the explanation of the Scriptures.

Figure 5. Title page from the 1597 edition of Chiara Matraini's *Lettere con la prima e seconda parte delle sue Rime*. The small oval on the lower right is the stamp of a library that once owned the volume. By permission of Houghton Library, Harvard University.

V

1597 VOLUME (BOOK C)

TRANSLATOR'S NOTE

Matraini's last book of poems was published by Nicolò Moretti in Venice in 1597, as *Lettere di Madonna Chiara Matraini gentildonna Lucchese, con la prima, e seconda parte delle sue Rime*. It was preceded two years earlier by a publication in Lucca, *Lettere della Signora Chiara Matraini, Gentildonna Luchese, con la prima, e seconda parte delle sue Rime*. This earlier volume (book B) was not authorized by Matraini, and none of it has been included here.

The 1597 volume begins with a series of eighteen letters which concern Matraini's poetry and her friendships. The last of the letters is addressed to the Virgin. I have translated only the first one, addressed to Cangenna Lipomeni, explaining a sonnet of Matraini's which she considered as basic to this book of poetry.

As with the 1555/56 book, I have selected two or three out of every five poems in the volume, in order, reflecting the sense of her narrative. I have translated primarily from the edition of Giovanna Rabitti, Chiara Matraini's *Rime e Lettere*, and have at times used a copy of the original as a prime source.

This book is very different from her first book of poems. Out of the eighty-seven poems published in this volume, only twenty-eight poems are carried over from the 1555/56 volume. Of the forty poems in part 1, the "in vita" sequence, fifteen are from her earlier book of poems (37.5 percent); of the forty-seven poems in part 2, the "in morte" sequence, only thirteen are from the earlier volume (28 percent). So Matraini has privileged the first part over the second, making the story of her falling in love and enjoying it much like her first book, while his death and her reaction to it are new and different in her third book.

In my selection of poems, I propose to the reader that Matraini created her life story, with what she defined at two different points in her poetic life as worth writing about. Her two *canzonieri* tell something about how the soul and the spirit function in life, where they get their energy and truth, how they move toward worthwhile ends. As her stories unfold and particularly as they inscribe their cardinal moments—in 1555/56, the death of the beloved; in 1597, the poet's spiritual conversion—the reader is confronted with a contrast in what is depicted as important and meriting consideration.

In narration, what happens is seen to be significant and important only in the end, in the place to which the action moves. Anything recounted earlier, as in the "past," has plot value only retroactively in light of the "future," the conclusion of the narration. As the reader reads, linearly, the significance is not immediately obvious. Only once the end has been reached is it possible to discover patterns in what came before, to tie together initially obscure, discrete episodes into configurations which cohere as a meaningful whole.

So my selection of poems between Matraini's first and last *canzonieri* is therefore a study of her meaning. In 1555/56, the meaning is that life is a love story, earthy and earthly, a love story that begins with enamorment and ends with the death of the loved person. In 1597, the meaning is that death is a love story, heavenly and Christian, beginning with the relinquishing of erotic love and finalized in salvation. My choice of her poetry is thus not only an attempt to describe the shapes and forms Matraini has constructed but also—and simultaneously—an attempt to show how she has conveyed meaning and to understand the profound meanings she has conveyed.

In fact, the story the poet relates is very diverse. In 1555/56, we have her triumph over her love for a man, over the woes and pleasures of life; whereas in 1597, we have the triumph of eternal life. No longer is she involved with a man, even as angel; she becomes involved with her poetry, her expression of it, and with God as Sun. In her later book of poems, she is liberated from earth and destined for the certitudes of salvation, of relations with the spirit world.

A more extended treatment of the differences between the 1555/56 and 1597 volumes is contained in *The Poetry of Chiara Matraini*, by Elaine Maclachlan, chapters 5 and 6.

TO MY READERS

You will perhaps be surprised to know, my most kindly readers, that first I sent into the light of day my Spiritual Meditations and the Considerations on the Seven Psalms of David, and next the worthy Praises of the Most Blessed Virgin, and now, last of all, I have published my youthful compositions, which, by reason, should have been the first. But if you knew how much persuasion was exercised by the prayers of my relatives and the exhortations of my friends, for my honor and my praise, you would not be surprised, nor would you blame me, if I have not followed that order in publishing my works to which I was obliged; but indeed I should be (and hope to be) kindly excused by you. So remain calm and happy.[1]

TO MADONNA CANGENNA LIPOMENI[2]
She declares to her the proper sense of her sonnet.

Here is the sonnet, my dear friend, which you requested from your Latona[3] with so much insistence, in which you will perceive how she persuades herself to leave the vain love of earthly and mortal things and turn to heavenly and divine contemplations.

> Return, soul of heaven, whitest moon,
> to your first circle, shining and beautiful,
> and renew with your most usual dawn
> the silver diadem which now grows dark.
>   Let the beloved Endymion go to the earth,
> to the black persistent shadow, hunting
> that prey which he delights in; and gather
> the eternal rays of your star to your brow.
>   Turn your beautiful eyes to your divine Sun,
> your true object, genuine and worthy,
> putting an abrupt halt to your swift stags.
>   Destroy with steady and honored indignation
> every wicked, evil fog that seeks to obscure
> your luminous heaven, clear and serene.
>   [Ritorna, alma del Ciel candida Luna,
> al primo giro tuo lucente e bella,
> e con l'usato albor tuo rinovella
> il diadema d'argento ch'or s'imbruna.
>   Lasc'ir per terra all'ombra atra, importuna,
> l'amato Endimïon, cacciando quella
> fera che più gli piace, e di tua stella
> eterni raggi alla tua fronte aduna.
>   Volgi i begli occhi al tuo divino Sole,
> proprio oggetto di te verace e degno,
> ponendo a' cervi tuoi veloci il freno.
>   Rompi con saldo ed onorato sdegno
> ogn'empia nebbia e vil ch'oscurar vuole
> il tuo lucido Ciel chiaro e sereno.]

But in order that you do not make a mistaken judgment as to its true intention, I will tell you what, in this sonnet of hers, Latona has really wanted to demonstrate, as I am always aware of every concern and work of hers. You must know, therefore, that since the moon is a true image and mirror of our soul, as we can amply demonstrate, our Latona at the first instance has appropriated her name in order to demonstrate how she must be in many ways similar to the moon. It is certain that as the moon has its light from the sun that shines upon us, so then our soul has the light of the intellect from the highest God; and as the moon at times has her light turned downward toward the earth and another time upward toward heaven, therefore Latona says:

> Return, soul of heaven, whitest moon,
> to your first circle, shining and beautiful,

Meaning: "Return, O my soul, after keeping for so long the light of the intellect turned toward low and earthly things, to gaze with it upon the infinite beauty of the supreme divine Sun, by which you were made famous and bright over all the stars." And following that metaphor, or rather simile, she adds that as the moon is a star of the first and lowest circle of all the heavenly spheres, so our soul is the clearest star of the first and most sublime circle of all the heavens, that is, of the empyrean heaven. Therefore she must turn to it with her circular motion and turn from her bodily nature, tarnished in the mire of earthly things, to the pure, candid intellectual nature, in order to contemplate the supreme and divine Sun that shines there. She follows then:

> and renew with your most usual dawn
> the silver diadem which now grows dark.

Meaning: "Renew with the usual light of the intellect, the silver diadem, that is, the venerated crown of the virtues, toward the higher part, as the moon does when she shines toward heaven. The diadem is darkened now, because it is in the shadow of your bodily desires."

> Let the beloved Endymion go to the earth,
> to the black persistent shadow, hunting
> that prey which he delights in; and gather
> the eternal rays of your star to your brow.

Here she demonstrates how she must let her delight in beloved earthly things go into the shadow of their vanity. The false pleasure of this world, in the guise of Endymion,[4] always tries to catch its wandering prey, that is, the roving appetites, totally deprived of reason; and the soul, finding itself deprived of that reason, is finally slain. "And of your star and your own intellectual light, which resides in the highest part of yourself, collect, or in truth gather eternal rays to your heavenly brow." But what else are the eternal rays of which our soul must make the diadem and crown, if not the lovely and clear cognitive virtues? By this she wants to demonstrate that the mind, or our intellect, must be served by the virtue of the true wisdom which renders its heavenly contemplation perfect, and she wants to demonstrate that reason must be served by prudence, so that it knows how to discern the true from the false, and therefore fantasy from true opinion, and will from justice, and hot-tempered power from fortitude. Then she follows:

> Turn your beautiful eyes to your divine Sun,
>   your true object, genuine and worthy,

Since the sun and moon are, or are said to be, the eyes of the heavens, so the reason and intellect are, or are said to be, the eyes of the heavenly and immortal soul. And, therefore, she tells her soul that because of the admirable and great operations of God, she ought to look at or contemplate with such eyes his supreme goodness, his divine beauty and infinite wisdom, as her true, proper, and worthy legacy.

> putting an abrupt halt to your swift stags.

This verse demonstrates that as the moon, with her right and natural reason, turns and guides her very swift stags and her bright and luminous carriage in their race (according to the imagination of the poets), thus she must change and brake her own swift desires which are always awake and ready to run headlong after the loved and vain pleasure and its feigned ghosts and false images. Thus she will not go astray from the true and straight path toward which she has been directed, so that she can ascend to her final and happy goal.

> Destroy with steady and honored indignation
>   every wicked, evil fog that seeks to obscure
>   your luminous heaven, clear and serene.

"Destroy," she says, "not with anger, which is a certain fury and heat of the blood that is born soon and soon dies, but with steady, stable, and hon- ored indignation, conceived by reason, against your mortal and treacherous enemies which are your own offending senses. Destroy and scatter the evil, wicked fog, I say, the troublesome and melancholy temptations, which want to darken your luminous heaven, clear and serene," meaning that the intellect begs heaven to be in the highest and most sublime part of our soul. And this has been said of the senses, for they are the sole, mighty cause of the rebellion of all our inferior powers from the rule of the higher powers, making them resistant to reason. It makes us raise the flesh against the spirit, whereby often we are transported by our great weakness and evil inclinations to do that which we should not and not do what we should.

This is what she has wished to demonstrate briefly in this sonnet of hers, and I commend myself to you.

COMINCIA LA PRIMA PARTE DELLE RIME DI MADONNA CHIARA MATRAINI, GENTILDONNA LUCCHESE.

C 1 (A 1, B 1)

Se lieta in verde età sola cantai
dell'interne mie fiamme i cari ardori,
la virtù, la beltà, gli eccelsi onori
di quell'alto mio Sol che tanto amai,   4
 ben dovea tutte vincer l'altre assai,
in mostrar quel, ch'altre celaron, fuori,
poiché co' suoi divini, almi splendori
vins'egli ogn'altro, ond'io sì chiara andai.   8
 Pero, s'oltr'al comune affetto, sempre
mi fu questo a virtù di gloria sprone,
che sol d'alti pensier l'anima cinse,   11
 scusimi appo ciascun sì caste tempre,
l'infinite vittorie, e le corone
d'Amore, che 'l saggio, il santo, e 'l forte vinse.   14

C 2 (A 6, B 2)

Con giusta meta il sol librava intorno
al secondo equinozio, e 'l tempo e l'ora
già dell'ugual bilance uscivan fora
per fare al nove dì lieto ritorno,   4
 quand'Amor, di sue grazie immense adorno,
altro Sol di beltà che 'l mondo onora
mostrommi, e di virtù ch'ad ora ad ora
fa dentro a l'alma un bel perpetuo giorno.   8
 Questi, non come il sol mai basso o torto
fa 'l suo vïaggio entro la quarta sfera
per produrre o nodrir cose terrene,   11
 ma dritto ed alto, con pensiero accorto
di fare in Cielo eterna primavera,
con l'alme e chiare sue luce serene.   14

C 4 (B 4)

Quai lampi a voi, di gloria ardenti e chiari,
apportar posso, o quai ghirlande or fregi

HERE BEGINS THE FIRST PART OF THE RHYMES OF MADONNA CHIARA MATRAINI, GENTLEWOMAN OF LUCCA

C 1 (A 1, B 1)

If happy in my green age, I sang alone
the dear passion of my inner flames,
the virtue, the beauty, the sublime honors
of that high Sun of mine whom I loved so much,   4
    indeed I had to conquer well all the others,
showing that which the other women hid,
because with his blessed divine splendors
he conquered all, making me, Chiara,[5] victorious.   8
    However, if beyond the common affection
I found this a spur to the virtue of glory
that encircled the soul with high thoughts only,   11
    may I be pardoned by all for such chaste feelings,
the infinite victories and crowns of Love
which conquered the wise, the holy, and the strong.   14

C 2 (A 6, B 2)

With right intent the sun was poised around
the second equinox, and already the time and hour
of its equal balance shone on the face of the earth,
to make the new day a happy return,   4
    when Love, adorned with his immense graces
showed me another Sun of beauty and of virtue,
honored by the world, which hour by hour
makes within my soul a perpetual sunny day.   8
    This Sun, not like the sun ever low or changing,
which makes his voyage within the fourth sphere
to produce or nourish earthbound things,   11
    but, straight and high with his thought designed
to make in Heaven an eternal springtime
with his immortal and clear, serene lights.   14

C 4 (B 4)

What flames burning and bright with glory
can I bring you, or what garlands or ornaments

degni de i vostri celebrati pregi,
ond'a voi lode sian del merto a pari?   4
   Troppo da' miei pensier vanno dispari,
e dal vostro valore e fatti egregi
le debol forze mie; pur alti e regi
sono i disir, ch'ho per voi dolci e cari.   8
   Questi adunque vi porgo e vi consacro
devota a terra, in basso, umile stile,
col core acceso d'alto affetto ardente,   11
   ove sculto l'essempio e 'l simolacro
di voi vedrete, oggetto almo e gentile
a l'ingegno, a la mano, a la mia mente.   14

C 6 (A 13, B 7)

   Alto mio Sol, se l'anima beata
che vi rivolge, a la mia stella desse
tanto del suo splendor, che pur vedesse
farsi un giorno da voi chiara e lodata,   4
   credo che con la mente innamorata
ne' raggi vostri (l'altre luci oppresse)
arderia sì, che de le fiamme stesse
vedreste nova luce al mondo nata.   8
   O felice suo corso, se le vostre
rote il guidasse ove l'eterna fronte
volgete voi da la mia mente stanca!   11
   Ma vedo in giro andar le sfere nostre
contrarie sì, che mentre a l'orizzonte
v'alzate voi, lei nel ponente manca.   14

C 8 (B 8)

   Se a voi tropp'alta e glorïosa appare
la vera laude, ch'io v'appendo e sacro,
vivo mio chiaro, ardente simolacro
degno di lode assai più belle e rare,   4
   a me par il contrario, e che dispare
vada d'assai lo stil mio rozzo ed acro
da' vostri merti, ond'io v'ergo e consacro
quant'affetto d'onore il cor può dare.   8

worthy of your renowned high qualities,
so that there will be praise equal to your merit? 4
    My weak attempts are too unlike my thoughts,
and far from your worth and excellent deeds,
though the desires that I have for you
are high and noble, most sweet and dear. 8
    These, therefore, I give and consecrate to you,
kneeling and devout, in a low, humble style,
my heart burning with deep affection, 11
    where you will see sculptured the example
and image of yourself, the dear, kind subject
for my talent, for my writing, for my mind. 14

C 6 (A 13, B 7)

    My Sun on high, if the blessed soul
which turns to you would give enough of its splendor
to my star, that it would even see itself
become one day greatly bright and praised, 4
    I believe that with my mind enamored
of your rays (the other lights overshadowed),
I would burn so much that in those same flames
you would see a new light born to the world. 8
    Oh, happy its course, if your wheels
would only guide it where you bend
your eternal brow from my tired mind! 11
    But I see the movement of our spheres
in contrary directions, so while on the horizon
yours is rising, mine descends in the west. 14

C 8 (B 8)

    If my true praise appears to you
too high and glorious, which I bring and consecrate,
my clear and ardent living image,
worthy of much more exquisite and rare praise, 4
    then to me it seems the opposite, and that
my style, rough and rude, is far distant
from your worth, wherefore I raise and consecrate
all the affection of honor my heart can offer you. 8

E temo che col tempo il mondo dica,
udendo la virtù vostra immortale
e 'l mio fioco cantare in basso stile: 11
     —Quest'ardiò troppo a tanta alta fatica
alzar la mente, e gir con deboli ale
a sì divino oggetto e sì gentile—.   14

C 10 (B 3)

     Cerchin pur altri in più pregiati marmi,
ed in fini metalli ed in colori,
l'amato volto indi goder di fuori,
fin che 'l tempo di sè non lo disarmi;   4
     ch'io dentro a l'alma vivo e bello parmi
scolpir mio dolce ben con vivi ardori,
e come reverente ivi l'onori
mostrarli in puri, affettüosi carmi.   8
     In quella il miro e lo contemplo, e come
altamente conviensi a' merti suoi
ed al bel foco mio, l'onoro ed amo.   11
     E se favor mi drà, seco il mio nome
chiaro più d'altro andar vedrà tra noi
sempre la gente, al segno alto ch'io bramo.   14

C 13 (B 12)

     Copri pur quanto sai di nebbie ed ombra
e di tenebre oscure, atre e d'orrori,
al sole, umida Notte, i suo' splendori,
e il volto tutto della terra adombra;   4
     chè 'l mio bel Sol ne scaccia e ne disgombra,
malgrado tuo, con suoi lucenti albori
ogni vil nebbia, ed apre or fronde or fiori
di virtù sempre, di cui l'alma ingombra;   8
     né pensar forse, invidïosa, mai
per fare a l'altro sol vergogna e scorno,
di turbar qui del mio l'interna luce.   11
     Fa' pur quanto che puoi dimora, o sai,
che mentre avrò 'l mio Sol chiaro per duce,
contra tua voglia avrò perpetuo giorno.   14

And I fear that with time the world will say,
hearing about your immortal virtue
in my feeble song of such a lowly style: 11
    "This woman dared too much to raise her mind
to such high labor, and with feeble wings
to approach so divine and noble an object."   14

C 10 (B 3)

    Let others try—in more prized sculptures,
and in pure bronzes, and in colorful paintings—
to enjoy the loved face from outside
as long as time yields not its sway,   4
    but I, within my soul, will try to sculpt
my sweet love alive with living passion
and, how reverently there I honor him
showing him in loving poetic verse.   8
    In my soul I see and contemplate him,
and as it is highly due to his worth
and to the beautiful fire of mine, I honor and love him.   11
    And if I am fortunate, people will clearly
see my name, more than others, become
famous for the high goal that I yearn for.   14

C 13 (B 12)

    Cover the sun as you can with fog and shades
and with heavy gloom, black and horrorful,
O misty Night, cover its splendors,
and shade the whole face of the earth with darkness;   4
    for my beautiful Sun dispels your blackness
and all dark fog, despite you, with his shining dawns,
and he brings forth now leaves and now flowers
with everlasting virtue, which fill the soul;   8
    and do not ever think, O envious Night,
that you cause the other Sun shame and disgrace
and thus disturb the internal light of mine.   11
    O Night, dwell as long as you wish or know,
for while I am led by my clear bright Sun
against your wish, I will have eternal daylight.   14

C 14 (A 59 e 79, B 9). STANZE

Almo mio Sol, che l'onorata fronte
di raggi ardenti d'ogni vera gloria
portate cinta, e con voglie alte e pronte
fate immortal di voi qua giù memoria,
tal che del Tempo e di Fortuna l'onte
sprezzate, e di lor degna, alta vittoria
avendo, sopra il bel carro lucente
del Ciel v'alzate con l'eterna mente;   8

se cantando di voi l'altere lodi
che mi fan sopra al Cielo alzare a volo,
posso tanto impetrar che da voi s'odi
questo mio dir, ch'a voi felice e solo
inchino e sacro con più saldi nodi
che stringa Amor da l'uno a l'altro polo,
spero, con dolci ed amorose tempre,
di farvi al mio bel foco arder mai sempre.   16

Ma chi mi drà la voce e le parole
da lodar voi, mio tanto alto soggetto?
Come potrà mai stella al chiaro Sole
aggiugner luce, o 'l mio basso intelletto
alzarsi in parte ov'arrivar non suole
spirto del mio più chiaro e più perfetto?
Tropp'alta impresa attendo, e via più innante
cerco salir del glorïoso Atlante.   24

Pur dirò sol che quanto dar potea
benigna stella in Ciel, tutto vi diede,
e che dalla più bella e chiara Idea
vi fe' Natura essempio, ove si vede
quella grazia e virtù, per cui dovea
fare Amor degne ed onorate prede
di quell'alme gentil, ch'a poco a poco
s'alzan da basso oggetto a divin foco.   32

Io 'l so, ché dalla vostra interna luce
tale è 'l foco gentil che in me s'accende,
che dell'alta Cagion sua prima luce,
ond'è norma celeste a chi più intende;
pensier non giunge ov'ei porta e conduce
se di nube mortal mai non s'offende,

C 14 (A 59 and 79, B 9). STANZAS

My beloved Sun, whose honored brow is
crowned with burning rays of every true glory
and with noble and prompt desires,
you render your memory immortal on this earth
so that you hold in contempt Time and Fortune,
and having a high and worthy victory over them,
you rise in the lovely shining carriage
of Heaven with your eternal mind;   8

    if by singing your proud praises
that make me fly beyond the skies,
I can so plead that you will hear my words
that I dedicate to you, alone and happy,
with the firmest ties with which Love binds
together from one pole to the other,
then I hope with sweet and loving tempering
to make you always burn at my beautiful fire.   16

    But who will give me the voice and words
to praise you, so high a subject?
How can a star ever add light to the clear
Sun, or how can my lowly intellect
rise to a place where even a spirit
more famous and perfect than mine cannot arrive?
I am trying too high an enterprise, and aiming
to climb even farther than the glorious Atlas.[6]   24

    So, I will say only that as much as a benign star
in Heaven could give, it gave you all,
and of the finest and brightest Idea
Nature made you an example; hence we see
that grace and virtue for which Love
was to make worthy and honored prey
of those noble souls, as little by little
they raise themselves from a lowly object to a divine fire.   32

    That I know, for from your internal light
such is the gentle fire that is lighted in me,
made radiant by its first high Cause,
whence it is a celestial rule to the one who understands it:
a thought does not arrive where it calls and leads
if it is not touched by a mortal cloud;

e s'io ne faccio pur talor querela,
vien dall'imperfezion che il ver mi cela.   40
    Ma quanto posso gire all'alta meta
che mi scopre il suo lume, andar m'ingegno,
né per volger di ciel, né di pianeta,
cercherò di cangiar l'alto disegno,
e se l'empia mia sorte agli occhi vieta
veder del proprio oggetto il caro pegno,
non è però che l'alto mio pensiero
non mi trasformi ognor nel suo bel vero.   48
    Quanto più col desio l'alma s'interna
nella cagion de gli alti miei desiri,
tanto nella maggior bellezza interna
d'un'in altra sembianza par ch'aspiri,
poi sormontando alla beltà superna
sovr'a tutt'altri luminosi giri,
visto quant'ogni bel men bello sia
di lei, la segue e tutte l'altre oblia.   56
    Così, co i sproni alla ragione e a' sensi
il fren, vengo ad amar, quanto amar lice,
l'alma vostra beltà, che fra gli accensi
miei spirti vive altera e vincitrice.
Fammi i be' lumi suoi ne l'alma intensi
gran frutto eccelso trar d'umil radice,
ch'è tal la virtù loro alma e gradita,
ch'a bellissimo oprar l'anima invita.   64
    Per questa scala, al Ciel volando poggia
l'alma sovente e 'n Dio si riconduce,
ché lasciato 'l terren suo stato, alloggia
nel vero fonte dell'eterna luce,
ove poi gode in sì beata foggia
l'infinità bontà che in lei riluce,
che, quanto far si può, fatta felice,
non s'erge in alto poi, ché più non lice.   72
    O di che gran pensier, di che bel foco
soavemente i' mi nodrisco ed ardo;
o qual dentro m'invola a poco a poco
e leva in alto a più soblime sguardo
di quell'alta beltà dov'io m'infoco
e ferir sento da celeste dardo:

and if sometimes I complain of it,
it is because of the imperfection that hides the truth from me.   40
    But as much as I can turn to the high goal
that his light shows me, I will strive to go,
nor by the turning of the sky, nor planet,
will I try to change the high purpose,
and if my cruel fate forbids my eyes
to see the dear token of the proper object,
it is not, however, that my high thought
does not transform me always into his beautiful truth.   48
    The more, with longing, the soul enters
the cause of my high desires,
the more in its greater internal beauty
it seems to aspire to a different appearance;
then rising to the heavenly beauty
above all the other shining circles,
it sees how much all beauty is less beautiful
than that beauty, follows it, and forgets all the others.   56
    Thus, with spurs to my reason and restraints
to my senses, I love, as much as is permitted,
your immense beauty that lives proud and winning
among my burning spirits.
So make beautiful lights deep in the soul,
and bring sublime fruit from a humble root,
for such is their virtue, sacred and pleasant,
that it invites the soul to its finest work.   64
    On this stairway, flying to Heaven, the soul
often rests, and to God it is returned,
for having left its earthly state, it resides
in the true source of eternal light,
where it is delighted in such a blessed way
by the infinite goodness which shines in it,
that, as much as it can, it is made happy,
and does not reach higher than it is permitted.   72
    Whether I am gently nourished and burned
with that great thought, with that glowing fire,
or if inside me it takes flight, little by little,
and rises high to a more sublime gaze
of that high beauty wherein I am inflamed
and feel myself wounded with a heavenly arrow,

io nol so dir, ma tal è il ben ch'io sento,
che non stimo fra noi maggior contento.   80

    Ché, da vostra bellezza alzando il piede
la mente a contemplar l'alto intelletto,
da cui deriva il bel che in voi si vede,
scorgo del bello e buono il più perfetto.
Così dall'alto vostro essempio riede
l'alma al suo prio nativo, almo ricetto,
che da grave e mortal sonno mi desta
e nuova fiamma entro 'l mio seno innesta.   88

    Felice l'alma ch'un bel foco accende,
e dolcemente l'arde e tienla in vita,
e con saldo desio mai sempre intende
a bellissimo oprare ed infinita
gloria cercando, tali i giorni spende,
che per cosa mirabile s'addita,
mostrando al vulgo cieco, errante, e vile
quanto lontan da sé volga 'l suo stile.   96

    Di tutti gli altri ben che sono al mondo
venuto il posseder, sazio è 'l desio;
ma di questo più sempre almo e giocondo
nasce 'l diletto, e da soave oblio
di sé, con un pensiero alto e profondo,
discerne il vero ben dal falso e rio,
mentre 'l suo albergo in disusata foggia
cangiando, in quel d'una bell'alma alloggia;   104

    dove, quasi nocchier saggio ed esperto
che in chiusa nave il nostro polo scorge,
si rivolge a sentier dritto ed aperto,
quest'anima gentil che ben s'accorge
dentr'al suo chiuso sen frale ed incerto,
del ben chiaro splendor che in lei risorge,
ond'il mar d'ogni error, gli scogli, e l'onde
fugge, e 'l segue con aure alme e seconde.   112

    Un'ombra, un fior caduco è questa forma
ch'al vulgo piace e poco tempo dura,
ma l'anima immortal che in noi s'informa
Tempo già mai né Morte non l'oscura.
Questa del vero ben seguendo l'orma,
che gli mostra di Dio la luce pura,

I cannot say, but such is the good I feel
that I cannot imagine among us a greater contentment.   80
    For, from your beauty, rising from base thoughts
in order to contemplate your high intellect
where your evident worth can be seen,
I discern the most perfect state of beauty and good.
Thus from your high example, the soul
returns to its first native, glorious shelter,
which awakens me from my heavy, mortal sleep
and sparks a new flame within my breast.   88
    Oh, happy the soul that lights a beauteous fire
and sweetly burns and keeps it alive,
and with firm desire forever aims
at doing good deeds and seeking infinite glory:
it spends its days, so that it is indicated
as a true wonder, showing the blind,
mistaken, and base common people
how distant from them its way appears.   96
    Of all the other goods in the world,
once we have possessed them, the desire is satisfied;
but of this, ever more sublime and joyful pleasure
is born, and from the gentle forgetfulness
of itself, with a high and deep thought
it discerns the true good from the false and wicked,
while changing its lodging in a new way,
and finds its place in a beautiful soul;   104
    where, like a wise and expert helmsman
who in a closed ship perceives our pole,
embarks on a right and open route,
so this gentle spirit well realizes
within its closed breast, fragile and uncertain,
the clear splendor rising in its soul,
whence it flees the sea of errors, the rocks and the waves,
and follows it with life-giving, propitious breezes.   112
    A shadow, a dying flower is this form
that delights people and lasts only briefly,
but the immortal soul that in us is informed
will not be overshadowed by Time or Death.
This soul, following the traces of true good
that shows the pure light of God,

richiamat' a voi il cor con dolci tempre,
che per troppo gioir par che si stempre.   160

C 17 (A 78)

    Empia Invidia crudel, che ne' miei danni
per cieco error così tacita entrasti,
come vilmente a' bei pensier contrasti
mentre fingi la voce, il volto, e' panni?   4
    Com'esser può che 'l tuo livor condanni
quel chiar'oprare, o lo nascondi o guasti
dinanzi al mio bel Sol, dove mandasti
il tuo fosco velen, sì che l'appanni?   8
    Ma scoprin d'ira pur l'inique fronti
fiere tempeste, e con rabbiosi denti
Saturno i figli suoi sempre divori,   11
    che sempre fian più manifesti e conti
a gli occhi miei que' divin raggi ardenti,
perch'io gli renda sempre eterni onori.   14

C 19

    Se nella fronte il cor, nel petto il foco
porto, e 'l martir ne gli occhi, e gravi omèi
per la lingua vi scopro, e i pensier miei
vi son sempre palesi in ciascun loco,   4
    perché prendete i miei tormenti in gioco,
dandomi sempre quel ch'io men vorrei
per guidardon del cor che a voi sol déi,
là dov'è scritto il bel nome ch'invoco?   8
    Deh, non sprezzate il pensier alto, ond'io
contemplo quel ch'a ogni bell'alma piacque
d'amar sempre e lodar con dolce canto.   11
    Non contrastate al ben, che dal desio
della sua perfezione eterna nacque,
ond'abbiate cagion d'amaro pianto.   14

C 20 (A 60, B 15). MADRIGALE

    Dalla più bella mano
ch'occhio dritto mortal vedesse mai

make my heart return to you with sweet sounds
because, for too much gladness, it is melting away.   160

C 17 (A 78)

    Cruel, wicked Envy, by blind mistake
and to my harm, you entered so silently;
how basely have you clashed with my lovely thoughts
while you feign his voice, his face, and his form?   4
    How can it be that your spite should condemn
that clear life, or hide or shatter it
before my beautiful Sun, where you sent
your wicked poison, to darken it wholly?   8
    But even though the vile face of wrath
uncovers fierce tempests, and Saturn[8] keeps
devouring his sons with his mad, rabid teeth,   11
    still ever more manifest and important
to my eyes will be those divine, burning rays
so that I may render to him eternal honor.   14

C 19

    If I carry my heart on my brow, my fire in my breast,
and my martyrdom in my eyes, and I discover
my speech indeed moans and my thoughts
are always disclosed to you everywhere,   4
    why do you take my torments for play,
giving me always what I would least wish
for reward of the heart, which to you only I gave,
there where the beautiful name I invoke is written?   8
    Alas, do not despise the high thought
whereby I contemplate what pleases every lovely soul:
always to love and praise with sweet song.   11
    Do not oppose the good, which was born
from desire of eternal perfection,
or you may have reason for bitter weeping.   14

C 20 (A 60, B 15). MADRIGAL

    By the most beautiful hand
that a fair mortal eye ever might see,

soavemente il cor sentii legarme,
e dalla pura neve
stringer le sparte fiamme in spazio breve.   5
O benedette l'ore
ch'al cor mandaron tanta alta dolcezza!
O fortunato ardore,
cui l'alma più d'ogn'altro bene apprezza!
Quando sarà quel giorno,
ch'io faccia a tanto ben già mai ritorno?   11

C 21 (A 34, B 16). MADRIGALE

Smarrissi il cor, ghiacciossi il sangue quando,
dipinto di pietà, l'almo mio Sole
udii, con dolci ed umili parole
dirmi e con un sospiro:—O mio sostegno,
mesto men vo, ma 'l cor ti lascio in pegno.—   5
In questo, l'aspro suo dolore accolto
sfogò per gli occhi, e 'mpalidì il bel volto.
Quel ch'io divenni allor, sasselo Amore,
e sallo bene ogni invescato core,
che quasi morta, in voce rotta e frale,
a gran pena formai:—Signor mio, vale!—   11
E più non potei dire,
ché mi senti' morire.

C 22 (A 38, B 17). CANZONE

Quant'è fallace e vario il nostro corso
e com'a' bei desir volgon le stelle
contrario il tempo, ch'al pensier si cela.
Ahi, quanto il mio disegno oggi trascorso
vedo da quel, che l'alte voglie e belle
aveano ordite alla mia nobil tela!   6
Libera credev'io poter la vela
ferma tener della mia ricca nave,
ed aver l'aure a' miei pensier seconde;
lassa, che sotto l'onde
la speme è gita, ed a giogo aspro e grave
l'alma mia quiete libera e soave.   12

softly I felt my heart being bound,
and by the purest snow
I felt the divided flames being contained rapidly.   5
Oh, blessed be the hours
which sent so fine a sweetness to my heart!
Oh, happy the burning passion
that the soul values more than any other good!
When will that day ever come
that I may ever return to so much good?   11

C 21 (A 34, B 16). MADRIGAL

My heart went astray, my blood turned to ice, when
painted with pity, I heard my beloved Sun
with sweet and humble words
tell me, and with a sigh, "O my support,
sadly I go, but I leave you my heart as a pledge."   5
His eyes then wept, and he surrendered
to the bitter grief, and became pale.
What I became then, Love only knows,
and every entangled heart knows it well:
that nearly dead, with a voice broken and frail,
with great sorrow I formed, "My lord, farewell!"   11
And more I could not say
for I felt myself die.

C 22 (A 38, B 17). SONG

How greatly deceptive and various is the course of our life,
and how the stars turn time, which is hidden
from our planning, against our fond desires!
And, oh, how greatly do I see my own design,
that I had mounted in great faith, and fine,
upon my noble loom ruined today and in shreds.   6
I had believed that I could hold
firm and steady the free sail of my rich ship,
and have the winds propitious to my plans.
But no, for under the waves
my hopes have gone; and my blessed peace of mind,
once sweet and free, under a rough and heavy yoke.   12

Ma, qual nocchier senza l'usate scorte
dritto non può guidarsi incontro a' venti,
quantunque il brami, e di fuggir li scogli,
    così non poss'io gir contra a ria sorte,
cieca, senza 'l mio Sol di raggi ardenti,
e col nudo voler frenar suo' orgogli;   18
    né posso fare ancor ch'io non mi dogli
di quell'empia cagione, aspra, importuna,
che mi tolse da gli occhi ogni mio giorno,
e il Sol, che d'ogn'intorno
fe' l'aër lieto, or fa mia mente bruna;
ch'or fuss'io spenta al latte ed a la cuna!   24

    Ma di me stessa, sola, ho da dolermi,
ché per troppo mirar persi la luce
ond'io potea veder gli eccelsi campi;
    or piango, e grido, e co'pie' lassi e 'nfermi
cerco cieca guidarmi e senza duce,
né sentier trovo che dal duol mi scampi.   30
    Ma s'avien mai che que' soavi lampi
riveggia, e le divine alte promesse
sian stabilite per voler divino,
per lungo, alto camino
seguirò l'orme sue nell'alma impresse,
perché più chiara ad alto fin m'appresse.   36

    Lassa, che parlo? Or se l'eterne rote
ferme non stanno, ma in contrario giro
volgon le stelle, e spesso a' nostri danni,
    quai promesse mortal, stabili, immote
trovar potransi, o lungi ogni martiro
aver nel lungo trapassar degli anni?   42
    Pur si deono schivare i certi danni,
e volger sempre a chiaro e divin segno,
con verissimi essempî, ogni consiglio.
Cade, qual rosa o giglio,
ogni nostro diletto e gran disegno,
se da salda virtù non ha sostegno.   48

    Dunque per l'orme di virtute intendo
seguir mia stella, ch'a bel fin mi scorge,

But, as a helmsman without his usual guides
cannot steer himself against the winds
as much as he desires, and flee the rocks,
    so I cannot move against my evil fate,
blind as I am; without my Sun of burning rays
and with my naked will alone rein in fate's pride;   18
    nor yet can I keep from lamenting
about that wicked cause, harsh and untimely,
which stole from my eyes every day of mine,
and the Sun which everywhere he turned
made the air bright but now makes my mind dark;
oh, that I were dead now in my cradle, a milk-fed babe!   24

    But of myself alone I must complain:
I stared too long, that is how I lost the light
which helped me see the heavenly fields.
    Now weeping and wailing, on weary feet and weak,
blind and with no leader, I try to guide myself,
yet find no path that will deliver me from pain.   30
    But if it ever happens that I may see
those sweet lights again, and if divine and fair decrees
are pledged by divine wish,
on the long high road
I will follow his footsteps sealed upon my soul,
so that more clearly I may approach my lofty goal.   36

    Alas, what am I saying? Now if the eternal wheels
will not stand still, and if against their proper way
the stars turn them, and often to our pain:
    what pledge of permanence stable and unmoved
can we find on earth, or how can we keep torment
distant from us in the long passing of the years?   42
    Yet certain pain is much to be avoided,
and we must always turn our every counsel
to bright and heavenly goals, based on true example.
Gone, like the rose or the lily,
are all our pleasures and our great plans at last
unless with good and steady strength we hold them fast.   48

    Thus I intend along the path of strength and virtue
to follow my star that guides me to a lovely goal,

ogni basso pensier posto in oblio;
　　né d'invidia o minacci il cor temendo,
lascerò 'l Sol, che da lontan mi scorge,
per li scogli contrarî al desir mio.　　　　　　　　　54
　　Tornin dunque i be' lumi, e 'l tempo rio
scaccin dall'onde, e con dolce aura e lieta
drizzin le vele al desïato porto,
anzi che sia risorto
il novo tempo, e 'l lucido pianeta
torni alla libra sua con giusta meta.　　　　　　　　60

　　Canzon, chi tua ragion facesse oscura,
dilli che non n'hai cura,
perché tosto averai chi dal bel velo
ti disciorrà, dov'io t'ascondo e celo.　　　　　　　64

C 23 (A 35, B 18)

　　Fera son io di questo ombroso loco,
che vo con la saetta in mezzo al core,
fuggendo, lassa, il fin del mio dolore,
e cerco chi mi strugge a poco a poco;　　　　　　　4
　　e, come augel che fra le penne il foco
si sente acceso, onde volando fuore
dal dolce nido suo, mentre l'ardore
fugge, con l'ale più raccende il foco,　　　　　　　8
　　tal io, fra queste fronde a l'aura estiva,
con l'ali del desio volando in alto,
cerco il foco fuggir, che meco porto.　　　　　　　11
　　Ma, quanto vado più di riva in riva
per fuggire 'l mio mal, con fiero assalto
lunga morte procaccio al viver corto.　　　　　　　14

C 24 (A 36, B 20)

　　Alti son questi monti, ed alti sono
li miei pensier, di cui l'alma s'ingombra:
questi, sol piante sterili gli adombra,
le mie speranze senza frutto sono.　　　　　　　　4
　　Scendon fonti da lor con alto suono,

with all lowly thoughts consigned to oblivion;
 nor shall my heart fear envy or threat,
nor will I give up the Sun that guides me from afar,
past the rocks that are contrary to my desire.   54
 So let the lovely lights return, let them drive the storms
out of the waves, and with sweet breeze and fair
set the sails straight for the port I seek,
before the new age
can arise, or the bright shining planet
can return to Libra[9] and its just destination.   60

 Song, if anyone should find your meaning obscure,
tell them that you do not mind;
for soon someone will come and free you
from the lovely veil wherein I conceal and hide you.   64

C 23 (A 35, B 18)

 A wild beast am I of this shady place,
and I go with an arrow in the center of my heart,
fleeing, alas, the end of my grief and pain,
yet I seek him who bit by bit destroys me;   4
 and, as a bird who among his feathers
feels the fire, so flying out of his sweet nest,
while he flees the fierce, impetuous heat,
he fans, with his wings, the hot fire more;   8
 so I, among these branches in the summer breeze,
with wings of desire flying up high,
seek to flee the fire which I bear in me.   11
 But as much as I go from here to there,
to flee my evil curse, with fierce assault,
a long death do I gain for my short life.   14

C 24 (A 36, B 20)

 Lofty are these mountains, and lofty are
my thoughts, with which my soul is burdened:
only sterile plants shadow these mountains,
just as my hopes remain without fruit.   4
 Deafening waters fall from them,

contrarî venti alle lor cime, ed ombra
di nubi stanno, e 'l duol da me disgombra
pianto e sospir, di cui sempre ragiono.   8
    Nemiche fere in essi, empie e rapaci,
s'annidan solo, e nel mio petto alberga
fiera doglia, che 'l cor m'ange e divora;   11
    godon pur questi le superne faci
qualor vil nebbia almo seren disperga,
ma non vedo mai 'l Sol che l'alma adora.   14

C 27

    Quel sì dolce di gloria ardente sprone,
ch'in le parti del cor profonde impresso
m'avete, oltra di quel c'ha il desir messo,
quant'al mio andar più duro il fren s'oppone,   4
    maledir mi fa i ceppi, e la prigione,
e gli altrui ingiusti torti, e 'l nostro sesso,
e 'l giogo, e le catene, c'hanno oppresso
il poter de l'ingegno e la ragione,   8
    che non mi lascian gire ov'io farei
fors'anco il nome mio, chiaro, immortale,
e voi n'andreste più superbo e altero.   11
    Deh, pur com'esser può che i pensier miei,
qual Dedalo, non trovino ancor ale
da fuggir questo laberinto fero?   14

C 30 (A 57)

    Lassa, non so qual nube il mio bel Sole
m'asconda e vieti il suo dolce ritorno,
per cui sì chiaro e lieto ogni mio giorno
solea mostrarsi più ch'altro non suole.   4
    Io pur ascolto e non odo parole
che mi faccino noto il suo soggiorno,
e temo, e spero, e ognor dentro e d'intorno
lo chiama l'alma che per lui si duole.   8
    Ohimè, dove son or quei chiari lumi,
che mi mostrâr con bei vestigi santi
di gir al Ciel con glorïosi passi?   11
    Lassa, non so: so ben che in doglie e pianti,

contrary winds at their summits, and they are
shadowed with clouds, and my grief brings on
tears and sighs, with which I am always burdened.   8
    Hostile beasts, wicked and rapacious,
lie only there, in my breast there lies
fierce sorrow, which devours my heart;   11
    but even they enjoy the supreme lights,
when the serene dawn clears the low fogs,
but I never see the Sun which my soul worships.   14

C 27

    That sweet blazing spur to glory
that you have deeply pressed into my heart,
beyond that which was placed by my desire,
finds a harder rein to oppose my course: 4
    this makes me curse shackles, and prisons,
and the unjust wrongs of others, and our sex,
and the yoke and chains which have oppressed
the power of my talent and my reason: 8
    these do not let me go where I would make
perhaps even my name both clear and immortal,
and then you too would go, more proud and majestic.   11
    Alas, how can it be that my thoughts,
like Daedalus,[10] do not yet find wings
to flee this fierce and loathsome labyrinth?   14

C 30 (A 57)

    Alas, I know not what cloud hides my lovely Sun
from me and forbids his sweet return,
whereby every day of mine once appeared
so clear and happy that the other days were shamed.   4
    I listen carefully and do not hear the words
that make known to me his place of lodging,
and I fear, and I hope, and always within and around
the soul that grieves for him calls to him.   8
    Oh, where are they now, those clear eyes
that showed me in that lovely holy path
the way to Heaven with radiant steps?   11
    Alas, I do not know: but I know that in pain and tears,

priva de gli alti suoi rari costumi,
gli occhi e l'alma a tutt'ore ardendo stassi.   14

C 33 (B 23)

    Vidi sgombrar dalle mie notti il velo,
ed ornarsi di gloria e splendor tutto
il mondo cieco e d'error fosco e brutto,
e mostrar nuove alte bellezze il Cielo;   4
    vidi l'acque fermarsi, e tremar Delo,
e d'immensa virtù nascer tal frutto
dolce sì, che 'l veleno avria distrutto
del grand'empio Piton nato di gelo,   8
    quando voi, Sol di luce ardente e vera,
scorsi, di gloria alteramente cinto,
apportar grazia desïata e nova;   11
    ond'ora è 'l sol da' vostri raggi vinto,
che sempre lieta mostran primavera,
e per cui chiara in me luce si trova.   14

C 34 (B 24)

    Ben ponno ormai del mio bel Serchio l'onde
superbe andare, e 'n chiari, alti concenti
cantar le Ninfe in grazïosi accenti,
con voci d'ogni onore alte e profonde,   4
    da poi che sopra a l'onorate sponde
s'odon sonar d'intorno a l'aere e venti
di voi il bel nome e le virtute ardenti,
con voci d'ogni onore alte e profonde.   8
    Ben poss'io dirmi ancor felice e chiara
stella, fra l'altre donne oggi illustrata
dal più bel Sol che di virtù risplenda.   11
    Ma più dir si potrà l'alma beata
poscia, s'al vostro essempio unico impara
ad oprar sì, ch'al sommo Bene ascenda.   14

C 36 (A 69, B 25). STANZA

    Sempre sperar si deve anzi la morte
che possa tornar lieto ogni suo giorno,

bereft of his high, rare ways of being,
my eyes and my soul will be forever burning.   14

C 33 (B 23)

I saw darkness disappear from my nights,
and saw all the blind world, dim with error,
become adorned with glory and splendor,
and Heaven showed new life, and lofty beauties.   4
I saw the waters cease to flow and Delos[11] tremble,
and such sweet fruit of immense virtue ripen
that the poison of the great, wicked Python,[12]
him that was born of ice, would have destroyed;   8
when you, O Sun of burning and true light,
I beheld, surrounded proudly with glory,
bringing new and desirable grace,   11
whence now the sun is conquered by your rays
which always show a happy springtime
and because of which there is clear light in me.   14

C 34 (B 24)

Well may the waves of my beautiful Serchio River[13]
flow proudly now, and in clear high harmonies
the Nymphs may sing in graceful accents,
with voices honoring high and deep,   4
since your lovely name and passionate virtues
high above its honored banks are heard,
sounding through the air and the winds
with voices honoring high and deep.   8
Well may I call myself a happy and clear star,
among the other women today, as I am lighted
by the most beautiful Sun shining with virtue.   11
But my soul is said to be the more blessed
when, following your unique example,
it learns to aspire to attain the highest Good.   14

C 36 (A 69, B 25). STANZA

One always has to hope until death
that every day may become joyful,

però ch'un valoroso animo e forte
rende al Tempo ed a Morte oltraggio e scorno,
né teme il grave duol che la sua sorte
gli fa sentir per lungo, agro soggiorno;
ond'avien poi, quando lo spera meno,
che vede il sol più chiaro e 'l ciel sereno.   8

C 37 (B 27). STANZA

Ridon or per le piagge erbette e fiori,
s'allegra il cielo e l'aure fresche intorno
spargon mille soavi e grati odori,
ché 'l mio bel Sol n'ha riportato il giorno
co' suoi chiari divini, almi splendori
che fan d'alte bellezze il mondo adorno,
e me lieta cantar con dolci e chiare
voci l'alta virtù sua singolare.   8

C 39 (B 28)

Già il ventesimo quinto anno rivolto
ha 'l Ciel, da poi che l'onorato affetto
fu per virtù d'Amor legato e stretto
nel bel nodo che mai non sarà sciolto.   4
E già venticinque anni ha che m'ha tolto
di rivedere il bel sembiante eletto,
ma non poteo già mai far che interdetto
mi fusse contemplare il divin volto,   8
qual con scarpello Amor di virtù impresse
sì forte nell'umana e nell'eterna
parte, che non fia mai per tempo estinto.   11
Così l'alto Motor del Ciel permesse
ch'un parlar breve, sol d'onestà cinto,
cagion fusse a grand'opra e sempiterna.   14

LA SECONDA PARTE DELLE RIME DI MADONNA CHIARA MATRAINI GENTIL DONNA LUCCHESE.

C 41 (B 29)

Ohimè l'alma beltade, ohimè il mio Sole,
ohimè de gli occhi miei la luce altera,

seeing that a worthy and strong spirit
repays Time and Death with outrage and scorn,
nor should we fear the heavy grief that our fortune
makes us feel for a long, harsh time;
for it happens then, when we hope for it least,
that we see the sun more clear and the sky serene.   8

C 37 (B 27). STANZA

Now grasses and flowers laugh on their slopes,
the sky is glad and the fresh breezes
scatter a thousand sweet and lovely fragrances,
because my beautiful Sun has brought back the day,
with its clear, divine, precious splendors.
They make the world lavish with true beauties
and make me joyful, singing, with sweet and clear
notes, his rare high virtues.   8

C 39 (B 28)

Already the heavens have counted the twenty-fifth year
since the deep and honored affection was,
by the act of Love, tied and tightened
in the lovely knot, never to be released.   4
And already, twenty-five years have gone by
that I have been forbidden to see my chosen one:
but never would I suffer my being refused
to contemplate his divine countenance.   8
By virtue of Love, it was still engraved
so strongly in my human and eternal soul
that never will it be eradicated.   11
Thus, the High Mover of the Heavens
let a short speech, girded with pure honesty,
become the cause of great, everlasting works.   14

THE SECOND PART OF THE RHYMES OF MADONNA CHIARA MATRAINI GENTLEWOMAN OF LUCCA.

C 41 (B 29)

Alas, my sublime beauty, alas, my Sun,
alas, the proud light of my eyes,

ohimè qual m'ha lasciata innanzi sera
fra quest'ombre mortali, orride e sole!   4
    Ed ohimè l'alte sue sagge parole,
quai l'anima d'udir già mai non spera
fin dopo morte, in quella ultima sfera,
là 've scorge 'l mio cor quanto si duole.   8
    Ma ben che senza te, dolce mia vita,
rimasta sia d'affanni e d'orror piena
ed ogni gioia abbi da me sbandita,   11
    non però fia che 'l duol che a morte mena
rompa 'l bel nodo, ov'a te sempre unita
starò, mentre ch'io viva in pianto e pena.   14

C 42 (B 30)

    O luci del mio cor fidate e care,
come da gli occhi miei vi dipartiste
tacite, e nell'occaso vi copriste
eternamente, senza mai tornare!   4
    Già non ponno veder più fosche, amare
notti quest'occhi, o sconsolate e triste,
di queste, ahi lassa, ch'al mio core apriste,
turbando l'ore mie serene e chiare.   8
    Ben conobbi il mio duolo e 'l vostro caso
(o speranze qui prese a' nostri danni):
ma chi può andare contr'al mortal suo corso?   11
    Piangete, occhi infelici, che rimaso
altro non v'è che lagrime ed affanni,
privi del vostro dolce, almo soccorso.   14

C 44 (A 88)

    Occhi miei, oscurato è il vostro Sole,
così l'alta mia luce è a me sparita
e, per quel che ne speri, è al Ciel salita;
ma miracol non è: da tal si vuole.   4
    Passò, com'una stella che in Ciel vole,
nell'età sua più bella e più fiorita.
Ahi dispietata Morte, ahi crudel vita
via men d'ogni sventura altra mi duole!   8

alas, that you have left me still alive
among these horrible mortal shadows!   4
    And alas, woeful me, your lofty and wise words
that my soul never hopes to hear again,
unless after my death, in that last circle
where my heart discerns the depths of grief.   8
    But verily, without you, my sweet life,
I am left full of unending sighs and horrors,
and my every joy is thrust away from me.   11
    The grief which leads to death will not undo
that lovely knot, where I will be tied to you
while I live in deep tears and affliction.   14

C 42 (B 30)

    O lights of my heart, trusted and dear,
how you did depart from my eyes, silently,
and in your setting were covered over
eternally, never more to return.   4
    And now these eyes of mine can bear to see
no more bitter dark nights, comfortless and sad
like these (ah, woe is me) you opened to my heart,
shattering my serene, clear, and limpid hours.   8
    Well have I learned my grief and your lot
(oh, hopes, here snatched away, to our loss!),
but who can go against one's mortal course?   11
    Weep, unhappy eyes, for there is nothing
left to you but your tears and anguish:
gone is your sweet, kind, everlasting help.   14

C 44 (A 88)

    My eyes, your Sun has been eclipsed
just as my great light has vanished from me,
and, I may hope, has risen to Heaven;
but a miracle it is not: God wants it so.   4
    He passed by as a star flies through the skies,
in his most lovely and most flowering age.
Ah, merciless Death, ah, cruel life,
no other misfortune can be more grievous!   8

Rimasta senza 'l lume ch'amai tanto,
vomene in guisa d'orbo, senza luce,
che non sa dove vada e pur si parte;   11
    così è il mio cantar converso in pianto.
O mia forte ventura, a che m'adduce:
veder l'alte speranze a terra sparte.   14

C 45 (A 82, B 32). CANZONE

Chiara, eterna, felice, e gentil alma,
che, fornito il tuo corso a mezzo gli anni,
volata sei fra l'anime beate,
    volgi la vista or da' superni scanni,
che mostrar mi solei sì chiara ed alma,
e mira in quanto duol l'alta pietate   6
    di te m'ha posto, e quelle luci amate
da te, colme vedrai di pianto amaro
bagnare il fido mio dolente petto,
però ch'ogni diletto,
ogni mia gioia e viver dolce e caro
tolto mi fu quando da me partita
facesti, fida mia benigna scorta.
Da indi in qua non passa un'ora sola
mai senza pianto, né altro mi consola
se non la speme sol che mi conforta,
diva mia forte, ardente calamita,
di rivederti in Cielo a meglior vita;
però che senza te, ch'ogni mia gioia
fosti, lassa, non so com'io non moia.   20

    Però ch'al tuo apparir, doglia e tormento
spariva, com'al sol sparisce ogn'ombra,
e rallegravi il cor, sì com'ei suole
    far doppo pioggia; or fosca nebbia ingombra
di noiosi pensieri ogni momento
l'alma, che senza te null'altro vuole;   26
    e quel ch'ognor via più m'affligge e duole,
è ch'io non posso o debbo ancor morire,
dubitando da te farmi più lunge.
Così mi frena e punge

So I, without the light I loved so much,
go on like a blind person, having no light:
I know not where I go and yet I move on;   11
    thus my singing is changed to weeping.
O my hard fortune, to this you lead me:
to see my high hopes strewn to the ground.   14

C 45 (A 82, B 32). SONG

Pure, eternal, joyous, and noble soul,
you who, ending your life in your mid years,
have flown among the blessed spirits,
    now turn your sight from the heavenly abode
that you once showed me, so bright and noble,
and observe in what grief the deep pity   6
    for you has placed me, and those beloved eyes
that you loved you will see full of bitter tears,
drenching my faithful mournful breast,
because every delight
every joy of mine and my sweet dear life
was taken away from me when you departed,
O my faithful, gracious guide.
Since then, there never passes a single hour
without weeping, nor does anything console me;
except the single hope that comforts me—
my strong, burning, magnetic power—
to see you in Heaven in a better life;
because without you, who were every joy of mine,
alas, I know not how I do not die.   20

Because when you appeared, grief and torment
disappeared, as the sun makes every shadow vanish,
and you made my heart rejoice, as the sun
    makes everything glad after a rain; now
a dark fog of worrisome thoughts burdens
my soul, which wants nothing but you;   26
    and what now still torments and grieves me
is that I cannot and must not yet die,
fearing that I would make myself more distant from you.
Thus my reason restrains me

or la ragione, ed ora il mio desire
pur mi sospinge: e tu di me non curi,
come sia spento in te quel caro affetto,
qual non vide mai sol pari né stella,
per quest'aspra del mondo atra procella.
Ne' tuoi saggi consigli ogni perfetto
giudicio intesi, e vidi esser sicuri
tutt'i miei passi, e per monti alti e duri
rendermi lieve, e 'n mar da' fieri venti
tôrmi, e dalle Sirene e lor concenti.   40

    Tu m'hai lasciata qui, senz'alma in vita,
la notte senza stelle e sole i giorni,
steril la terra e 'l Ciel turbato e negro,
        e pien di mill'oltraggi e mille scorni
vegg'ov'io miri, e la virtù sbandita,
e quanto scorsi già bello ed allegro   46
        veggio al tuo dipartir languido ed egro.
Valore e cortesia per terra giacque
quel dì che mi lasciasti in doglia e pianto,
né mai più riso o canto
s'udio, ma ciascun mesto, afflitto tacque,
con pianti che potean rompere i sassi
per la pietade, e gravi alti sospiri;
né più sereno giorno il Cielo aperse:
Parnaso un nembo oscuro ricoperse,
e' fonti e fiumi da' lor proprî giri
voltârsi a dietro addolorati e lassi
per ascosi sentieri orridi e bassi,
nella tua morte, e voci alte e funeste
d'udîr fra l'ombre, lagrimose e meste.   60

    Or, quanto a me, non ha più bene il mondo
senza te, la mia stella e 'l mio conforto
che fosti all'alma travagliata e stanca.
    Tu 'l sai, ch'essendo a me celato e morto,
nulla veggio più chiaro o più giocondo
in questa vita lagrimosa e manca,   66
        né vedrò fin che questa chioma bianca
non sia 'ncor tutta, e 'l vital nodo sciolto,

and wounds me, and now my desire
still spurs me on: but you care for me not at all,
as if that lovely affection is dead in you,
which never saw a sun like it, nor star,
through this harsh black tempest of the world.
In your wise opinions I understood
each perfect judgment and saw all my steps
secure, and through tall and rough mountains
I was made light, and in the seas I was saved
from the wild winds and from the Sirens and their songs.   40

    You have left me here, living without my soul,
in nights without stars and days without sun,
the earth barren and the sky gloomy and black,
    and full of a thousand abuses and contempt
I see wherever I glance, and virtue abandoned;
and all that I perceived glad and joyous   46
    I see languishing and faint at your departure.
Worth and courtesy were destroyed on the earth
that day when you left me in grief and weeping.
No more laughter and song were heard,
but everyone was hushed, heavy of heart, and afflicted
with weeping that could move stones
to compassion, and deep mournful sighs.
No more did Heaven open a serene day:
a dark storm cloud covered Parnassus,[14]
and the springs and rivers turned back
from their headlong course, sorrowful and weary,
in hidden paths, horrid and lowly
in your death, and deep, funereal voices
were heard among the shades, tearful and gloomy.   60

    Now, as for me, the world has no more worth
without you, O my star and my comfort
that you were to my troubled, tired soul.
    This you know, that with you buried and dead to me,
I see nothing more clear and more joyous
in this tearful and wanting life,   66
    nor will I see it until these locks of hair
are all white, and this knot of life is untied

che mi ritiene in questo basso incarco.
Ahi Ciel invido e parco,
Ciel oggi a impoverirmi in tutto vòlto,
perché non festi in un medesmo punto
ch'un medesmo sepulcro ambi chiudesse,
dovendo a tanto mal rimaner viva,
e del morto mio ben spogliata e priva?
Forse per far ch'a' suoi gran merti avesse
eguale il pianto, e mai da me digiunto
non fusse il duol ch'al cor morendo impresse?
Per ch'io non resterò di pianger mai
ma tanto 'l piangerò quanto l'amai.   80

   Deh, se come ti calse, ora ti cale
di me, che vivo in tenebre e martiri,
porgemi la tua casta e fida mano,
   e trammi dalle lagrime e sospiri
ond'io mi sfaccio, ché ben vedi quale,
poi che ti festi, ohimè, da me lontano,   86
   sia qui 'l mio stato ed ogni pensier vano
del mio morir ch'io bramo e ch'io vorrei;
né d'altro non aver più non m'incresce,
fuor di te solo, ond'esce
dal cor ogn'altra voglia e desir miei.
Né fera è in selva, o pesce in acqua, o in ramo
augello, o in arbor fronde, ovvero in terra
erba, o pietra si giace entro la rena,
che testimon non sia della mia pena.
Tu, Re del Cielo, a cui nulla si serra,
prego che mandi l'alma che tant'amo
pietosa a ricondurmi al fin ch'io bramo,
dove m'aspetti ad esser teco unita,
omai lasciando questa mortal vita.   100

   Canzon, colma di pianto, in veste oscura,
fra le pompe funebri e meste andrai,
là 've è spento 'l mio Sole, ingegno, ed arte;
   ed a lui, c'ha di me la meglior parte,
con parole di duol grave dirai:
—Mentre 'l bel nome tuo, ch'ogn'altro oscura,   106

which keeps me in this low mortal state.
O Heaven, envious and miserly,
today aiming in every way to impoverish me,
Heaven, why did you not arrange that in the same moment
the same tomb should embrace both of us;
why do I remain alive to such evil,
so truly deprived and bereft of my dear dead one?
Perhaps so that his great merits would have
tears to equal them and never would be separated
from me the grief he laid upon my heart by dying?
Because I will not stop weeping ever,
and my tears for him will equal my love.   80

    Ah, if as much as you cared then,
you care for me now that I live in darkness and tortures,
offer me your chaste and faithful hand,
    and free me from the tears and sighs
with which I am undone, for you see clearly,
since you have gone, alas, far away from me,   86
    for this is my life, and how vain my thoughts are
about my death that I yearn and wish for;
for I do not regret not having anything else
outside of you alone, because any other wish
of my desire departs from my heart.
No beast in the woods, nor fish in water, nor bird
on a branch, leaf on a tree, nor even blade in the earth,
nor stone lying in the sand,
that does not witness my pain.
O King of the Heavens, from whom nothing is shut away,
I pray you to send the soul that I love so well,
to lead me, merciful, to the end I yearn for,
where you wait for me to be joined with you,
leaving now this mortal life.   100

    Song, overflowing with tears, dark in dress,
you will go among the sadness of the funereal displays,
there where my Sun, my talent, and art are dead;
    and to him, who has the better part of me,
with words of grave grief you will say:
"While your lovely name, overshadowing all others,   106

vivrà nel mondo e questa pietra dura
che ti cinge sarà, colei che tanto
t'amò col spirto avrà sospiri e pianto—.
Poi sopra il lembo, e' suoi begli occhi spenti,
e la bocca onde uscian note sì chiare,
versa d'immenso duol lagrime amare,
fin che di questa spoglia i' mi disarme
e dolce l'oda e lieto a sé chiamarme.   114

C 47 (B 34)

Ahi come presto, libera e spedita,
sazia di questo ben fallace e 'ndegno,
anima bella, dal terrestre regno
sei veloce anzi tempo al Ciel salita!   4
    Or vegg'io ben come l'umana vita
è polve ed ombra; e quasi sol, ch'a sdegno
avendo il nostro dì, cangia disegno,
onde fa qui da noi tosto partita,   8
        tu fuor d'ogni tempesta hai preso il porto
e col celeste tuo Nocchier ti vivi,
godendo l'aura sua lieta e tranquilla.   11
        Ma io qual nave in mar, per camin torto
rimasta son, con gli occhi in tutto privi
di te, chiara del Cielo alma favilla.   14

C 50 (B 35)

Io pur ascolto e non odo novella
della mia fida scorta che nel Cielo,
fuor del suo chiaro e bel corporeo velo,
gode il Fattor d'ogni lucente stella.   4
    Io pur ascolto a sé mi chiami e ch'ella
tutt'accesa di puro, ardente zelo,
volga a me i suoi begli occhi, ov'ancor celo
la casta fiamma mia, lucente e bella,   8
        e dica a me pietosa:—Ormai ti chiamo
a sentir del mio eterno, alto diletto,
e consolar le tue notti dolenti—.   11
        O felice quel dì, se al fin ch'io bramo

will live on in the world, and this hard stone
encircles you, she who so much loved you
in her spirit will have sighs and weeping."
Then on his shroud, his beautiful eyes now dead,
and the mouth which breathed such clear notes,
you will pour bitter tears of immense grief,
until I am freed of my mortal remains,
and I hear him sweetly and joyfully calling to me.   114

C 47 (B 34)

Oh, how fast you, O my beautiful soul,
free and quick, sated with this treacherous world,
have arisen from the earthly reign
rapidly to Heaven, far before your time!   4
Now I see clearly how human life
is dust and shadow; and like the sun,
which disdaining our day, changes its course
whence it soon departs from us.   8
You, leaving every storm, have found your harbor
and with your heavenly Helmsman are living now,
enjoying his joyous, tranquil breezes.   11
But I, like a ship on the sea, am left
wandering in error, with my eyes bereft of you,
you who are the clear, noble light of Heaven.   14

C 50 (B 35)

I listen carefully and yet hear no news
of my faithful guide, who is in Heaven,
no longer veiled in his precious, clear body
but now loving the Maker of every shining star.   4
I listen carefully, while wholly burning
with pure, blazing zeal, he calls me near
and turns his fair eyes to me where I hide
the chaste flame, shining and beautiful;   8
and says to me, with pity, "Now I call you
to partake of my eternal, high pleasure
and comfort you in your sorrowful nights."   11
Oh, happy that day, if to the end I desire

mi trarrà seco al desïato aspetto,
là 've si fanno gli angeli contenti.   14

C 51 (A 84)

    Vago augeletto mio, caro e gentile,
che dolcemente canti e sfoghi il core
mercé sperando aver del tuo dolore,
non lungi assai dal bel fiorito Aprile,   4
    ma io già mai col mio dolente stile,
in ch'io piango e mi doglio, a più liet'ore
giugner non spero, o 'ntepidir l'ardore
ch'io sento, o m'oda la bell'alma umile.   8
    Tu la tua amata e dolce compagnia
troverai forse in aere, in ramo, o in terra;
io la mia dove o quando, i' non saprei.   11
    Te la tua sente; ma chi dolce apria
mio core e speme, è spento oggi, e sotterra,
né le mie voci ascolta o' pianti miei.   14

C 52 (A 37, B 36)

    L'aura soave mormorando torna,
la terra ornando di novelli fiori
e, spargendo lontan soavi odori,
le rive e' colli di be' rami adorna.   4
    Né 'l bel lume del cielo oltra soggiorna
a far noti di sé gli antichi onori;
cantan gli augelli i lor felici amori,
ogni cosa s'allegra e lieta torna.   8
    Ma da me, lassa, un lagrimoso verno
non parte mai, ché, lunge al mio bel Sole,
oscura e mesta i' vivo in tristo averno;   11
    né trovo scampo alle mie doglie sole,
ché sì fiero è 'l martir nel core interno,
che Ragion non può far ch'io mi console.   14

C 53 (B 47)

    Tu dunque, figlio, sei morto, che solo
eri qui della mia vita conforto,

he will draw me with him, to the desired place,
there where the angels are made content.   14

C 51 (A 84)

   Wandering little bird, dear and gentle,
you who sweetly sing and open your heart,
have hope of finding pity for your sorrow,
so close to the fine flowering April,   4
      but I, with my sorrowful ways
in which I weep and grieve, never hope
to arrive at happier hours, nor quell the passion
I feel, nor hope that his humble soul hears me.   8
      You will find your sweet beloved
companion in the air, on a branch, or on the ground;
I do not know where or when I will find mine.   11
      Your own love hears you, but the one who sweetly
opened my hopes and my heart is dead today and buried,
and he does not hear my words or my cries.   14

C 52 (A 37, B 36)

   The soft breeze which murmuring returns,
adorning the earth with spring flowers
and, sprinkling afar those soft smells,
brightens the banks and hills with colorful boughs.   4
      Nor does the light of heaven linger
to make the ancient glory apparent;
the birds sing their happy, serene loves
and everything returns now merry and bright.   8
      But for me, alas, a tear-filled winter
never departs, because far from my beautiful Sun,
I live, dark and melancholy, in a wretched hell;   11
      nor do I find escape from my lonely sorrows
because so fierce is the martyrdom in my heart
that the power of Reason cannot console me.   14

C 53[15] (B 47)

   You then, my son, are dead, you
who alone were the comfort of my life,

e del mio legno travagliato il porto,
e d'ogn'orrida mia tempesta il polo?   4

    Ahi come presto al Cielo alzato a volo
ti sei, lasciando me per questo torto
camin, dov'or dubbiosa e stanca porto
questa mia vita fral carca di duolo.   8

    Ma poiché così piacque al tuo Fattore,
pregal che tempri almeno il dolor mio,
che col pianger non turbi il tuo diletto;   11

    e vien talor con filiale amore
a consolarmi, onde quest'aspro e rio
dolor volghi in più caro e santo affetto.   14

C 55 (B 39)

    —Deh, come il Tempo se ne fugge e vola
e di noi sempre se ne porta il meglio—
dicemi spesso il mio fidato speglio
com'ogni mortal cosa ne invola!   4

    Né dal pigro mio sonno anco una sola
volta, doppo molt'anni, i' mi risveglio,
ben ch'io mi veggia il crin canuto e veglio,
e fuggir la beltà che ne consola.   8

    In questo parla con la mente e dice
un pensier che di tema il cor mi punge:
—Non tardare a trovar securo albergo,   11

    ché chi col Tempo i passi non aggiunge,
qual pellegrino stanco ed infelice,
a mezza notte il dì si trova a tergo.—   14

C 57 (A 94, B 41)

    Fra le dubbie speranze e il van dolore,
d'ombre e sogni gran tempo invan nodrita,
fuor del dritto sentier l'alma smarrita,
vagando, andata è dietro al cieco errore.   4

    Ma Tu del Cielo eterno, alto Motore,
la cui somma pietà larga e infinita,
precorre a nostre offese in darci aita,
tra' a meglior corso il disvïato core,   8

and the harbor of my tormented ship,
and the safe haven in every dreadful storm? 4
Ah, how quickly you have flown to Heaven,
leaving me here in this twisted path
where now, doubtful and weary, I bear
this my frail life, heavy with grief. 8
But since your Maker wanted it so,
entreat Him to lessen at least my suffering,
so with my tears I may not disturb your joy; 11
and come perhaps with a son's love
to soothe me, so that this bitter, wretched
grief I may turn to a dearer, more holy affection. 14

C 55 (B 39)

"Alas, how Time flies away and flees
and always carries away the best part of us,"
my trustworthy mirror often says to me,
"and how time steals every mortal thing." 4
Nor from my sluggish sleep do I wake up,
a single time, after these many years,
even though I see my hair turned white and aged
and I see the beauty flee which comforted me. 8
Thus the mirror bespeaks my mind
and says a thought that pierces my heart,
"Do not tarry to find a secure lodging: 11
whoever does not match her steps with Time,
as a pilgrim, weary and unhappy,
will find the day behind her at midnight." 14

C 57¹⁶ (A 94, B 41)

Among the doubtful hopes and the vain sorrow,
nourished in vain with shadows and dreams,
my lost soul, wandering far from the right path
has followed the blind, wrong direction. 4
But You of the Heavens, eternal high Mover,
whose supreme piety, wide and infinite,
runs before us to give aid when we err,
lead the forlorn heart to a better path 8

e svelli omai dell'alma ogni radice
della speranza debole e fallace
che mi fe' vaneggiar fra tanti affanni;   11
   sì che, se al cominciar dell'infelice
guerra pers'il camin d'ogni mia pace,
almen ritorni a Te ne gli ultim'anni.   14

C 58 (B 43)

   Mentre la nave mia colma d'oblio
solcando andava in questo mar di pianto
e stava a udir delle Sirene il canto,
scôrta dal vago suo cieco desio,   4
   Tu solo, immenso, alto, e pietoso Iddio,
dal Ciel mandasti il tuo bel lume santo,
che sgombrò delle nebbie oscure il manto
onde me non vedeva e 'l fallir mio.   8
   Grazie dunque ti rendo, ed infiniti
preghi ti porgo, che 'l mio stanco legno
con la sant'aura tua conduchi al porto.   11
   Fa' che stian sempre i miei pensieri uniti
a Te solo, e 'l mio cor, l'opra, e l'ingegno,
sì che non resti al fin dell'onde assorto.   14

C 60 (B 50)

   Già comincia a scoprirsi il bel sereno
de' miei tranquilli giorni, e a poco a poco
ad accenders'il cor di novo foco
pien di dolcezza, senz'alcun veleno.   4
   Già comincia a raccôr l'anima il freno,
e volger i desiri a meglior loco,
e del mondo sprezzar diletto e gioco,
ed empier d'alte imagini il suo seno.   8
   Poi che voi, fida mia celeste scorta,
dimostrato m'avete il bel sentiero
che ne conduce a ben vero ed eterno,   11
   così per vostro aiuto ancora spero
lasciar via cieca, perigliosa, e torta
e condurmi a fin lieto e sempiterno.   14

and remove now from my soul every source
of the weak and fallacious hope that
made me go raving in so much anguish; 11
 so that, if at the outset of the unhappy
war I lost the path of every peace of mine,
at least I may return to You in my last years. 14

C 58 (B 43)

 While my ship laden with forgetfulness
was making headway in this sea of tears
and was intent on hearing the Sirens' song,
led by its uncertain blind desire, 4
 You alone, O immense, high and merciful God,
from Heaven sent your precious holy light,
that cleared the curtain of the dark mists
which kept me from seeing myself and my failure. 8
 Thanks therefore I give You, and infinite
prayers I offer You, that you will lead my tired
ship to the harbor with your holy breeze. 11
 Make my thoughts ever be united
to You alone, and my heart, my work and talents,
so that I will not be drowned in the waves. 14

C 60 (B 50)

 The beautiful serenity of my tranquil days
is already beginning to appear, and little by little
my heart begins to grow bright with a new fire
full of sweetness, without any poison at all. 4
 My soul is beginning to stop evil ways
and to turn my desires to a better place,
to despise the pleasures and play of the world,
and to fill my breast with high images, 8
 since you, my faithful heavenly escort
have showed me the true pathway
which leads to a true and eternal good. 11
 Thus through your help I still hope
to leave the blind, perilous, and twisted way,
that I may be led to the joyous, everlasting end. 14

C 64 (A 74, B 52)

Mai fuor di libertà, dolce né cara
cosa non fu né fia bella o gradita,
onde il buon Cato prima uscir di vita
volse, che servitute empia ed amara.   4
    Felice quel ch'all'altrui essempio impara,
e la grazia di Dio larga, infinita
apprezza, e tien solo al suo giogo unita
l'anima, ove di gire al Ciel s'impara.   8
    Io, da che sciolta e rotta è la catena,
là dov'io fui sì strettamente avvolta,
non fia già mai ch'io sia più per entrarve,   11
    ch'ombre diverse e spaventose larve
mi stan d'intorno al cor, con sì gran pena
qualor vi penso, ch'a fuggir m'han volta.   14

C 65

Se per vero trovar diletto e pace,
lungi dal porto la speranza mia
seguio tempesta perigliosa e ria
nel mar del cieco mio desire audace,   4
    volghisi or, con tranquilla aura vivace,
l'anima al sommo Sol dond'uscì pria,
qual sopra al Cielo a sé dritto l'invia,
accesa di sua pura, ardente face;   8
    ed al chiaro splendor de' santi rai,
purgata da ogni bassa ombra terrena,
seco le voglie sue sempre al Ciel erga,   11
    e quasi angel celeste ed immortale,
volando sopra i venti, apra e disperga
le nebbie, ond'io smarrita e cieca andai.   14

C 66

Come potrò senz'alma e senza vita
viver qui, senza voi, fra tanto duolo,
ch'esser solevi il mio conforto solo,
gentil mia prezïosa margherita?   4

C 64 (A 74, B 52)

 Never was there, nor shall there be,
a prize more sweet and dear than freedom:
so the good Cato[17] wished to take his own life
rather than bear his wicked, bitter slavery.   4
 Happy are those who learn from example,
and who value the grace of God, so wide and infinite,
and keep their soul ever united to its yoke,
and learn to travel upon the path to Heaven.   8
 I, since the chain is loosed and broken,
there where I was so tightly bound and confined,
may it never be again that I need to enter there: 11
 for many shadows and frightening ghosts
abide there, around my heart, with such great pain
when I think of them, that I am bound to flee.   14

C 65

 If, far from the straight harbor,
my hope of finding true pleasure and peace
is pursued by a dangerous foul tempest
in the sea of my bold, blind desire,   4
 may my soul, with tranquil living breezes,
turn to the supreme Sun whence it first came,
who up to Heaven sends it straightaway,
burning with its pure and blazing torch,   8
 and in the clear splendor of its holy rays,
cleansed of all its lowly earthly shadows,
it raises to Heaven its own wishes,   11
 and as a celestial, immortal angel
flying above the winds, it opens and scatters
the fogs where I was straying, lost and blind.   14

C 66

 My most gentle precious pearl,[18]
how can I, without my soul and life,
live here, without you, in the midst of grief,
you, who used to be my only comfort?   4

Lungi or da me, quest'anima smarrita
seguirà sempre voi ch'onoro e colo,
quasi stella che segue il nostro polo,
se tanto però fia da voi gradita.   8

Deh graditela in parte, e quel bel nodo
d'amor, ch'ambe ne strinse, ognor più forte
si faccia entro 'l bel vostro amato seno;   11

ch'io con più fisso e con più saldo chiodo
v'avrò nel cor, vivendo e dopo morte,
s'amor per morir mai non venga meno.   14

C 70 (B 61)

Come talora suol la verginella,
visto lontan le vïolette e' fiori,
che tratta dal desio de' be' colori
corre per côrli, leggiadretta e snella,   4

a cui giunta dipoi non può far ch'ella,
sentendo i lor soavi e cari odori,
ponga fine al desio, ch'entro e di fuori
l'accese a contemplar cosa sì bella;   8

così l'alma, da Dio fatta gentile,
spera trovar dentr'al bel viso altrui
quel divino splendor ch'appar di fuore,   11

ma quanto più s'accosta al suo simile
per appagare in parte i desir sui,
tanto s'accende di più intenso ardore.   14

C 72 (B 67)

Ben che voi, sacro ed onorato Monte,
passiate di grandezza Olimpo e Atlante,
e di Saturno l'alta stella errante
con la celeste e glorïosa fronte,   4

non sdegnate però, dal vivo fonte
ch'irriga di virtù le vostre piante,
mandar ad altri di quell'acque sante
che fanno aver del Tempo a scherno l'onte;   8

ma con l'altere idee vostre divine

Now far from me, this lost spirit
will always follow you, whom I honor and esteem,
like a star which follows our north pole,
if this should be pleasing to you.   8

    Ah, accept it in part, and let that dear knot
of love, which both of us tied, still stronger
be tied within your dear beloved heart;   11

    for I, with a more fixed and steady nail,
will have you in my heart, in life and after death,
if dying should not ever diminish love.   14

C 70 (B 61)

    There is a time when a fair young maiden
who has seen the violets and flowers from afar
and is enticed by desire for the bright colors
runs, winsome and slender, to gather them up,   4

    and she reaches them and can no longer
pick them; she smells their sweet and gentle scents
and there ends her desire: burning inside and out,
simply from gazing at their beauty.   8

    Thus the soul, ennobled by God,
hopes to find, within the fair face of another,
that divine splendor which outside is seen: 11

    but the more the soul nears its likeness,
to satisfy in part its desire,
the more it burns with a more intense heat.   14

C 72 (B 67)

    However much, sacred and learned Monte,[19]
you are greater than Olympus or Atlantis,[20]
and the distant errant star of Saturn[21]
with its heavenly and glorious appearance,   4

    you do not disdain, from the living spring
which waters your flowers[22] with so much virtue,
to send to others those holy waters,
that they may deride the passage of Time;   8

    but with your own divine, lofty thoughts

invitate a cantar le più bell'alme
d'intorno a quello in chiari, alti concenti.   11

    Ond'io con voglie ardenti, umili e chine
spero gustarne e glorïose palme
apportar lieta alle più strane genti.   14

C 73 (A 72)

    Quando formò di voi la bella figlia,
Cangenna mia gentil, l'alma Natura
tutt'arte, ingegno, ed ogn'estrema cura
pose ne' be' sembianti e nelle ciglia.   4

    Ogni maravigliosa maraviglia
restò ammirata allor oltra misura,
quando il parto gentil, ch'ogn'altro oscura,
vide, e quel bel ch'a null'altro assimiglia.   8

    Venere e Giove con benigni aspetti
si miravano in Ciel, cantando a prova
le Grazie in terra e' più felici Amori.   11

    Così a lei sempre più benigni affetti
mostrin le stelle, e 'n lei tal virtù piova,
che merti in terra e 'n Cielo eterni onori.   14

C 75

    Vivo Sole immortal, che da quest'ombre
levato al Ciel, di bei raggi immortali
di tua gloria t'adorni e tanto sali,
che d'ogni van pensier tutto ti sgombre,   4

     se mai nube mortal qui non adombre
il tuo splendor, ma spieghi ognor più l'ali
de l'opre eccelse a pensier alti eguali,
e d'immenso piacer l'alma s'ingombre,   8

     apri l'alme tue luci altere e belle
a la mia notte, ond'io contempli e miri
di tue chiare virtù l'ardenti stelle;   11

     ch'io prego poi che 'l bel dove che aspiri
sempre mai lieto ti si mostri, e quelle
luci dond' ardi a te rivolghi e giri.   14

invite the most worthy souls around
to sing with clear high harmony. 11
    So that I, with humble burning wishes,
hope to enjoy them, and joyously bring
palms of glory to the strangest of people. 14

C 73 (A 72)

    When blessed Nature fashioned from you,
my gentle Cangenna,[23] your lovely daughter,
she placed all art, every talent and care
in her beautiful appearance and form. 4
    Every marvelous marvel stood
then in admiration beyond measure
when it saw the newborn babe, which eclipses all,
and that beauty which resembles nothing else. 8
    Venus and Jove with kind faces looked at
each other in Heaven, while on earth the Graces,
along with the joyous Loves, were singing together. 11
    Thus may the stars show her their kind affection,
and in her may be poured such virtue
that she will have eternal honors on earth and in Heaven. 14

C 75[24]

    Living immortal Sun, who from these shadows
was raised to Heaven, you adorn yourself
with immortal rays of glory and rise so high
that you are totally freed of every vain thought. 4
    A mortal cloud here does not ever shade
your splendor, but keeps on spreading out the wings
of your best works, high and equal to your thoughts,
and with immense pleasure binds up your soul. 8
    May you open your lovely proud lights
to my night, so that I may contemplate
the blazing stars of your shining virtues, 11
    and may my prayers ever be that the beauty
you search for be shown to you ever joyous,
and may those lights where you burn be upon you. 14

C 77 (B 58)

Poi che l'antico Prometeo formata
ebbe di terra qui l'umana gente,
ascese al Cielo e una favilla ardente
tolse dall'alta sua rota infocata;   4
    e con sì degna preda alma e pregiata,
ritornato dal Cielo immantenente,
die' vita a quella e spirito lucente,
del cui splendor sarà sempre illustrata.   8
    Tal io, volendo dar spirito e vita
de' miei concetti alle figliuole morte,
convien che al Sol del gran Mobile ascenda,   11
    e della gloria sua, larga, infinita,
una scintilla del suo lume apporte
in esse, ond'io con lor chiara risplenda.   14

C 79 (B 69)

Dolce, ch'e tuoi pensier sì dolcemente
discopri al suon della tua dolce lira,
mentre ch'Apollo di sua grazia spira
nella tua chiara e sempiterna mente,   4
    se mai non fian quelle dolci aure spente
della tua gloria, e 'l grato odor che spira
de le grand'opre tue che 'l mondo ammira,
ma sempre un Sol ti mostri almo e lucente,   8
    fammi gustar di quel soave tanto
fiume dell'acque tue chiare e profonde,
che spargon di te sempre eterni onori;   11
    donami di tue note un dolce canto,
sì che l'alto desio ch'in me s'asconde,
dimostri al Sol de' tuoi chiari splendori.   14

C 82 (B 55)

L'alta mente di Dio grande ed immensa,
che di quant'ha creato il fin prevede,
scorge dalla sua eterna e stabil sede
ciò ch'a noi copre oscura nebbia e densa;   4

C 77 (B 58)

When the ancient Prometheus[25] had
formed here the human race from clay,
he rose to the Heavens and a burning spark
he ensnared from its high flaming wheel,   4
    and with that noble and honored prize
he returned from the Heavens straightaway
and gave it life and that shining spirit
by whose splendor it will always be enshrined.   8
    So I, wishing to give spirit and life
of my concepts to my lifeless daughters,[26]
must rise to the Sun of the Moving Heaven,   11
    whence I may bring a spark of his light
and of his glory, so wide and infinite,
so that I may be resplendent, Chiara,[27] and clear.   14

C 79 (B 69)

Sweet Dolce,[28] who so sweetly reveal
your thoughts to the sound of your sweet lyre,
while Apollo[29] inspires with his grace
songs in your clear, everlasting mind,   4
    if those sweet auras of your glory will never
be forgotten, and the reputation inspired
by your great works which the world admires,
and you always appear a Sun, sublime and bright,   8
    make me taste, sweet Dolce, that gentle
river of your waters, so clear and deep,
which ever spread your eternal honors,   11
    grant me a sweet song of your notes
so that the high desire that is concealed in me
may show to the Sun your clear splendors.   14

C 82 (B 55)

The high mind of God, great and immense,
which foresees the end of all that he creates,
discerns from his eternal and unmoving abode,
that which for us is covered by dark, dense fog;   4

né vuol che ingegno uman, che indarno pensa
salir tant'alto col suo fragil piede,
intenda 'l fine ov'il principio riede
nel cerchio alto maggior, ch'apre e dispensa;   8
    ma che fisso al suo centro ov'ei s'annida,
miri qua giù la sua bontà infinita
ch'ogni cosa a buon fin volge e governa.   11
    Questa fie sol di noi fidata guida
a seguir lieta e glorïosa vita
in Ciel cara, beata, e sempiterna.   14

C 85 (B 75)

    Speme del sommo Ben, che 'l dolce e chiaro
fonte del mio gioir cresci ed inondi,
l'erbe m'infiori e gli arboscei m'infrondi,
e purghi ogni mio dolce almo d'amaro,   4
    sali innanzi al gran Sol, mai non avaro
de' suoi raggi beati al cor profondi,
ed ergi ivi il pensier, che non affondi
il nettar dolce, prezïoso, e caro.   8
    Ivi canta 'l bel foco, ove 'l mio ghiaccio
fia trasformato, entro nell'alma assiso,
e lieta ogn'ombra ne discaccia e 'l gelo,   11
    tanto ch'io possa alla sua grazia in braccio,
altera stella, sovr'alzarmi al Cielo,
e quasi angel volar nel Paradiso.   14

C 86 (MEDITATIONI SPIRITUALI 12, B 73). CANZONE

    Padre del Ciel, se 'l mio gran pianto amaro
può dell'immensa tua somma pietade
impetrar di mie colpe ancor perdono,
    non m'esser, prego, di tua grazia avaro,
ch'io piango e 'l pianto che da gli occhi cade
è proprio ancor di Te verace dono.   6
    Padre, tu sai ch'io sono
tua figlia pur da Te creata, e ch'io,
se sarò dalla tua grazia sbandita
in questa mortal vita,

nor wishes that human wisdom, which thinks
it can move so high with its fragile footstep,
can understand the end where the beginning resides
in the highest circle, wherein he reigns and bestows;   8

but that fixed in the center where he nests,
he directs his infinite goodness toward us,
so that all is aimed and governed to good end.   11

This alone must be our trustworthy guide:
to follow in Heaven a joyous and glorious life,
one that is loved, blessed, and everlasting.   14

C 85 (B 75)

Hope of the supreme Good, you who increase
and fill the sweet, clear source of my joy
and make my flowers bloom, my shrubs green,
and who cleanse my sweet soul of all bitterness,   4

may you rise before the great Sun, never
miserly of its rays, which shine deep
in the heart, and there may you raise your thoughts,
that the sweet, precious nectar may not disappear.   8

There the lovely fire sings, where my ice,
which is now within my soul, will be transformed,
and it gladly banishes every shadow and cold,   11

so that I, as a beauteous star on high,
may rise to Heaven, held by his grace,
and like an angel fly to Paradise.   14

C 86 (SPIRITUAL MEDITATIONS 12, B 73). SONG

Heavenly Father, if my heavy bitter weeping
from your immense supreme pity
can still beseech pardon for my sins,
do not be, I pray you, miserly with your grace:
for I weep, and the tears that fall from my eyes
are still a true gift from you.   6

Father, you know that I am
your daughter even created by you, and that
if I am banished from your grace
in this mortal life,

il tuo crudo Avversario iniquo e rio
sarà dell'opra tua, fra tanta guerra,
vittorïoso, ov'ei si chiude e serra.   13

    Ben mi potresti dir, Padre cortese,
che perdonato m'hai già molte volte
e che molte di nuovo ancor t'ho offeso,
        onde non son da Te, lassa, più intese
le voci mie, né da' mesti occhi tolte
son le lagrime e 'l pianto indarno speso.   19
        Ma sai che mai conteso
non ti piacque che fusse ad umil core
il perdonar, sì come già imponesti
a Pietro; e però questi
preghi vogli accettar, tanto maggiore
di lui mostrando la tua gran clemenza,
quant'è più propria a tua divina essenza.   26

    Già conosco, Signor, che cieca e frale,
senz'avedermi unqua del proprio fallo,
lasciando Te, son corsa alla mia pena;
        ma so poiché 'l tuo amore è tanto e tale,
che purgherà 'l mio error senza intervallo,
e romperà del mondo ogni catena;   32
        e so che se con piena
voce il sangue d'Abel gridò vendetta
e l'impetrò, se 'l tuo sempre più forte
griderà che da morte
mi scampi al Padre tuo, da Lui disdetta
non fia la grazia sua per mia salute
ond'a Lui gloria sia sempre e virtude.   39

    Ben so, giusto Signor, che non aspetti
ch'eschi da me dal cieco laberinto
de' vani affetti miei, com'io v'entrai;
        perché di lacci avvilippati e stretti
ho' piedi avvolti e 'l mio cor lasso e vinto,
ond'impossibil fia d'uscirne mai,   45
        se miracol non fai
simile a quel che già mostrasti a Pietro,

your harsh Adversary, wicked and evil,
will be victorious over your work
in this war, in which he hides.   13

    You could certainly tell me, gracious Father,
that you have already forgiven me many times
and that many times over I still have offended you,
    so that, alas, my words are not perceived
by you, nor from my sad eyes are the tears
gathered and all the weeping proffered to no avail.   19
    But you know that you never wished forgiveness
to be denied to a humble heart,
as you once commanded Peter;[30]
and may you still accept
these prayers, as they
show your infinite mercy greater than his,
as it is more proper to your divine essence.   26

    I already know, my Lord, that blind and weak,
without ever being aware of my own offense,
leaving you, I have run to my punishment;
    but I know that your love is so great
that it will cleanse my unending affliction
and will break every worldly chain;   32
    and I know that, if with full voice
the blood of Abel[31] shouted and begged
for revenge, your even stronger blood
will shout to your Father
to keep me from death; he will not refuse
his holy grace for my salvation
so that glory and power will be his forever.   39

    Truly I know, righteous Lord, that you do not expect
me to leave on my own the blind labyrinth
of my vain passions, as I entered it;
    because my feet are bound with chains
entangled and tight, and my heart is slack and overcome,
whence it is truly impossible for me to depart,   45
    if you do not create a miracle
like the one that you once showed to Peter,[32]

in trarmi di sì orribile prigione.
Dunque fa' che perdone
a me, Padre, ti prego, e volgi a dietro
tuo giusto sdegno, e carità ti volga
a perdonarmi, e del mio mal ti dolga.   52

    Già sai che non potea fuor de l'Egitto
uscir senza Mosé 'l popolo ebreo
mentre 'l superbo Faraon regnava,
    ma stava a maneggiar la terra afflitto
tutti i suoi giorni, nel suo stato reo,
né da se stesso a sé rimedio dava.   58
    Tal io sotto la prava
legge dell'error mio, forte nimico,
non poss'uscir né rilasciarlo a tergo,
se Tu, a cui inalzo ed ergo
ogni sperar, non mi ti mostri amico
col trarmi del mio error dal fango vile,
a volger l'alma a Te tutta e 'l mio stile.   65

    Tu vedi, alto Nocchier saggio e celeste,
ch'io son qual nave in mar senz'alcun vento,
e che mover me stessa unqua non posso
    se non secondo l'onde ognor di queste
fallaci voglie, a cui soggiacer sento
lo spirto, di valor spogliato e scosso,   71
    se da Te non è mosso
e tirato al tuo lieto a divin porto,
prima che cieco altrui desire il mene
ove l'impie Sirene
l'abbian nell'alto mar profondo assorto.
Scopriti dunque, omai, Luce divina,
e quest'anima al Ciel scorgi e 'ncamina.   78

    So ben che non aspetti, eterno Padre,
che 'l talento del dono il qual m'hai dato,
spenda qui per tua gloria e per mia lode;
    o 'l seme delle tue sante e leggiadre
grazie, ch'in me ponesti, via portato
da gli augelli non sia dell'empia frode;   84

in drawing me out of such a horrible prison.
Therefore, pardon me,
Father, I beg you, and turn
your just anger away from me, and find
charity to forgive me, and have pity for my evil ways.   52

You already know that without Moses[33]
the Hebrew people could not leave Egypt
during the reign of the haughty Pharaoh,
    but, tormented, they continued to work the land
all their days, in their wretched state,
nor could they by themselves find a remedy.   58
    So I, under the perverse
law of my delusion, my invincible enemy,
cannot depart from it, nor leave it behind,
if you, to whom I raise and exalt
every hope, do not show yourself a friend,
and draw me away from the mire of my error,
to turn all my soul to you, and my art.   65

You see, wise and heavenly Helmsman,
that I am like a ship on the becalmed sea
and that I cannot even stir myself,
    if not according to the waves of these
deceptive wishes, to which I feel my spirit
succumb, its valor stripped and shattered,   71
    if it is not moved by you
and drawn to your joyous, divine harbor,
before another's blind desire leads it
to where the wicked Sirens[34]
can drown it in the deep sinking sea.
Thus, O divine Light, reveal yourself
and make this soul be contrite and walk toward Heaven.   78

I know well that you do not expect, eternal Father,
my talent, which is a gift you gave me,
to be spent here for your glory and my praise;
    or the seed of your holy, fair
graces, which you placed in me, to be
carried away by the birds of cruel deceit;   84

o chi del mal si gode
rida che dalle spine oppressa i' sia,
perché sai ben ch'io son cieca e impotente,
né bisogna ch'io tente
senza 'l tuo aiuto andar per dritta via,
né di trovar salute altra fra noi
che la tua sola, onde salvar mi puoi.   91

Ben mi potresti dir, mia speme e vera,
ch'alla porta del cor già tante e tante
volte hai battuto col tuo Spirto interno,
    ma come sorda e malaccorta ch'era,
mai non apersi alle tue luci sante,
ond'in me non entrasti, o Sole eterno.   97
    Ma dimmi, alto e superno
Re delle stelle, onnipotente e vero,
Tu sol ch'hai del mio cor le chiavi in mano,
perché del mio pensiero
non apri 'l seno e scacci ogn'amor vano?
Già non hai, Signor mio, per me sì poco
speso, che 'l perdermi abbi a scherzo e gioco.   104

Togli, secondo l'alte tue promesse,
Signor, da me questo mio cor di pietra,
e rendimelo poi tenero e molle;
    rompi e scaccia le nebbie oscure e spesse
di questo senso van che sì m'arretra,
che 'l veder la tua luce mi si tolle.   110
    Però che Tu sol puolle
col tuo santo spirar mandar disperse,
e la mia lunga notte e senza luce,
alto mio Sole e Duce,
render chiara qual dì già mai s'aperse,
e far che 'l mio terren sterile e asciutto
produca ancora a Te qualche bel frutto.   117

E se Tu, mia benigna e ferma speme,
argumentando ancor, volessi dire
che più volte in tua grazia ebbi ricetto,
    ma non durai perfino a l'ore estreme

or whoever enjoys evil
to laugh when I am oppressed by thorns,
because you know well that I am blind and powerless
and I am helpless to try,
without your help, to walk on the right path,
nor can I find another salvation here in this world
than yours alone, whence you can save me. 91

You might say to me, my true hope,
that at the door of my heart you have knocked
so many times with your inner Spirit,
but as I was deaf and heedless,
I never opened to your holy lights,
so that you did not enter, O eternal Sun. 97
But tell me, high and heavenly
King of the stars, omnipotent and true,
you alone who handles the keys to my heart,
why do you not open
the womb of my thought and banish all its vain love?
You have not, my Lord, invested in me
so little that my loss is a game to you. 104

Lord, according to your high promise,
remove from me this my heart of stone
and deliver it to me, tender and yielding;
break and banish the dark, thick clouds
of the vain feeling that holds me back
and prevents me from seeing your light. 110
Because you alone can disperse
those clouds with your holy breath,
and my long, lightless night,
my high Sun and Leader,
you alone can render clearer than any day,
and make my barren and dry soil
yield again some beautiful fruits for you. 117

And if you, my kind-hearted, steadfast hope,
still reasoning, were to say that I
have found shelter again and again in your grace
but that it did not endure to my last hours

perch'io ne volsi, misera, partire
e seguir ben fallace ed imperfetto,   123
    direi ch'ancor disdetto
non mi debbe esser gire infino al fine
per questo; ond'io, Signor, grazia ti chieggio:
mentre che 'l dritto veggio,
possa con opre altere e pellegrine,
fuggendo 'l crudo ed infernale scempio,
mostrar delle tue grazie al mondo essempio.   130

    Già dicesti, Signor, chïunque ha fede
in Te che sempre ha Teco vita eterna,
piena di santa e desïata pace;
    dunque, poichè mia speme ha in Te sua sede
posta, Tu sol m'insegna e mi governa,
ch'io vo' sol quel ch'a Te diletta e piace.   136
    Ahi Padre alto e verace,
com'esser potria mai che tanta offesa
facessi a l'amor tuo perfetto e santo,
nell'indurarti tanto
contra ad anima umil ch'a Te sia resa,
s'altro mostran le faci ardenti e chiare
che nel tuo corpo altrui non puoi celare?   143

    Dunque in Te creder sempre
voglio, e por tutta in Te la mia speranza
che possi e vogli al gran bisogno aitarme,
e per me prender l'arme
della divina tua somma possanza
contra 'l nemico mio, donde vittoria
io ne riporti, e Tu trïonfo e gloria.   150

C 87 (B 77). MADRIGALE

    Sì come al tuo volere eterno piacque,
Padre, senza principio, e senza fine,
che al mio nascer Davina
pria fussi detta, e poscia a le sacre acque
CHIARA fussi nomata,   5

for I, alas, wished to leave you
and follow my fallacious and imperfect way,   123
    I would say that still I should not
be prevented from arriving at the end
for this; whence I, O Lord, ask your grace:
while I can see the path,
may I, with proud and crusading works,
fleeing the cruel, infernal chaos,
show the world an example of your graces.   130

    O Lord, you said once that whoever has faith
in you will always have eternal life,
full of holy and desired peace.
    Thus since my hope has placed its foundation
in you, may you alone teach and govern me,
for I want only what delights and pleases you.   136
    O high and truthful Father,
how could it ever be that my great offense
against your perfect and holy love
would make you so harsh
against this humble soul which has returned to you,
if the clear and burning flames show something different,
which you cannot conceal from others in your body.   143

    Therefore in you I wish
to believe always, and place all my hopes in you,
that you are able and want to help me in my great need
and to take up arms for me
in your divine supreme power
against my enemy, whence I may gain
victory, and you triumph and glory.   150

C 87³⁵ (B 77). MADRIGAL

    As it pleased your eternal wish,
Father, without beginning and without end,
that at my birth I was first called
Davina, and then at the sacred waters
I was named CHIARA, the clear one;   5

e del tuo Santo Spirito illustrata,
così prego, che al fine
d'esta vita meschina,
mi chiami (eletta in Ciel) divina, e chiara
risplenda, a la tua luce immensa, e cara.   10

and by your Holy Spirit I was enlightened,
thus I pray, that at the end
of this wretched life,
you call me (chosen to live in Heaven) divine,
and that I may shine clear in your overwhelming light.　　　10

VI

SPIRITUAL DIALOGUES

TRANSLATOR'S NOTE

Spiritual Dialogues was published by Fioravante Prati in Venice in 1602, late in Matraini's life, though it was probably written earlier. It contains a picture of a considerably aged Matraini. It can be found in Venice at the Biblioteca Nazionale di San Marco and at the Widener Library at Harvard University, in microfilm.

Spiritual Dialogues relates four imaginary conversations between "Theophila," who was Matraini herself, and "Philocalio," who was the son of "Cangenua," probably Cangenna Lipomeni, her lifelong friend. The dialogues proclaim Matraini's everlasting adherence to the search for salvation. This journey was not easy: the way was rough and not clear, always ready to be forgotten for the pleasures of this world. But the struggle for illumination represented for Matraini, speaking as Theophila, the highest Good, and was divine.

The volume also contains three sermons and eight poems of Matraini's; the last of them is her sonnet to Santa Chiara (Saint Clare), which concludes the book and was her last published poem.

THE AUTHOR TO HER READERS

> Out of the shadow of the dark, horrid death,[1]
> my Cynthia appeared to her beautiful Sun,
> more than ever she was Clear and bright, thus
> she follows him wherever his light leads.
>
> She fears not to wander on the path; as escorts
> she has her honored virtue and decency,
> nor does she ever repent or regret loving him:

1. Chiara Matraini, *Dialoghi Spirituali* (Venice: Fioravante Prati, 1602), 7.

his loving was given by destiny, so worthy of her.

 Indeed, the more she is absent from her Sun,
the more she is shining Clear and bright,
since nothing mortal casts her in its shade,
 nor do her eyes have any other object
than to do well, and she aspires only to reach
her beautiful Sun, who drives out every other light.

 [Dall'ombra dell'oscura horrida morte
Uscita la mia Cinthia al suo bel Sole
Chiara (più che mai torna) e come suole,
Il segue ovunque la sua luce apporte.

 Ne'l sentier, teme errar; ch'ha per sue scorte
Virtute, et honestà, ch'honora, e cole,
Ne mai d'amarlo, unqua, si pente, o duole
Sì degn'a lei 'l suo amor fu dato in sorte,

 Anzi quant'è più dal suo Sole assente,
Tanto più Chiara e lucida risplende
Poi ch'altra mortal cosa non l'adombra,

 Ne ad altro oggetto ha le sue luci intente
Ch'a ben oprar, nè ad altro aspira o intende
Ch'al suo bel Sol, ch'ogn'altro lume sgombra.]

To Gentle and Curious Readers:[2]
Insofar as books are printed, they pass through the hands of many people,
among whom there may be those who, with the power of their intellect, can-
not understand all things, and in particular, obscure things, which sometimes
they take wrongly, or mistakenly. Therefore, I have wished to explain here
the preceding Sonnet. You must, therefore, know that the Author, in the first
four verses, has appropriated for herself the name of Cynthia, that is, the
Moon, for certain imitations and similarities taken by her. She says that when
Cynthia, or really the Moon, leaves a certain thick, dark cloud, she takes the
light from the Sun. So, coming out from the shadow of death, that is, from a
grave illness, she returns to her beautiful Sun ever more clear and bright.

 By the Sun, she understands the study of the good sciences, which she
left behind because of this illness, and she calls it the Sun also because it has
always illuminated her mind to achieve the things fitting and proper to her.
She adds that she wants to follow it wherever its beautiful light leads, that
is, as far as the human intellect may arrive. She then indicates, saying that in

2. Ibid., 8.

following this, her Sun, she is not afraid to lose her path or way, for she has chosen for her most faithful escorts virtue and decency, which she cherishes and honors.

She adds that she never regrets or is sorry for loving so high and noble a subject as the Sun, considering how much her most honorable love is worthy of praise. It is instilled in the soul by a rare grace, by the most benign God. She follows the metaphor or the simile of Cynthia, the Moon, saying that the farther Cynthia is from the Sun, the more she shines, because she has left all earthly shadows behind her, which kept her from being completely illuminated by the Sun. Thus, the Author wants to demonstrate that the further she goes in separating herself from bodily and earthly delights, which oppose the sight of the intellect, the more she shines with the clear and true light of the knowledge of the most high and divine things that she has studied. Then no shadow of these delights may obstruct the sight of her clear and most beautiful splendor.

FIRST DIALOGUE

The speakers are Theophila and Philocalio.[3]

THEOPHILA: May God be with you, Philocalio. Right now I was about to knock on your door when you came out.[4]

PHILOCALIO: And what did you want, Lady Theophila?

THEOPHILA: I wanted Lady Cangenua,[5] your mother and my dear friend.

PHILOCALIO: She's not at home, but it cannot be very long until she returns from the villa with my lord father. Now, if you wish to wait for her you can enjoy yourself here in our garden.

THEOPHILA: I am glad to accept your invitation, to comfort the soul a little, as I am oppressed by many grave and unceasing thoughts.

PHILOCALIO: Well, come on in.

THEOPHILA (she enters): Oh, what breeze of earthly paradise I feel here.

PHILOCALIO: How do you like it, Lady Theophila?

THEOPHILA: Truly, I do not believe that one can find in this world a

---

3. These names are chosen to present her philosophy. Theophila means love of God. Philocalio means love of beauty.

4. Matraini, *Dialoghi Spirituali*, 10.

5. The name Cangenua most likely refers to her old friend Cangenna Lipomeni, who had a son.

more graceful, more beautiful, or more delightful garden for the senses than this. But for my mind's delight, I would not change the small garden of my study for this spacious and lavish one, full of the world's most chosen and fruitful plants.

PHILOCALIO: Oh, what pleasure or delight can you have there? Being always alone and almost, one can say, without light?

THEOPHILA: What do you mean, alone and without light? Indeed, I have there, always, at any hour that I want it, that agreeable company of most excellent spirits, which I desire and wish for most. They yield greater and more useful light to the eyes of the intellect and reason to distinguish the true from the false than the clear rays of this most bright Sun which we have shining above us.

PHILOCALIO: And this garden of yours, upon what soil have you made it grow?

THEOPHILA: Upon the soil of books, sown with many varied and generous writings, and fertile with the most noble virtues and wisdom. Other earth is broken with the iron hoe or with the plow, but this earth, with a more dignified tool, moves and is turned over with the sharpness and effort of the intellect.

PHILOCALIO: Then what water do you give it?

THEOPHILA: Sometimes with the water of the fountain of Parnassus, sometimes with the water from the river of eloquence (whenever I am able to obtain it), both of which produce excellent and beautifully perfumed fruits of true wisdom. Here, O Philocalio, forever under gentle and temperate airs, from day to day, there are born worthy and virtuous plants and fragrant flowers, the scents of which sometimes are spread throughout all the parts of the universe because they have fastened their roots in immortality.

PHILOCALIO: It would therefore certainly be noble and praiseworthy to keep the seeds of such rare and excellent plants.

THEOPHILA: Right you are: but as you know, there are few wise men who try to gather and preserve them within the treasury of their memory. Remember what Petrarch said in that sonnet:

> Gluttony, sleep, and the pillows of indolence
> have banished every virtue from the world,
> so that whoever wishes to make a river of eloquence
> flow is pointed at as a strange thing.[6]

6. This is derived from Petrarch's *Rime sparse*, 7, but she combines two quatrains and changes "Elicona" to "eloquenza." The original Petrarch reads:

(La gola, il sonno, e l'otiose piume
Hanno dal mondo ogni virtù sbandita
Che per cosa mirabile s'addita
Chi vuol far d'eloquenza nascer fiume.)

. . .

THEOPHILA:[7] . . . However, we often say, "If we follow nature as our guide, we will never go astray."[8]

PHILOCALIO: I don't think that this saying ought to be for everyone.

THEOPHILA: Why not?

PHILOCALIO: Because there are many, indeed, the majority of men, who follow their nature and yet go very far astray.

THEOPHILA: "All beauties with which the earth is adorned / Issue with goodness from the hands of the Eternal Master."[9]

PHILOCALIO: Yes, but what do you mean by that?

THEOPHILA: I mean that the man who errs does so by the use of his senses instead of his own nature. The most benign God adorned him with a reasonable nature, creating him in Heaven in his own image and likeness, gifted with an intellect and reason, to be a companion of the birds in Heaven, but above the fishes of the sea and the beasts of the land. But although man finds himself the most noble, perfect creature

---

La gola e 'l sonno et l'oziose piume
ànno del mondo ogni vertù sbandita,
ond' è dal corso suo quasi smarrita
nostra natura vinta dal costume;

et è sì spento ogni benigno lume
del ciel per cui s'informa umana vita,
che per cosa mirabile s'addita
chi vol d'Elicona nascer fiume.

Robert M. Durling's translation reads: "Gluttony and sleep and the pillows of idleness / have banished from the world all virtue, / and our nature, conquered by custom, / has almost ceased to function; / and so spent is every benign light of heaven / by which human life should be shaped, that / whoever wishes to make a river flow from Helicon / is pointed at as a strange thing." Robert M. Durling, *Petrarch's Lyric Poems* (Cambridge: Harvard University Press, 1976), 42–43, poem 7. He adds, to "make a river flow from Helicon" means to bring about the renewal of poetry. Matraini has chosen her lines to make her point.

7. Matraini, *Dialoghi spirituali*, 15.

8. In the original Matraini uses the Latin: "Naturam ducem si sequamur nunquam aberrabimus." In Latin, the word *aberrabimus* expresses the idea of both "mistaking" and "going astray, getting lost, wandering with no clear destination."

9. The Italian reads: "Tutte le cose di che'l mond'è adorno / Uscir buone di man del mastro eterno."

in this world of ours, there are certain imperfections in him which cause unhappiness and which cannot be found in any other living creature, not even in the heavens where the most perfect and sensible bodies are found. For all other things follow their purposes, in their natural way, according to the order given them by God, unhindered by any opposition. But man has within himself a contradiction which continually deters him and turns him away from the true and rightful path. Reason demonstrates this path to him at every hour, which, with the help of divine grace, would lead him to his most perfect happy goal if he were to obey its commandment. But almost every time he departs from the rightful path, to his shame and harm he is brought to his ultimate ruin. Although the intellect by its nature looks for the truth, and the will desires and loves the good as its own, nevertheless most men, deceived by the appearance of false good, do not look for and do not follow the end of perfection, toward which they are directed by God and ordered by nature.

PHILOCALIO: Why does this take place more in man than in all other living things?

THEOPHILA: Because all other living things have only one driving force, the appetite, by which they are moved to seek their goal without any opposition. But man has two: the first is in the appetite, the other in reason. Since these are different and distinct by nature, man lets himself be guided in two divergent ways. And because the senses are instruments of the soul, bringing to man delightful things, however harmful they may be, he desires and wishes them, and so by accident he does what he should not do by nature. Wherefore he comes to be like the Aesop's dog, which left his prey to follow his own shadow, thinking it was better than his prey. Therefore, O Philocalio, follow your nature and do not do as some ignorant people do: though they may have infinite things surrounding them from which they can partly learn the infinite power of him who miraculously has made them, still they close their eyes of intellect and reason, and sleep throughout their lives in the ugly sloth of their idleness and vileness. Instead, turn your noble, elevated talents to the honored study of the good sciences. . . .

FROM THE SECOND DIALOGUE

THEOPHILA: . . . and in this contemplation we feel measureless contentment, a conquest of all those things that we can desire, and we obtain all that we ask for, we understand as much as we yearn to know, and we live always beautiful, young, and joyful.[10] Being a lover and being loved in mutual, chaste, and reciprocal love; without annoyance or suspicion of envy or jealousy; always having delights, mirth, and pleasures for untold ages; and other things more worthy and of greater excellence: these things we cannot think of, much less express, because we are blind and mortal. And in short, the true and perfect happiness of man does not consist in the pleasures of the body or of the entire world, not in riches, not in powers, not in glory and honors, not in moral virtues, nor in the works of prudence and the other virtues, but alone in the action of the intellect, which is engaged in the contemplation of the truth. In sum, this is a Good really belonging only to man, whose aim is the Greatest Good, which we seek out gladly. It is a Good which is desirable in and of itself, a perfect state gathered together from all the Goods which are found in those who are united with God through their intellect, in the contemplation of him, and not in other things, calming the mind, which is insatiable for all human things.

PHILOCALIO: A great desire is born in my soul to reach this highest, most perfect happiness which you have spoken of to me.

THEOPHILA: As they say in a proverb, "Desire and love were born of a single childbirth."

PHILOCALIO: And what do you mean by that?

THEOPHILA: I mean that if your potential intellect is enlightened by the active intellect, your will power, which loves everything that pleases the intellect, can lead from the potential to the active achievement which your intellect desires, with the help of God.

PHILOCALIO: And the will power, what is it?

THEOPHILA: It is the function of the body, which works according to what the will power wants, which is reasonable and just, causing honest effects and excellent operations. These are the true means to obtain and achieve those things that the intellect knows and the will power loves and wishes.

PHILOCALIO: And what are these works?

THEOPHILA: To make yourself weary in fleeing and resisting vices, which, as if they were our adverse and capital enemies, pursue us to kill us. And to follow virtues, which provide us with arms against them, to save us. However, it would not help for the intellect to know the good and for our free will to love and desire it, if we do not exercise ourselves in virtuous works to acquire the known and loved good. But because we

10. Matraini, *Dialoghi spirituali*, 32.

do not love what we do not know as good, in the same way we do not hate what we do not recognize as its opposite and mortal enemy. So it is of the greatest necessity to have knowledge of the vices in order to know how to despise and flee from them, just as it is necessary to know the beautiful virtues in order to follow them. . . .

THIRD DIALOGUE

PHILOCALIO: May God save you, my Lady Theophila, and may he make you his friend in Heaven, as you show yourself by your name[11] on earth.[12]

THEOPHILA: May God make you always passionate about virtues and sciences, as your beautiful name[13] demonstrates clearly.

PHILOCALIO: Then it is true, as you said to me the other day, that both Love and desire were born in one childbirth; so I love them and desire them, although they are not yet mine.

THEOPHILA: That which Love and desire cannot achieve in the acquisition of a noble subject, no force in the entire world can accomplish; wherefore it is said in a proverb, "Nothing is difficult for the mind which wants [to attain it]."[14] So, Philocalio, open the window of your intellect to the Sun of divine grace, if you want its form to enter there; because as Saint Augustine has said, "He who created you without you will not save you without you,"[15] meaning that grace is not given except to those who are predisposed to it and able to receive it.

PHILOCALIO: It seems to me difficult to receive this grace if it does not exist in us already, because even if we have the free will to be able to turn ourselves to the good, as well as to the evil, we do not have the power by ourselves to follow the good (because of the sin of our first parents) unless by grace and divine generosity.

THEOPHILA: That is true, so far as the operation of divine grace is concerned, but there are many things which instinctively invite us to do good works.

PHILOCALIO: And what are they?

THEOPHILA: First, the law of nature, which is written in the heart

---

11. See above, note 3.
12. Matraini, *Dialoghi spirituali*, 46.
13. See above, note 3.
14. The Latin (which Matraini uses) reads: "Animo volenti, nihil difficile est."
15. The Latin (which Matraini uses) reads: "Qui creavit te sine te, non salvabit te sine te."

of man and which says: "Do unto others as you would have them do unto you,"[16] and so forth. The second is reason, which tells and shows us all those things which are delightful, useful, and virtuous. Third is the written law and the law of grace, which tells us we must love God and our neighbor for the love of God, who is the highest good. Grace is not given except to those who, with the three laws mentioned above, make themselves able and disposed to receive it. But you should not close the eyes of your intellect and reason to the light of the Sun, which God makes shine upon evil as well as upon good men. When it is time for combat, do not throw down your weapons if you do not want to be captured, wounded, or killed. For he who fails to ply the oars through the tempest is often drowned and remains underwater. Therefore, Philocalio, be quick to learn the good doctrine and true wisdom and to operate virtuously, recognizing the wonderful gifts which you have received from the most high God and the infinite duties you have toward him, and as a true judge of our greatest good you will exercise the most noble part of your soul in wisdom and in virtue. . . .

. . . There follows finally Charity,[17] which is an intense, alive, and inflamed love, united with right will power, distant from all earthly things, united and joined inseparably with God, burning with the pure fire of His divine spirit. Charity is above everything that we love according to our senses, is excellent above all other loves; it is the summit of all good works, the aim of divine precepts, the life of true virtues, the fortress of those who battle against the world, the invincible weapon of all good minds, the crown and triumph of victory. Without Charity nothing is pleasing to God, and with it nothing can displease Him. Charity is fruitful for the penitent, delighted with those who continue with good works, victorious for martyrs, and glorious for those who persevere. It is a love and a delight by which a person loves God for himself and his neighbor for God. It is a force that embraces, clasps, and binds the beloved God with the spirit that loves Him. It is that virtue, finally, by which we desire to see and enjoy God himself with infinite delight and everlasting joy.

Charity is similar to the Dawn, because it follows forever the clear, joyful day of divine eternity; it is also like Noah's Ark, in which, if you do not find yourself, you remain without true life. It is a tree that bears

---

16. The Latin (which Matraini uses) reads: "Quae vultis ut faciant vobis homines, & vos facite."

17. Matraini, *Dialoghi spirituali*, 56.

delicious fruits, and, in sum, it is the key that opens the sublime gates of Paradise. It is a Regal crown, which adorns the head of our soul; it is the Queen of all the other virtues and more similar to God than all of them. Its beauty is greater than that of any other virtue, just as the splendor of the star of Venus is greater than that of all other stars, except that of the Sun, from which all the other stars take light, as all graces emanate only from God. Of this great virtue the blessed Bernard[18] has said, "Charity is like a good mother: she soothes the ill, she keeps the older ones busy, she corrects the troubled ones; showing different attitudes to different ones, she loves everyone just like her own child; when she scolds she is mild, when she encourages she is simple, she is fierce when she needs to be, heals without pain, knows how to be angry with patience, how to shame with humility. She is the one who is mother to men as well as to angels, who brings peace not only to the earthly but also to the heavenly things; she is the one who, by appeasing God toward men, reconciled men with God."[19]

Oh, happy is that soul, Philocalio, that within the stormy sea of this world has the mast of faith, the safety plank of hope, and the rudder of charity in its ship, and will not listen to the Sirens of worldly pleasures, which hold sway over our feelings in such a way that often we are miserably drowned by them. . . .

FROM THE FOURTH DIALOGUE

THEOPHILA: . . . Remember always that everything you know, think, speak, or write should be done for the glory of the most high God, which consists of inner faith and outer reverence.[20] The Salvation of the soul consists of abstaining from all evil and approaching the good, and Charity consists of helping your neighbor with deeds and consoling him with words. May you always aim for these three objects, which feather the wings of your soul, giving them a gentle breeze of

---

18. Bernard of Clairvaux (1090–1153) was a Cistercian monk who emphasized his devotion to the Virgin in his writings.

19. Matraini uses the Latin: "Bona mater charitas; quae sive foveat infirmos, sive exerceat provectos, sive arguat inquietos, diversis diversa exhibens, sicut filios diligit universos; cum arguit mitis est, cum blanditur simplex est, piae solet saevire, sine dolore mulcere; patienter novit irasci, humiliter in dignari, Ipsa est quae hominum mater & angelorum non solum quae in terra, sed etiam quae in caelo sunt pacificat; ipsa denique Deum homini placans, hominem Deo reconciliavit."

20. Matraini, *Dialoghi spirituali*, 71.

divine grace, and make us spread our wings for flight to the supreme
celestial nest of the true immortal glory.

End of the fourth and last Dialogue.

Only beginning, without beginning, everlasting
Moving Force, who in your Final Cause, only without Finality,
move both human and divine things
to your holy and eternal will:
let my inner affection
be expressed for your glory,
finally giving me victory,
so that to your blessed and desired light,
my soul be made in Heaven CHIARA, clear, and beatified.[21]

(Principio sol, senza principio, eterno
Motor, che al fin di te, sol senza fine,
Muovi le cose humane, e le divine,
Al tuo santo voler, e sempiterno,
Deh fa, che questo interno
Espresso affetto mio sia per tua gloria,
Dandome al fin vittoria,
Tal, che all'alma tua luce, e desiata,
Sia fatta in Ciel da te CHIARA, e beata.)

꒦

21. The word CHIARA, in upper case, is as it was published in the Matraini volume.

TO SAINT CLARE[22]

Clare, bright flame of love, so divine and burning
that you went so high to the source
of your humble, pure, and eternal mind
that your divine sparks and chaste thoughts
will never be extinguished:
but as a Phoenix, forever alive
before the rays of the eternal Sun,
you will be, Saint Clare,
on earth and in Heaven,
a shining example and mirror, where we learn
to love God alone above all things.
O Clare in Heaven, happy and glorious:
I beg you to be my guide to God,
when I am living, and then when I am dead.

(A SANTA CHIARA

CHIARA fiamma d'Amor divino ardente,
Che tanto in alto alla cagione andasti
Dell'humile tua pura eterna mente,
Che mai non fiano spente
Di te l'alme faville, e pensier casti,
Ma qual Fenice suole
Davanti a' raggi dell'eterno Sole
Sempre mai viva, e CHiara
In terra, e 'n Ciel sarai,
Un chiaro essempio, e speglio, ove s'impara
Ad amar solo Iddio sopr'ogni cosa.
O CHiara in Ciel felice, e gloriosa
Prego, che sii mia scorta;
A Dio, vivendo, e poi ch'io sarò morta.)

22. This poem appears after the sermons and poems in her *Spiritual Dialogues*. Saint Clare of Assisi (1194–1253) was a follower of Saint Francis of Assisi.

APPENDIX
DERIVATIVE LINES IN MATRAINI'S POETRY

In Matraini's day, it was considered a mark of poetic prowess to be able to work a line from another poet's work into one's own new poem, particularly if the line in question was a well-known one. The concept of plagiarism lay in the future. The information presented below is not intended in any way to detract from Matraini's work but instead to provide a glimpse into what her influences were and what she considered poetically important in the work of others.

Of the 46 (out of 99) translated poems in this volume from Matraini's book A (1555/56), 30 of them contain lines which seem to have been derived from the *Rime sparse* of Petrarch or from Bembo's poem 142. In these 30 poems, a total of 153 individual lines may be identified as derivative. Some of this overlapping, of course, is to be expected, since the three poets traveled the same poetic landscape of love, loss, and death. Of these 153 lines, 62 lines (about 40 percent) come from a single poem, the clearly derivative A 82. Poem A 88 contributes another 14 lines (roughly 10 percent). Poem A 10 contributes 9 lines, and A 38 another 7. In other words, 4 poems account for about half of the derivative lines. The remaining 63 lines are distributed in lesser numbers among the remaining 26 poems.

Of the 46 (out of 87) translated poems from book C (1597), 27 have seemingly derivative lines. In these 27, a total of 145 lines may be identified as derivative. However, when one discounts those book C poems which were republished from book A, only 44 lines from 15 poems seem to be derivative. The influence of Petrarch is clearly diminished in the newly published book C poems, yet is still present. For example, in C 50, 7 of the 14 lines appear to have been influenced by Petrarch, and the first line of the sonnet is almost exactly the first line of Petrarch's poem 254. These new poems contain lines similar to only 52 of Petrarch's lines taken from 49 of his poems, whereas 136 of his lines from 94 of his poems are in book A. The influence of Petrarch is most strongly visible in those poems which exist in both volumes.

The tables below contain a detailed comparison of all derivative lines which I discovered. Please note that these figures apply only to the Matraini poems translated in this volume. Of particular note is poem A 88 which was republished with minor changes as C 44, in which each line of the sonnet comes (some with small differences) directly from an individual line somewhere in Petrarch. The first 4 lines of this sonnet are also almost identical to the first 4 lines of Vittoria Colonna's sonnet 58.[1] It is noteworthy that the lines which come from Petrarch come from a wide cross-section of his work and are rather evenly spread over almost half of his total of 366 poems. An example is A 94/C 57, which makes use of single lines from Petrarch's numbers 1, 21, 224, 234, 264, and 270. Clearly Matraini was familiar with the broad spectrum of Petrarch's work. The most lines taken from any one of Petrarch's poems are 5 lines taken from his poem number 23. Nowhere did I discover that more than 2 lines in a row of Petrarch's found their way into Matraini's work.

In order to reach the conclusions above, I obtained (downloaded) a database of Petrarch's *Rime* from the Italian Internet site "Liber Liber."[2] With this database in hand, I selected several key words from each line of Matraini work and when necessary reduced them to the root form of the word, then searched for them in the Petrarch database. Particular care had to be used with accented words. (A method of "wildcarding" accent marks would have been most helpful, but that was not available.) Most searches yielded nothing. Some finds were questionable, containing only a few words in common or frequently used expressions which might be found in any poet's work. Then there was the occasional gem, a line that was identical or very close to it. When a line of any possible significance was found, I checked the database version of Petrarch's line against the same line as published in *Petrarch's Lyric Poems* by Durling.[3] The database was found to have a number of minor errors, particularly with punctuation and accent marks, sometimes with spelling. Therefore, the line that appears in this appendix is the line as published in Durling, which is considered to be the more reliable source.

Another poem of particular note is A 82, which was shortened, reworked, and republished as C 45. Here the work of Pietro Bembo becomes a major influence. I obtained a database copy of Bembo's *canzone* 142[4] in a manner similar to that described above. Matraini's lines 14 and 95 almost exactly

1. Vittoria Colonna, *Rime*, ed. Alan Bullock, in Scrittori d'Italia, no. 270 (Rome-Bari: Laterza, 1982).

2. http://www.liberliber.it.

3. Francesco Petrarch, *Petrarch's Lyric Poems*, ed. and trans. Robert M. Durling (Cambridge: Harvard University Press, 1976).

4. http://www.classicitaliani.it.

match those same line numbers in Bembo's poem. Here, also, is one of the few places where more than 2 consecutive derivative lines are present in Matraini's work. In A 82, lines 81–88 appear to be a reworking of Bembo's lines 81–88. The same lines carry over into C 45, lines 41–48.

A small number of lines from the poems embedded in Matraini's prose works also seem to have their roots in Petrarch, but there were not a significant enough number of them to warrant inclusion here.

Table 1 compares lines from Matraini's book A poems (1555/56) with those of Francesco Petrarch, Pietro Bembo, and Vittoria Colonna. For the most part, individual lines are shown, sometimes line pairs, and occasionally multiple lines of 3 or more. Table 2 is in all ways similar to table 1, except that it compares lines from Matraini's book C (1597).

TABLE 1 **Derivative Lines from Book A**

Author initials	Poem number	Poem type[1]	Line number	Line text[2]
CM	A 6	So	5	quand'Amor diemmi assalto, e a bel soggiurno
FP	23	Ca	21–22	I' dico che dal dì che 'l primo assalto mi diede Amor
CM	A 10	Ca	1	Poiché tacer non posso
FP	325	Ca	1	Tacer non posso, et temo non adopre
CM	A 10	Ca	30	com'a l'alta speranza si conface
FP	72	Ca	65	qual a l'alta speranza si conface
CM	A 10	Ca	33	cangerei solo a un ragionare, a un canto
FP	264	Ca	53	un mover d'occhi, un ragionar, un canto
CM	A 10	Ca	48	credetti in parte disfogare il core
FP	92	So	8	quanto bisogna a disfogare il core
CM	A 10	Ca	54	lo mio desir e 'l Tempo si dilegua
FP	73	Ca	21	or m'abbandona al tempo et si dilegua
CM	A 10	Ca	77–78	da la tempesta e da' contrarî venti, ch'a' due lumi ch'ha sempre il nostro polo
FP	73	Ca	48–49	a' duo lumi ch' à sempre il nostro polo, così ne la tempesta
CM	A 10	Ca	76	Come nocchier già stanco
FP	151	So	2	fuggio in porto giamai stanco nocchiero
CM	A 10	Ca	82	fuggendo al suo apparir angoscia e duolo
FP	71	Ca	97	Fugge al vostro apparire angoscia et noia CM's A 10 and FP's 73 both have 93 lines.
CM	A 14	Ma	3	che m'arde e strugge dentro a dramma a dramma
FP	18	So	4	che m'arde et strugge dentro a parte a parte

(continued)

TABLE 1 *Continued*

Author initials	Poem number	Poem type[1]	Line number	Line text[2]
CM	A 20	So	14	anzi che le sia trônco arbore o sarte
FP	272	So	13	il mio nocchier, et rotte arbore et sarte
CM	A 21	So	3	colm'ambe di ineffabile dolcezza
FP	116	So	1	Pien di quella ineffabile dolcezza
CM	A 28	Ma	4–5	mi dicea con parole rare nel mondo o sole
FP	37	Ca	86–87	et l'accorte parole rade nel mondo, o sole
CM	A 28	Ma	14	non mai ne l'odorifero orïente
FP	337	So	2	l'odorifero et lucido oriente
CM	A 29	So	10	vertù risplende dal mar Indo al Mauro
FP	269	So	4	dal borea a l'austro o dal mar indo al mauro
CM	A 33	So	14	ch'ogni basso pensier posi in oblio
FP	351	So	8	ch' ogni basso pensier del cor m'avulse
FP	325	Ca	45	che me stesso e 'l mio mal posi in oblio
CM	A 35	So	9	tal io, fra queste frondi a l'aura estiva
FP	279	So	1–2	Se lamentar augelli, o verdi fronde mover soavemente a l'aura estiva
CM	A 37	So	1	L'aura gentil, che mormorando torna
FP	194	So	1	L'aura gentil che rasserena i poggi
CM	A 37	So	4	le rive e' colli di be' rami adorna
FP	9	So	6	le rive e i colli, di fioretti adorna
CM	A 38	Ca	2–3	e come a' be' desir volgon le stelle contrario il tempo, ch'al pensier si cela
FP	12	So	12	Et se 'l tempo è contrario ai be' desiri
CM	A 38	Ca	20	de l'empia e vïolenta mia Fortuna
FP	331	Ca	8	a l'empia et violenta mia fortuna
CM	A 38	Ca	23	fe l'aër lieto, or fa mia mente bruna
FP	223	So	2	et l'aere nostro et la mia mente imbruna
CM	A 38	Ca	24	ch'or foss'io spenta al latte ed alla cuna
FP	359	Ca	36	ch' or fuss'io spento al latte et a la culla
CM	A 38	Ca	28	or piango e grido, e co' pie' lassi e 'nfermi
FP	105	?	76	De' passati miei danni piango et rido
CM	A 38	Ca	61	Canzon, chi tua ragion facesse oscura
FP	119	Ca	106	Canzon, chi tua ragion chiamasse oscura
CM	A 40	So	1	Viva mia bella e dolce calamita
FP	135	?	30	ad una viva dolce calamita
CM	A 41	So	2	il Cielo, e 'l ragionar cortese e santo

(*continued*)

TABLE 1 *Continued*

Author initials	Poem number	Poem type[1]	Line number	Line text[2]
FP	270	Ca	81	l'abito onesto e 'l ragionar cortese
CM	A 41	So	6	il cor che ne portò nel suo bel manto
FP	313	So	8	lei ch' avolto l'avea nel suo bel manto
CM	A 41	So	9	Io, ch'odo le dolcissime parole
FP	165	So	10	s'accordan le dolcissime parole
CM	A 43	So	1	Quando fia 'l dì ch'io vi riveggia ed oda
FP	253	So	2	or fia mai il dì ch' i' vi riveggia et oda
CM	A 43	So	7	tanto martir ne l'anima rinfresca
FP	55	?	3	fiamma et martir ne l'anima rinfresca
CM	A 43	So	11	misurata allegrezza i' non avrei
FP	71	Ca	64	misurata allegrezza
CM	A 44	Se	1	Freschi, ombrosi, fioriti e verdi colli
FP	243	So	1	Fresco ombroso fiorito et verde colle
CM	A 44	Se	2	dov'or si siede dolcemente a l'ombra
FP	125	Ca	22	ove si siede a l'ombra
CM	A 44	Se	20	e lieta andava più di giorno in giorno
FP	85	So	2	et son per amar più di giorno in giorno
CM	A 48	So	7	ch'io non vi veda con mirabil arte
FP	107	So	13	che 'l mio avversario con mirabil arte
CM	A 57	So	5	Io pur ascolto e non odo parole
FP	254	So	1	I' pur ascolto, et non odo novella
CM	A 57	So	7	e temo, e spero: ognor dentro e d'intorno
FP	134	So	2	e temo et spero, et ardo et son un ghiaccio
FP	252	So	2	et temo et spero, et in sospiri e 'n rime
CM	A 57	So	11	di gir al Ciel con glorïosi passi
FP	306	So	2	di gire al Ciel con gloriosi passi
CM	A 57	So	13	Lassa, non so: so ben ch'in doglie e pianti
FP	252	So	7	(lasso, non so che di me stesso estime)
FP	255	So	3	a me doppia la sera et doglia et pianti
FP	332	DS	5	vòlti subitamente in doglia e 'n pianto
CM	A 60	Ma	6	O benedette l'ore
FP	284	So	13	sospira et dice:—O benedette l'ore
CM	A 65	So	5	quella vostra ineffabile dolcezza
FP	116	So	1	Pien di quella ineffabile dolcezza
CM	A 65	So	11	virtù risplende dal mar Indo al Mauro
FP	269	So	4	dal borea a l'austro o dal mar indo al mauro
CM	A 66	Ca	29	a l'Infido pastor sovra il suo grembo

(continued)

TABLE 1 *Continued*

Author initials	Poem number	Poem type[1]	Line number	Line text[2]
FP	126	Ca	42	una pioggia di fior sovra 'l suo grembo
				CM's A 66 has the same 68-line format as FP's 126. CM's A 66 lines 29-33 has "grembo," "lembo," and "nembo" rhyming, whereas FP's 126, lines 42-46, rhymes "grembo," "nembo," and "lembo."
CM	A 66	Ca	63–65	ond'io mi trasformai da quel ch'io sono, facendomi di chiara fonte
FP	23	Ca	38–39	et duo mi trasformaro in quel ch' i' sono, facendomi d'uom vivo
CM	A 72	So	3	tutt'arte, ingegno, ed ogni estrema cura
FP	193	So	14	Arte, Ingegno, et Natura e 'l Ciel po fare
CM	A 72	So	8	vide, e quel bel ch'a null'altro simiglia
FP	160	So	4	che sol se stessa et nulla altra simiglia
CM	A 72	So	9	Venere e Giove con benigni aspetti
FP	325	Ca	65	Venere e 'l padre con benigni aspetti
CM	A 73	So	4	correndo il sol le sue vie lunghe e torte
FP	37	Ca	24	guinto il vedrai per vie lunghe et distorte
CM	A 77	So	9	Or hai fatto l'estremo di tua possa
FP	326	So	1	Or ài fatto l'estremo di tua possa
CM	A 78	So	1	Empia Invidia crudel, che ne' miei danni
FP	12	So	7	e 'l viso scolorir che ne' miei danni
CM	A 78	So	2	per cieco error così tacita entrasti
FP	172	So	3	per qual sentier così tacita intrasti
CM	A 78	So	4	mentre fingi la voce, il volto, e' panni
FP	282	So	14	a l'andar, a la voce, al volto, a' panni
CM	A 78	So	12	che sempre fian più manifesti e conti
FP	23	Ca	120	e parlo cose manifeste et conte
CM	A 81	So	2	e l'angelico riso, che solea
FP	292	So	6	e 'l lampeggiar de l'angelico riso
CM	A 81	So	3	far chiara e dolce l'aura fosca e rea
FP	223	So	12	Vien poi l'aurora et l'aura fosca inalba
CM	A 81	So	9	U' la virtute, il portamento altero
FP	267	So	2	oimè il leggiadro portamento altero
CM	A 81	So	10	l'andar celeste, i be' costumi santi
FP	213	So	7	l'andar celeste e 'l vago spirto ardente
CM	A 81	So	11	ch'eran mia scorta in questo camin cieco
FP	73	Ca	5	sia la mia scorta e 'nsignimi 'l camino

(continued)

TABLE 1 *Continued*

Author initials	Poem number	Poem type[1]	Line number	Line text[2]
CM	A 81	So	14	lume de gli occhi miei non è più meco
FP	276	So	14	lume degli occhi miei non è più meco
CM	A 82	Ca	2	che, fornito il tuo corso a mezzo gli anni
FP	254	So	14	et fornito il mio tempo a mezzo gli anni
PB	142	Ca	37	e s'ella non si tronca a mezzo gli anni
CM	A 82	Ca	3	volata sei fra l'anime beate
FP	313	So	14	fuor de' sospir, fra l'anime beate
CM	A 82	Ca	4	volgi la vista or da' superni scanni
FP	126	Ca	32	volga la vista disiosa et lieta
CM	A 82	Ca	9	bagnare il fido mio dolente petto
FP	23	Ca	27	lagrima ancor non mi bagnava il petto
CM	A 82	Ca	11	ogni mia gioia e viver dolce e caro
PB	142	Ca	19	caro a me stesso: or teco ogni mia gioia
CM	A 82	Ca	14	Da indi in qua non passo un'ora sola
PB	142	Ca	14	da indi in qua né lieto, né securo
CM	A 82	Ca	24	Tu 'l sai s'io 'l dissi; e quel che di negarme
PB	142	Ca	78	Tu 'l sai, che, poi ch'a me ti sei celato
CM	A 82	Ca	29	potria bastare a consolarmi mai
PB	142	Ca	26	che del mio duol bastasse a consolarme
CM	A 82	Ca	31	dove scorgi la piaga alta e profonda
FP	342	So	4	pensando a la sua piaga aspra et profonda
CM	A 82	Ca	40	et or m'ho in odio e vo cieca e depressa
FP	134	So	11	et ò in odio me stesso et amo altrui
CM	A 82	Ca	41–42	Dinanzi al tuo apparir, doglia e tormento spariva, come al sol sparisce ogn'ombra
FP	235	So	12	ov' altrui noie, a sé doglie et tormenti
PB	142	Ca	41–42	Dinanzi a te partiva ira e tormento, come parte ombra a l'apparir del sole
CM	A 82	Ca	54	ver' me, cui sol non vide mai né stella
FP	135	Ca	70	simil giamai né sol vide né stella
CM	A 82	Ca	67	di far sempre mai in due le voglie stesse
FP	158	So	4	per far sempre mai verdi i miei desiri
CM	A 82	Ca	79–80	si rimase ella. O cruda, acerba sorte! O dispietata, inesorabil Morte!
FP	217	So	11	tal fu mia stella et tal mia cruda sorte
FP	332	DS	7	Crudele, acerba, inesorabil Morte
FP	300	So	12	Quant' a la dispietata et dura Morte
FP	324	Ma	4	Ahi dispietata Morte, ahi crudel vita!

(*continued*)

TABLE 1 *Continued*

Author initials	Poem number	Poem type[1]	Line number	Line text[2]
PB	142	Ca	74–75	O disavventurosa acerba sorte! O dispietata intempestiva morte!
CM	A 82	Ca	81–88	Tu m'hai lasciato senza l'alma in vita, la notte senza stelle e sole i giorni, la terra scossa e 'l Ciel turbato e negro, e pien di mill'oltraggi e mille scorni veggio ov'io miri, e la virtù sbandita, e quanto scorsi già bello ed allegro or veggio al tuo partir languido ed egro. Valore e cortesia per terra giacque
PB	142	Ca	81–88	Tu m'hai lasciato senza sole i giorni, le notti senza stelle, e grave et egro tutto questo ond'io parlo, ond'io respiro: la terra scossa, e 'l ciel turbato e negro, e pien di mille oltraggi e mille scorni mi sembra in ogni parte quant'io miro. Valor e cortesia si dipartiro nel tuo partir, e 'l mondo infermo giacque
CM	A 82	Ca	85	veggio ov'io miri, e la virtù sbandita
FP	96	So	6	porto nel petto et veggio ove ch' io miri
FP	7	So	2	ànno del mondo ogni vertù sbandita
CM	A 82	Ca	89	quel dì che ne lasciasti in doglia e pianto
FP	332	DS	5	vòlti subitamente in doglia e 'n pianto
CM	A 82	Ca	90	né mai più riso o canto
FP	249	So	11	e 'l riso e 'l canto a 'l parlar dolce umano
FP	268	Ca	79	non t'appressare ove sia riso o canto
CM	A 82	Ca	94	né più sereno giorno il Cielo aperse
FP	325	Ca	69	Il sol mai sì bel giorno non aperse
CM	A 82	Ca	95	Parnaso un nembo eterno ricoverse
PB	142	Ca	95	Parnaso un nembo eterno ricoperse
CM	A 82	Ca	101	Or, quanto a me, non ha più bene il mondo
PB	142	Ca	58	Or, quanto a me, non ha più un bene al mondo
CM	A 82	Ca	102–3	senza te, la mia stella e il mio conforto che fosti a l'alma travagliata e stanca
FP	73	Ca	51	sono il mio segno e 'l mio conforto solo
PB	142	Ca	63–64	fosti de l'alma travagliata e stanca: la mia sola difesa e 'l mio conforto
CM	A 82	Ca	104	Tu il sai, ch'essendo a me celato e morto
PB	142	Ca	78	Tu 'l sai, che, poi ch'a me ti sei celato
CM	A 82	Ca	106	in questa vita lagrimosa e manca
FP	46	So	5	Però i dì miei fien lagrimosi et manchi

(continued)

TABLE 1 *Continued*

Author initials	Poem number	Poem type[1]	Line number	Line text[2]
CM	A 82	Ca	111	Cielo oggi a impoverirmi in tutto vòlto
PB	142	Ca	106	destin a impoverirmi in tutto volto
CM	A 82	Ca	113	ch'un medesmo sepolcro ambi chiudesse
FP	264	Ca	65	et temo ch' un sepolcro ambeduo chiuda
PB	142	Ca	155	un'ora et un sepolcro ne chiudesse
CM	A 82	Ca	115	e del morto mio ben spogliata e priva
FP	294	So	5	L'alma d'ogni suo ben spogliata et priva
CM	A 82	Ca	118–19	perch'io tregua non vo' col pianto mai, e tanto il piangerò quanto l'amai
PB	142	Ca	144–46	Tregua non voglio aver col mio dolore, infin ch'io sia dal giorno ultimo giunto; e tanto il piangerò, quant'io l'amai
CM	A 82	Ca	120	Chi mi darà le voci, o chiaro spirto
PB	142	Ca	174	Chi mi dà il grembo pien di rose e mirto
CM	A 82	Ca	124	O quai corone dar di lauro o mirto
FP	270	Ca	65	la qual dì et notte più che lauro o mirto
CM	A 82	Ca	127	con le Ninfe del Serchio (ahi duro scempio)
FP	23	Ca	10	ben che 'l mio duro scempio
CM	A 82	Ca	128	lacere tutte e pien di morte il volto
PB	142	Ca	103	lacero il petto e pien di morte il volto
CM	A 82	Ca	132	Così s'udîr per l'alte selve ombrose
FP	162	So	7	ombrose selve ove percote il sole
CM	A 82	Ca	137	e gir con mesta e lagrimosa fronte
FP	102	So	7	rise fra gente lagrimosa et mesta
CM	A 82	Ca	140–41	Venner poi le tue caste e pie sorelle colme di pianto e con le treccie sparse
FP	343	So	9	O che dolci accoglienze et caste et pie!
FP	53	Ca	22	securamente, et ne le trecce sparte
PB	142	Ca	121–22	Qual pianser già le triste e pie sorelle, cui le trecce in sul Po tenera fronde
CM	A 82	Ca	142	e' cari figli, e' frati, e 'l padre antico
PB	142	Ca	102	cadde, grave a se stesso, il padre antico
CM	A 82	Ca	143–44	gridando:—Ahi sordo Ciel, nemiche Stelle, Destino ingiusto e di pietà nemico
PB	142	Ca	104–5	E disse:—Ahi sordo e di pietà nemico, destin predace e reo, destino ingiusto
CM	A 82	Ca	154	Così detto, da gli occhi il tristo umore
FP	216	So	5	In tristo umor vo li occhi consumando
CM	A 82	Ca	160	assiso in alta e glorïosa sede

(*continued*)

TABLE 1 *Continued*

Author initials	Poem number	Poem type[1]	Line number	Line text[2]
FP	347	So	3	assisa in alta et gloriosa sede
CM	A 82	Ca	170	t'accende l'alma, e più soavi accenti
FP	283	So	6	post' ài silenzio a' più soavi accenti
CM	A 82	Ca	171	vedi di Ninfe più leggiadre e belle
FP	268	Ca	45	Più che mai bella et più leggiadra donna
FP	323	Ca	62	pensosa ir sì leggiadra et bella Donna
CM	A 82	Ca	179–80	Deh, se come ti calse, ora ti cale di me, che vivo in tenebre e martiri
FP	359	Ca	24	che son rimaso in tenebre e 'n martiri
PB	142	Ca	181–83	Se come già ti calse, ora ti cale di me, pon dal ciel mente, com'io vivo, dopo 'l tu' occaso, in tenebre e 'n martiri
CM	A 82	Ca	185–87	sia la mia vita ed ogni pensier vano del morir mio ch'io bramo e ch'io vorrei; né d'altro non aver più non m'incresce
FP	35	So	11	sia la mia vita, ch' è celata altrui
FP	170	So	5	Fanno poi gli occhi suoi mio penser vano
PB	142	Ca	187–89	fa la mia vita, e tutti i miei desiri sono di morte, e sol quanto m'incresce è ch'io non vo più tosto al fin ch'io bramo
CM	A 82	Ca	193	che testimon non sia della mia pena
PB	142	Ca	196	che non sia testimon del mio cordoglio
CM	A 82	Ca	194	Tu, Re del Ciel, cui null'asconde o serra
FP	365	So	6	Re del Cielo, invisibile, immortale
PB	142	Ca	197	Tu Re del ciel, cui nulla circonscrive
CM	A 82	Ca	196	pietosa a ricondurmi al fin ch'io bramo
PB	142	Ca	189	è ch'io non vo più tosto al fin ch'io bramo
CM	A 82	Ca	202	con lui, che tien di me la miglior parte
PB	142	Ca	140	di me la viva e miglior parte ha seco
CM	A 82	Ca	203	e sopra il lembo e 'l suo bel viso santo
FP	135	Ca	43	sì mi trasporta che 'l bel viso santo
FP	252	So	5	Or fia giamai che quel bel viso santo
CM	A 84	So	1	Vago augelletto puro, almo e gentile
FP	353	So	1	Vago augelletto, che cantando vai
CM	A 84	So	2	che dolcemente canti e sfoghi il core
FP	225	So	11	sedersi in parte et cantar dolcemente
FP	92	So	8	quanto bisogna a disfogare il core
FP	293	So	10	pur di sfogare il doloroso core
CM	A 84	So	7	giugner non spero, o 'ntepidir l'adore

(*continued*)

TABLE 1 *Continued*

Author initials	Poem number	Poem type[1]	Line number	Line text[2]
FP	270	Ca	28	cosa seguir che mai giugner non spero
CM	A 84	So	8	ch'io sento, o m'oda la bell'alma umile
FP	184	So	1	Amor, Natura et la bella alma umile
CM	A 84	So	9	Tu la tua dolce, amata compagnia
FP	222	So	6	dogliose per sua dolce compagnia
FP	300	So	10	ànno or sua santa et dolce compagnia
CM	A 84	So	12	Te la tua sente; ma chi dolce apria
FP	206	?	37	Ma s' io nol dissi, chi sì dolce apria
CM	A 88	So	1–4	Occhi miei, oscurato è il vostro Sole, così l'alta mia luce è a me sparita e, per quel che ne speri, è al Ciel salita; ma miracol non è: da tal si vuole
VC	58	So	1–4	Occhi miei, oscurato è il nostro sole: così l'alta mia luce a me sparita è, per quel ch'io ne speri, al ciel salita; ma miracol non è, da tal si vuole
FP	275	So	1	Occhi miei, oscurato è 'l nostro sole
FP	327	So	6	così l'alta mia luc' è a me sparita
FP	91	So	3	et, per quel ch' io ne speri, al ciel salita
FP	207	Ca	42	ma miracol non è, da tal si vole
CM	A 88	So	5	Passò, com'una stella ch'in Ciel vole
FP	233	So	13	passò quasi una stella che 'n ciel vole
CM	A 88	So	6	ne l'età sua più bella e più fiorita
FP	278	So	1	Ne l'età sua più bella et più fiorita
CM	A 88	So	7	Ahi dispietata Morte, ahi crudel vita
FP	324	Ma	4	Ahi dispietata Morte, ahi crudel vita
CM	A 88	So	8	via men d'ogni sventura altra mi duole
FP	267	So	11	via men d'ogni sventura altra mi dole
CM	A 88	So	9	Rimasa senza il lume ch'amai tanto
FP	292	So	10	rimaso senza 'l lume ch' amai tanto
CM	A 88	So	10–11	vomene in guisa d'orbo, senza luce, che non sa ove si vada e pur si parte
FP	18	So	7–8	vommene in guisa d'orbo, senza luce, che non sa ove si vada et pur si parte
CM	A 88	So	12	così è 'l mio cantar converso in pianto
FP	332	DS	34	così è 'l mio cantar converso in pianto
CM	A 88	So	13	O mia forte ventura, a che m'adduce
FP	207	Ca	77	O mia forte ventura, a che m'adduce
CM	A 88	So	14	colpa d'Amor, non già difetto d'arte

(continued)

TABLE 1 *Continued*

Author initials	Poem number	Poem type[1]	Line number	Line text[2]
FP	74	So	14	colpa d'Amor, non già defetto d'arte
				Every line of A 88 comes originally from individual lines in Petrarch's *Rime sparse* The first 4 lines also closely parallel Colonna's sonnet 58. Colonna also copied lines from Petrarch, but not the same ones as Matraini.The similarity in all lines except for 11, 12, and 14 has been pointed out by Luciana Borsetto in "Narciso ed Eco," in *Nel cerchio della luna* (Venice: Marsilio, 1983).
CM	A 93	So	6	quasi raggio di sol ch'in vetro fera
FP	95	So	10	come raggio di sol traluce in vetro
CM	A 93	So	14	sposa eletta di Dio figliuola e madre
FP	366	?	46	madre, figliuola et sposa
CM	A 94	So	1	Fra le dubbie speranze e 'l van dolore
FP	1	So	6	fra le vane speranze e 'l van dolore
CM	A 94	So	2	d'ombre e sogni gran tempo invan nudrita
FP	1	So	10	favola fui gran tempo, onde sovente
CM	A 94	So	4	lungi a me stessa, è stata in lungo errore
FP	224	So	4	un lungo error in cieco laberinto
CM	A 94	So	9	e svelli omai de l'alma ogni radice
FP	264	Ca	24	et del cor tuo divelli ogni radice
CM	A 94	So	10	della speranza debole e fallace
FP	21	So	6	vive in speranza debile et fallace
CM	A 94	So	11	che mi fe' vaneggiar fra tanti affanni
FP	270	Ca	25	che mi fa vaneggiar sol del pensero
FP	234	So	6	In tanti affanni: di che dogliose urne

[1] "So" indicates a sonnet, "Ca" indicates a *canzone*, "Ma" indicates a madrigal, "Se" indicates a sestina, "DS" indicates a double sestina, and in a small number of cases a question mark indicates a poem that does not fit into these types.

[2] In a few cases, text here is my own explanatory material.

TABLE 2. **Derivative Lines from Book C**

Author initials	Poem number	Poem type[1]	Line number	Line text[2]
CM	C 14	St	13	inchino e sacro con più saldi nodi
FP	196	So	12	Torsele il tempo poi in piú saldi nodi
CM	C 14	St	15	spero, con dolci ed amorose tempre
FP	359	Ca	37	per non provar de l'amorose tempre
CM	C 14	St	16	di farvi al mio bel foco arder mai sempre
FP	182	So	12	l'altra non già: ché 'l mio bel foco è tale
CM	C 14	St	26	benigna stella in Ciel, tutto vi diede
FP	240	So	11	quanto mai piovve da benigna stella
CM	C 14	St	34	tale è 'l foco gentil che in me s'accende
FP	72	Ca	66	et al foco gentil ond'io tutto ardo
CM	C 14	St	35	che dell'alta Cagion sua prima luce
FP	360	Ca	143	potea levarsi a l'alta cagion prima
CM	C 14	St	43	né per volger di ciel, né di pianeta
FP	50	Ca	28	né per volger di ciel né di pianeta
CM	C 14	St	49	Quanto più col desio l'alma s'interna
FP	327	So	11	ove nel suo Fattor l'alma s'interna
CM	C 14	St	74	soavemente i' mi nodrisco ed ardo
FP	207	Ca	39	et di ciò insieme mi nutrico et ardo
CM	C 14	St	82	la mente a contemplar l'alto intelletto
FP	116	So	6	la mente a contemplar sola costei
CM	C 14	St	89	Felice l'alma ch'un bel foco accende
FP	71	Ca	67	Felice l'alma che per voi sospira
CM	C 14	St	94	che per cosa mirabile s'addita
FP	7	So	7	che per cosa mirabile s'addita
CM	C 14	St	103	mentre 'l suo albergo in disusata foggia
FP	48	So	7	perché fai in lei con disusata foggia
CM	C 14	St	108	quest'anima gentil che ben s'accorge
FP	31	So	1	Questa anima gentil che si diparte
CM	C 14	St	122	d'una in altra sembianza, col governo
FP	360	Ca	142	d'una in altra sembianza
CM	C 14	St	138	di sue virtuti, in queste parte e 'n quelle
FP	299	So	2	volgea il mio core in questa parte e 'n quella
CM	C 17	So	1	Empia Invidia crudel, che ne' miei danni
FP	12	So	7	e 'l viso scolorir che ne' miei danni
CM	C 17	So	2	per cieco error così tacita entrasti
FP	172	So	3	per qual sentier così tacita intrasti
CM	C 17	So	4	mentre fingi la voce, il volto, e' panni
FP	282	So	14	a l'andar, a la voce, al volto, a' panni

(*continued*)

TABLE 2 *Continued*

Author initials	Poem number	Poem type[1]	Line number	Line text[2]
CM	C 17	So	12	che sempre fian più manifesti e conti
FP	23	Ca	120	e parlo cose manifeste et conte
CM	C 19	So	4	vi son sempre palesi in ciascun loco
FP	50	Ca	74	tu non vorrai mostrarti in ciascun loco
CM	C 19	So	5	perché prendete i miei tormenti in gioco
FP	129	Ca	18–19	de la mia donna, che sovente in gioco gira 'l tormento ch'i' porto per lei
CM	C 19	So	6	dandomi sempre quel ch'io men vorrei
FP	206	?	19	S'i' 'l dissi mai, di quel ch'i' men vorrei
CM	C 19	So	14	ond'abbiate cagion d'amaro pianto
FP	135	Ca	21	d'amaro pianto che quel bello scoglio
CM	C 20	Ma	6	O benedette l'ore
FP	284	So	13	sospira et dice:—O benedette l'ore
CM	C 22	Ca	2–3	e com'a'bei desir volgon le stelle contrario il tempo, ch'al pensier si cela
FP	12	So	12	Et se 'l tempo è contrario ai be' desiri
CM	C 22	Ca	23	fe' l'aër lieto, or fa mia mente bruna
FP	223	So	2	et l'aere nostro et la mia mente imbruna
CM	C 22	Ca	24	ch'or fuss'io spenta al latte ed a la cuna
FP	359	Ca	36	ch'or fuss'io spenta al latte et a la culla
CM	C 22	Ca	28	or piango, e grido, e coi' pie' lassi e 'nfermi
FP	105	?	76	De' passati miei danni piango e rido
CM	C 22	Ca	61	Canzon, chi tua ragion facesse oscura
FP	119	Ca	106	Canzon, chi tua ragion chiamasse oscura
CM	C 23	So	9	tal io, fra queste frondi a l'aura estiva
FP	279	So	1–2	Se lamentar augelli, o verdi fronde mover soavemente a l'aura estiva
CM	C 27	So	1	Quel sì dolce di gloria ardente sprone
FP	147	So	1	Quando 'l voler, che con due sproni ardenti
CM	C 27	So	7	e 'l giogo, e le catene, c'hanno oppresso
FP	89	So	10	dissi:—Oimè, il giogo et le catene e i ceppi
CM	C 30	So	5	Io pur ascolto e non odo parole
FP	254	So	1	I' pur ascolto, et non odo novella
CM	C 30	So	7	e temo, e spero, e ognor dentro e d'intorno
FP	134	So	2	e temo et spero, et ardo et son un ghiaccio
FP	252	So	2	et temo et spero, et in sospiri e 'n rime
CM	C 30	So	11	di gir al Ciel con glorïosi passi
FP	306	So	2	di gire al Ciel con gloriosi passi

(continued)

TABLE 2 *Continued*

Author initials	Poem number	Poem type[1]	Line number	Line text[2]
CM	C 30	So	12	Lassa, non so: so ben che in doglie e pianti
FP	252	So	7	(lasso, non so che di me stesso estime)
FP	255	So	3	a me doppia la sera et doglia et pianti
FP	332	DS	5	vòlti subitamente in doglia e 'n pianto
CM	C 37	St	1	Ridon or per le piagge erbette e fiori
FP	239	Se	31	Ridon or per le piagge erbette et fiori
CM	C 37	St	6	che fan d'alte bellezze il mondo adorno
FP	70	?	41	Tutte le cose di che 'l mondo è adorno
FP	119	Ca	82	ch' à di voi il mondo adorno
CM	C 39	So	1–2	Già il ventesimo quinto anno rivolto ha 'l Ciel
FP	122	So	1	Dicesette anni à già rivolto il cielo
CM	C 41	So	3	ohimè qual m'ha lasciata innanzi sera
FP	302	So	8	et compie' mia giornata inanzi sera
CM	C 42	So	6	notti quest'occhi, o sconsolate e triste
FP	331	Ca	35	ché tal morì già tristo et sconsolato
CM	C 44	So	1–4	Occhi miei, oscurato è il vostro Sole, così l'alta mia luce è a me sparita e, per quel che ne speri, è al Ciel salita; ma miracol non è: da tal si vuole
VC	58	So	1–4	Occhi miei, oscurato è il nostro sole: così l'alta mia luce a me sparita è, per quel ch'io ne speri, al ciel salita; ma miracol non è, da tal si vuole
FP	275	So	1	Occhi miei, oscurato è 'l nostro sole
FP	327	So	6	così l'alta mia luc' è a me sparita
FP	91	So	3	et, per quel ch' io ne speri, al ciel salita
FP	207	Ca	42	ma miracol non è, da tal si vole
CM	C 44	So	5	Passò, com'una stella ch'in Ciel vole
FP	233	So	13	passò quasi una stella che 'n ciel vole
CM	C 44	So	6	nell'età sua più bella e più fiorita
FP	278	So	1	Ne l'età sua più bella et più fiorita
CM	C 44	So	7	Ahi dispietata Morte, ahi crudel vita
FP	324	Ma	4	Ahi dispietata Morte, ahi crudel vita
CM	C 44	So	8	via men d'ogni sventura altra mi duole
FP	267	So	11	via men d'ogni sventura altra mi dole
CM	C 44	So	9	Rimasta senza il lume ch'amai tanto
FP	292	So	10	rimaso senza 'l lume ch' amai tanto

(*continued*)

TABLE 2 *Continued*

Author initials	Poem number	Poem type[1]	Line number	Line text[2]
CM	C 44	So	10–11	vomene in guisa d'orbo, senza luce, che non sa dove vada e pur si parte
FP	18	So	7–8	vommene in guisa d'orbo, senza luce, che non sa ove si vada et pur si parte
CM	C 44	So	12	così è 'l mio cantar converso in pianto
FP	332	DS	34	così è 'l mio cantar converso in pianto
CM	C 44	So	13	O mia forte ventura, a che m'adduce
FP	207	Ca	77	O mia forte ventura, a che m'adduce
CM	C 44	So	14	veder l'alte speranze a terra sparte
FP	331	Ca	46	or mie speranze sparte
				Every line of C 44 comes originally from individual lines in Petrarch's *Rime sparse*. The first 4 lines also closely parallel Colonna's sonnet 58. Colonna also copied lines from Petrarch, but not the same ones as Matraini. The similarity in all lines except for 11, 12, and 14 has been pointed out by Luciana Borsetto in "Narciso ed Eco," in <u>Nel cerchio della luna</u> (Venice: Marsilio, 1983).
CM	C 45	Ca	2	che, fornito il tuo corso a mezzo gli anni
FP	254	So	14	et fornito il mio tempo a mezzo gli anni
PB	142	Ca	37	e s'ella non si tronca a mezzo gli anni
CM	C 45	Ca	3	volata sei fra l'anime beate
FP	313	So	14	fuor de' sospir, fra l'anime beate
CM	C 45	Ca	4	volgi la vista or da' superni scanni
FP	126	Ca	32	volga la vista disiosa et lieta
CM	C 45	Ca	9	bagnare il fido mio dolente petto
FP	23	Ca	27	lagrima ancor non mi bagnava il petto
CM	C 45	Ca	14	Da indi in qua non passa un'ora sola
PB	142	Ca	14	da indi in qua né lieto, né securo
CM	C 45	Ca	19–20	però che senza te, ch'ogni mia gioia fosti, lassa, non so com'io non moia
PB	142	Ca	19–20	caro a me stesso: or teco ogni mia gioia è spenta, e non so già, perch'io non moia
CM	C 45	Ca	21–22	Però ch'al tuo apparir, doglia e tormento spariva, com'al sol sparisce ogn'ombra
FP	235	So	12	ov' altrui noie, a sé doglie et tormenti
PB	142	Ca	41–42	Dinanzi a te partiva ira e tormento, come parte ombra a l'apparir del sole
CM	C 45	Ca	34	qual non vide mai sol pari né stella
FP	135	Ca	70	simil giamai né sol vide né stella

(*continued*)

TABLE 2 *Continued*

Author initials	Poem number	Poem type[1]	Line number	Line text[2]
CM	C 45	Ca	41–48	Tu m'hai lasciata qui, senz'alma in vita, la notte senza stelle e sole i giorno, steril la terra e 'l Ciel turbato e negro, e pien di mill'oltraggi e mille scorni vegg'ov'io miri, e la virtù sbandita, e quanto scorsi già bello ed allegro veggio al tuo dipartir languido ed egro. Valore e cortesia per terra giacque
PB	142	Ca	81–88	Tu m'hai lasciato senza sole i giorni, le notti senza stelle, e grave et egro tutto questo ond'io parlo, ond'io respiro: la terra scossa, e 'l ciel turbato e negro, e pien di mille oltraggi e mille scorni mi sembra in ogni parte quant'io miro. Valor e cortesia si dipartiro nel tuo partir, e 'l mondo infermo giacque
CM	C 45	Ca	45	vegg'ov'io miri, e la virtù sbandita
FP	96	So	6	porto nel petto et veggio ove ch' io miri
FP	7	So	2	ànno del mondo ogni vertù sbandita
CM	C 45	Ca	49	quel dì che mi lasciasti in doglia e pianto
FP	332	DS	5	vòlti subitamente in doglia e 'n pianto
CM	C 45	Ca	50	né mai più riso o canto
FP	249	So	11	e 'l riso e 'l canto a 'l parlar dolce umano
	268	Ca	79	non t'appressare ove sia riso o canto
CM	C 45	Ca	54	né più sereno giorno il Cielo aperse
FP	325	Ca	69	Il sol mai sì bel giorno non aperse
CM	C 45	Ca	55	Parnaso un nembo oscuro ricoperse
PB	142	Ca	95	Parnaso un nembo eterno ricoperse
CM	C 45	Ca	60	d'udîr fra l'ombre, lagrimose e meste
FP	102	So	7	rise fra gente lagrimosa et mesta
CM	C 45	Ca	61	Or, quanto a me, non ha più bene il mondo
PB	142	Ca	58	Or, quanto a me, non ha più un bene al mondo
CM	C 45	Ca	62–63	senza te, la mia stella e 'l mio conforto che fosti all'alma travagliata e stanca
FP	73	Ca	51	sono il mio segno e 'l mio conforto solo
PB	142	Ca	63–64	fosti de l'alma travagliata e stanca: la mia sola difesa e 'l mio conforto
CM	C 45	Ca	64	Tu 'l sai, ch'essendo a me celato e morto
PB	142	Ca	78	Tu 'l sai, che, poi ch'a me ti sei celato
CM	C 45	Ca	66	in questa vita lagrimosa e manca
FP	46	So	5	Però i dì miei fien lagrimosi e manchi

(*continued*)

TABLE 2 *Continued*

Author initials	Poem number	Poem type[1]	Line number	Line text[2]
CM	C 45	Ca	71	Ciel oggi a impoverirmi in tutto vòlto
PB	142	Ca	106	destin a impoverirmi in tutto volto
CM	C 45	Ca	73	ch'un medesmo sepulcro ambi chiudesse
FP	264	Ca	65	et temo ch' un sepolcro ambeduo chiuda
PB	142	Ca	155	un'ora et un sepolcro ne chiudesse
CM	C 45	Ca	75	e del morto mio ben spogliata e priva
FP	294	So	5	L'alma d'ogni suo ben spogliata et priva
CM	C 45	Ca	80	ma tanto 'l piangerò quanto l'amai
PB	142	Ca	146	e tanto il piangerò, quant'io l'amai
CM	C 45	Ca	81–82	Deh, se come ti calse, ora ti cale di me, che vivo in tenebre e martiri
FP	359	Ca	24	che son rimaso in tenebre e 'n martiri,
PB	142	Ca	181–83	Se come già ti calse, ora ti cale di me, pon dal ciel mente, com'io vivo, dopo 'l tu' occaso, in tenebre e 'n martiri
CM	C 45	Ca	87	sia qui 'l mio stato ed ogni pensier vano
FP	170	So	5	Fanno poi gli occhi suoi mio penser vano
CM	C 45	Ca	95	che testimon non sia della mia pena
PB	142	Ca	196	che non sia testimon del mio cordoglio
CM	C 45	Ca	96	Tu, Re del Cielo, a cui nulla si serra
FP	365	So	6	Re del Cielo, invisibile, immortale
PB	142	Ca	197	Tu Re del ciel, cui nulla circonscrive
CM	C 45	Ca	98	pietosa a ricondurmi al fin ch'io bramo
PB	142	Ca	189	è ch'io non vo più tosto al fin ch'io bramo
CM	C 47	So	6	è polve ed ombra; e quasi sol, ch'a sdegno
FP	294	So	12	Veramente siam noi polvere et ombra
CM	C 50	So	1	Io pur ascolto e non odo novella
FP	254	So	1	I' pur ascolto, et non odo novella
CM	C 50	So	3	fuor del suo chiaro e bel corporeo velo
FP	264	Ca	114	antiveder per lo corporeo velo
CM	C 50	So	5	Io pur ascolto a sé mi chiami e ch'ella
FP	36	So	14	et di chiamarmi a sé non le ricorda
CM	C 50	So	6	tutt'accesa di puro, ardente zelo
FP	336	So	4	tutta accesa de' raggi di sua stella
FP	182	So	1	Amor che 'ncende il cor d'ardente zelo
CM	C 50	So	8	la casta fiamma mia, lucente e bella
FP	33	So	4	rotava i raggi suoi lucente et bella
CM	C 50	So	11	e consolar le tue notti dolenti

(continued)

TABLE 2 *Continued*

Author initials	Poem number	Poem type[1]	Line number	Line text[2]
FP	282	So	2	a consolar le mie notti dolenti
CM	C 50	So	12	O felice quel dì, se al fin ch'io bramo
FP	349	So	9	O felice quel dì che del terreno
CM	C 51	So	1	Vago augelletto mio, caro e gentile
FP	353	So	1	Vago augelletto, che cantando vai
CM	C 51	So	2	che dolcemente canti e sfoghi il core
FP	225	So	11	sedersi in parte et cantar dolcemente
FP	92	So	8	quanto bisogna a disfogare il core
FP	293	So	10	pur di sfogare il doloroso core
CM	C 51	So	7	giugner non spero, o 'ntepidir l'adore
FP	270	Ca	28	cosa seguir che mai giugner non spero
CM	C 51	So	8	ch'io sento, o m'oda la bell'alma umile
FP	184	So	1	Amor, Natura et la bella alma umile
CM	C 51	So	9	Tu la tua amata e dolce compagnia
FP	222	So	6	dogliose per sua dolce compagnia
FP	300	So	10	ànno or sua santa et dolce compagnia
CM	C 51	So	12	Te la tua sente; ma chi dolce apria
FP	206	?	37	Ma s' io nol dissi, chi sì dolce apria
CM	C 52	So	1	L'aura gentil, che mormorando torna
FP	194	So	1	L'aura gentil che rasserena i poggi
CM	C 52	So	4	le rive e' colli di be' rami adorna
FP	9	So	6	le rive e i colli, di fioretti adorna
CM	C 53	So	5	Ahi come presto al Cielo alzato a volo
FP	345	So	13	con li angeli la veggio alzata a vol
CM	C 53	So	13	a consolarmi, onde quest'aspro e rio
FP	34	So	5	dal pigro gelo et dal tempo aspro et rio
FP	262	So	7	appare in vista, è tal vita aspra et ria
CM	C 55	So	3	dicemi spesso il mio fidato speglio
FP	361	So	1	Dicemi spesso il mio fidato speglio
CM	C 55	So	5	Né dal pigro mio sonno anco una sola
FP	53	Ca	15	Non spero che giàmai dal pigro sonno
CM	C 55	So	9	In questo parla con la mente e dice
FP	264	Ca	19	L'un penser parla co la mente, et dice
CM	C 57	So	1	Fra le dubbie speranze e il van dolore
FP	1	So	6	fra le vane speranze e 'l van dolore
CM	C 57	So	2	d'ombre e sogni gran tempo invan nodrita
FP	1	So	10	favola fui gran tempo, onde sovente
CM	C 57	So	4	vagando, andata è dietro al cieco errore

(*continued*)

TABLE 2 *Continued*

Author initials	Poem number	Poem type[1]	Line number	Line text[2]
FP	224	So	4	un lungo error in cieco laberinto
CM	C 57	So	9	e svelli omai dell'alma ogni radice
FP	264	Ca	24	et del cor tuo divelli ogni radice
CM	C 57	So	10	della speranza debole e fallace
FP	21	So	6	vive in speranza debile et fallace
CM	C 57	So	11	che mi fe' vaneggiar fra tanti affanni
FP	270	Ca	25	che mi fa vaneggiar sol del pensero
FP	234	So	6	In tanti affanni: di che dogliose urne
CM	C 58	So	1	Mentre la nave mia colma d'oblio
FP	189	So	1	Passa la nave mia colma d'oblio
CM	C 58	So	7	che sgombrò delle nebbie oscure il manto
FP	270	?	36	et sgombrar d'ogni nebbia oscura et vile
CM	C 65	So	11	seco le voglie sue sempre al Ciel erga
FP	346	So	13	ond'io voglie et pensier tutti al Ciel ergo
CM	C 65	So	12	e quasi angel celeste ed immortale
FP	323	Ca	52	veder forma celeste et immortale
FP	339	So	6	Forme, altere celesti et immortali
CM	C 66	So	3	ch'esser solevi il mio conforto solo
FP	73	Ca	51	sono il mio segno e 'l mio conforto solo
CM	C 66	So	6–7	seguirà sempre voi ch'onoro e colo, quasi stella che segue il nostro polo
FP	321	So	11	che per te consecrato onoro et colo
FP	73	Ca	48	a' duo lumi ch' à sempre il nostro polo
CM	C 70	So	8–9	così l'alma, da Dio fatta gentile, l'accese a contemplar cosa sì bella
FP	23	Ca	121	L'alma ch' è sol da Dio fatta gentile
FP	268	Ca	27	perché cosa sì bella
CM	C 70	So	11	quel divino splendor ch'appar di fuore
FP	140	So	11	ivi s'asconde, et non appar più fore
CM	C 73	So	3	tutt'arte, ingegno, ed ogni estrema cura
FP	193	So	14	Arte, Ingegno, et Natura e 'l Ciel po fare
CM	C 73	So	8	vide, e quel bel ch'a null'altro simiglia
FP	160	So	4	che sol se stessa et nulla altra simiglia
CM	C 73	So	9	Venere e Giove con benigni aspetti
FP	325	Ca	65	Venere e 'l padre con benigni aspetti
CM	C 86	Ca	1	Padre del Ciel, se 'l mio gran pianto amaro
FP	62	So	1	Padre del ciel, dopo i perduti giorni
CM	C 86	Ca	13	vittorïoso, ov'ei si chiude e serra

(continued)

TABLE 2 *Continued*

Author initials	Poem number	Poem type[1]	Line number	Line text[2]
FP	300	So	5	Quanta ne porto al Ciel che chiude et serra
CM	C 86	Ca	41	ch'eschi da me dal cieco laberinto
FP	224	So	4	un lungo error in cieco laberinto
CM	C 86	Ca	76	l'abbian nell'alto mar profondo assorto
FP	132	So	11	mi trovo in alto mar senza governo
CM	C 86	Ca	77	Scopriti dunque, omai, Luce divina
FP	151	So	5	né mortal vista mai luce divina
CM	C 86	Ca	89	senza 'l tuo aiuto andar per dritta via
FP	261	So	7	ivi s'impara, et qual è dritta via
CM	C 86	Ca	96	mai non apersi alle tue luci sante
FP	108	So	3	ver me volgendo quelle luci sante
FP	350	So	14	sol per piacer a le sue luci sante
CM	C 86	Ca	113	e la mia lunga notte e senza luce
FP	18	So	7	vommene in guisa d'orbo, senza luce
CM	C 86	Ca	121	ma non durai perfino a l'ore estreme
FP	140	So	13	se non star seco infin a l'ora extrema
FP	295	So	5	Poi che l'ultimo giorno et l'ore extreme
CM	C 86	Ca	136	ch'io vo' sol quel ch'a Te diletta e piace
FP	290	So	1	Come va 'l mondo! or mi diletta et piace
CM	C 86	Ca	145–46	voglio, e por tutta in Te la mia speranza, che possi e vogli al gran bisogno aitarme
FP	366	?	105–6	Vergine in cui ò tutta mia speranza, che possi et vogli al gran bisogno aitarme
CM	C 86	Ca	147	e per me prender l'arme
FP	2	So	11	che potesse al bisogno prender l'arme

[1] "So" indicates a sonnet, "Ca" indicates a *canzone*, "Ma" indicates a madrigal, "Se" indicates a sestina, "DS" indicates a double sestina, "St" indicates a stanza, and in a small number of cases a question mark indicates a poem that does not fit into these types.

[2] In a few cases, text here is my own explanatory material.

NOTES

CHAPTER ONE

1. Chiara Matraini, *Rime e Lettere*, ed. Giovanna Rabitti (Bologna: Commissione per i testi di lingua, 1989).

2. "Se lieta e verde, *chiara*, alta cantai" and "ond'io sì *chiara* andai": throughout, Matraini makes the joyous pun on *chiara* meaning "clear, renowned" and her given name.

3. Phaeton was the son of the sun god Helios and Clymene. He begged his father to let him drive his chariot across the heavens, but he was too weak to check the horses; they bolted and approached the earth, ready to set it on fire. Zeus killed him and he fell into the river Eridanus. Phaeton is honored for his daring attempt to drive the chariot of the sun.

4. Icarus was the son of Daedalus; when his father was imprisoned by King Minos and constructed artificial wings for them to escape, Icarus was so bold that he drew near to the sun. The wax of his wings melted, and he was drowned in the Aegean Sea. Icarus is remembered for his pride in daring to fly.

5. The Indus Sea of South Asia and the Mauritanian Sea of West Africa came to represent the far reaches of the civilized world.

6. The "bright shining planet" is Venus. Libra is the constellation into which Venus returns; here it means her deserved freedom.

7. "Qual si fe' Glauco . . ." See Dante, *Paradiso*, 1.68. Glaucus was a fisherman in Boeotia. He achieved immortality either by tasting the grass which had revived a hare he had almost captured, or by tasting part of the divine herb which Cronos had grown. In either case, he was made immortal by such tasting.

8. Dante's rhyming words for his sestina 44 are *ombra, colli, erba, verde, petra, donna*. In the sestina above, Matraini uses *colli, ombra, giorno, erba, verde, mirto*. Four of these are common to Dante and Matraini. It is of note that this sestina of Matraini's has more Dantesque rhyme words than any other sestina of the period. Her third rhyme word, *giorno*, is in a sestina of Petrarch's (22), but more probably is taken from Dante's "Al poco *giorno*," where it appears in the emphatic position of closure of the hemistich.

Mirto appears only in Matraini as a rhyme word—and it is the last word of the entire composition, sealing it as her own utterance.

9.   The Serchio River is a stream which flows through the outskirts of Lucca.

10.   Delia is Artemis, the moon, sister of Apollo; their names, Delia and Delos, come from their birthplace on the island of Delos. This may be a *senhal* for her lover.

11.   See above, note 5.

12.   Androgeo is the *senhal* for her loved one.

13.   Pan is the Greek god of woods and fields, flocks and herds, quite perfect for Androgeo.

14.   Lappato is a river which flows from Pescia to Lucca.

15.   Cangenna Lipomeni clearly was a prized friend to Chiara Matraini and is mentioned a number of times in her work.

16.   Saturn was the Roman name for Cronos, the youngest son of Heaven and Earth and leader of his brothers, the Titans. He married Rhea, and learning that he was fated to be overcome by his children, he devoured all of his male children except Zeus.

17.   To Matraini, suicide would have represented a damnable sin.

18.   Sirens, in Greek mythology, were women who sang beautiful songs and lured sailors to their death.

19.   Arachne was a Lydian woman who was superb in the art of weaving. She challenged Athena to compete with her and was so excellent that Athena destroyed her work. When Arachne in despair tried to hang herself, the rope was changed into a spider web, with Arachne herself the spider. She entered the domain of the gods with her web of marvelous worth.

20.   Parnassus is the highest part of a mountain range in Greece, north of Delphi, receiving the full rays of the sun during the heat of the day. It is sacred to Apollo and the Muses.

21.   See above, note 9.

22.   See above, note 12.

23.   The Nymphs were young and beautiful female spirits who were believed to inhabit the seas, fresh water, mountains, or grottoes. They were used to signify the participation of the deities in earthly matters.

24.   Alecto was one of the Furies, or to use their Greek name, the Erinyes or Eumenides. They were the spirits of punishment: no sacrifices or prayers could exempt them from punishing their object of persecution.

25.   Rhadamanthus was the son of Zeus and Europa and the brother of King Minos of Crete. Fearing his brother, he fled to Boeotia, where he married Alcmene. He was a very just man: when he died, he was made the judge of the afterlife, and no man could dispute his claims.

26.   Nero (37–68) was the sixth emperor of Rome; his full name was Claudius Caesar Nero. In the tenth year of his reign (64), Rome was nearly destroyed by fire: it burned for six days and seven nights. It was generally believed that Nero himself had

started the fire: he watched the conflagration from a high tower and was said to have been singing the song "The Destruction of Troy." Nero accused the Christians of setting the fire and executed a great number of them.

27.   This poem also appears in chapter 3 of her *Spiritual Meditations*, as part of her reflections before the Greater Power speaks.

28.   The identity of M. L. is unknown.

29.   Pietro Bembo (1470–1547) was the arbiter of Italian Renaissance literature. His writings, both poetry and prose, advocated a strict adherence to Petrarch and Boccaccio. He wrote the *Asolani*, a book about love which was founded upon Neoplatonic and courtier traditions. See *Gli Asolani*, trans. Rudolf B. Gottfried, Indiana University Publications Humanities Series no. 31 (Bloomington: Indiana University Press, 1954; reprint, Freeport, NY: Books for Libraries Press, 1971).

30.   Mario Equicola (1470–1525) worked for Isabella d'Este and for Federico Gonzaga; he composed *De natura de Amore* in Latin, on the model of Ficino, praising love.

31.   Apelles (fourth century BCE) was the court painter to Alexander the Great; he was famous for his painting of Venus, the goddess of love and fertility.

CHAPTER FIVE

1.   Vi marauigliarete forse, benignissimi Lettori, che hauendo mandate primieramente in luce le spirituali meditationi, e le considerationi fatte sopra de i sette salmi di Dauit, e di poi le degne lodi della beatissima Verginc, hora in vltimo habbia fatto stampare queste mie giouenili compositioni, le quali più ragioneuole era, che douessero esser le prime; ma, se voi saperete quanto di forza habbino le preghiere de parenti, e l'essortationi de gli amici, i quali à ciò fare, per mio honore, e per mia lode m'hanno sospinta, voi non vi marauiglierete, nè mi biasmerete, se non hò seruato quell'ordine, che douea nel mandar fuori l'opre mie; ma più tosto ne douerò (com'io spero) esscrne da uoi, benignamente, scusata, però restate quieti, e felici. Chiara Matraini, *Lettere con la prima e seconda parte delle sue Rime* (Venice: Moretti, 1597), n.p.

2.   This is the first of her letters in the 1597 edition of her poems. It appeared in the 1595 edition, as letter number 2.

3.   Latona is the Latin name of Leto, the mother of Apollo and Diana.

4.   Endymion is the beautiful youth beloved of Diana.

5.   The word *chiara* is to be understood as meaning both "clear" or "bright" and her name, Chiara.

6.   Atlas was a Titan who at first was guardian of the pillars of heaven and later was forced by Zeus to uphold the sky with his head and hands. This was because he had supported the Titans in their scheme against Zeus.

7.   Avernus means the infernal regions.

8.   See chap. 1, note 16

9.   See chap. 1, note 6.

10.   Daedalus was the father of Icarus; when he was imprisoned by King Minos in

the labyrinth of the Minotaur, he constructed artificial wings to escape and flew away to Sicily. His son, however, drew near to the sun, which melted the wax, and was drowned in the Aegean Sea.

11.   Delos is the small Greek island reputed to be the birthplace of Apollo, the sun god, and Diana, goddess of the moon.

12.   Python was a huge serpent, or dragon, with poisonous teeth; it guarded Delphi and was killed by Apollo.

13.   See chap. 1, note 9.

14.   See chap. 1, note 20.

15.   This poem was written for Matraini's son, Federigo, who most likely died between 1571 and 1575. The two of them had argued about her dowry, but perhaps they got over that hurdle, for she wrote this upon his death.

16.   This poem also appears in chapter 3 of her *Spiritual Meditations*, as part of her reflections before the Greater Power speaks.

17.   Cato the Younger was a Roman patriot and Stoic philosopher. He was born in Rome in 95 BCE and committed suicide at Utica, in North Africa, in 46 BCE, when he learned of the victory of Caesar.

18.   Her "pearl," frequently used in poetry, is her lover.

19.   Monte is the name Matraini uses for Benedetto Varchi, a name for his place of origin, which was Montevarchi. It was a common Renaissance usage to name people for their birthplace.

20.   Olympus and Atlantis are here used to mean places of importance. Olympus was the fabled place of the gods, especially Apollo and the Muses. Atlantis was an island which disappeared, the place of wisdom and honor.

21.   Saturn, a planet of the solar system, was in Matraini's time generally thought to be like a wandering star.

22.   "[Y]our flowers" refers to the poems he wrote.

23.   Cangenna Lipomeni clearly was a faithful friend to Matraini, but that is all we know about her.

24.   This sonnet accompanied a letter written to M. Annibal Tosco, dated Genoa, 1562, in the Aldine collection of letters (see the Biblioteca Nazionale Centrale of Florence Pal. 12.-11.1.2). It has been partly altered in Matraini's book. I am indebted to Giovanna Rabitti for this source.

25.   Prometheus was a Titan who created the first man from clay and also stole fire from the wheel of the chariot of the gods, to give it as a gift to people. The fire was interpreted to be the flame of divine inspiration for poets and other creative minds.

26.   Her "lifeless daughters" refers to her poems.

27.   See above, note 5.

28.   This sonnet is to Lodovico Dolce, a poet who admired Matraini and included her entire first book of poems in his book for the Aldine Press, the *Rime di diversi signori napolitani e d'altri* (Venice, 1556). His name, Dolce, means sweet or soft in Italian.

29.   Apollo was the god of the sun and the inspiration for poets.

30.   See Acts 12: 8–11.

31.   Abel was the younger brother of Cain and slain by him. His blood cried from the ground for revenge, and the Lord heard it and banished Cain. See Genesis 4:1–15.

32.   Saint Peter, the apostle, died in about 64 CE.

33.   Moses saved the Hebrews from Pharaoh; he led them out of Egypt into the Promised Land. His story is told in Exodus.

34.   Sirens, in Greek mythology, were women who sang beautiful songs and lured sailors to their death.

35.   This madrigal is given here at it was printed in the 1597 volume of Matraini's poems. I have added "the clear one" to emphasize that her name means "clear" or "bright."

SERIES EDITORS'
BIBLIOGRAPHY

PRIMARY SOURCES

Alberti, Leon Battista (1404–72). *The Family in Renaissance Florence*. Trans. Renée Neu Watkins. Columbia, SC: University of South Carolina Press, 1969.

Arenal, Electa, and Stacey Schlau, eds. *Untold Sisters: Hispanic Nuns in Their Own Works*. Trans. Amanda Powell. Albuquerque, NM: University of New Mexico Press, 1989.

Astell, Mary (1666–1731). *The First English Feminist: Reflections on Marriage and Other Writings*. Ed. and Introd. Bridget Hill. New York: St. Martin's Press, 1986.

Atherton, Margaret, ed. *Women Philosophers of the Early Modern Period*. Indianapolis, IN: Hackett Publishing Co., 1994.

Aughterson, Kate, ed. *Renaissance Woman: Constructions of Femininity in England: A Source Book*. London and New York: Routledge, 1995.

Barbaro, Francesco (1390–1454). *On Wifely Duties*. Trans. Benjamin Kohl in Kohl and R. G. Witt, eds., *The Earthly Republic*. Philadelphia: University of Pennsylvania Press, 1978, 179–228. Translation of the preface and book 2.

Behn, Aphra. *The Works of Aphra Behn*. 7 vols. Ed. Janet Todd. Columbus, OH: Ohio State University Press, 1992–96.

Blamires, Alcuin, ed. *Woman Defamed and Woman Defended: An Anthology of Medieval Texts*. Oxford: Clarendon Press, 1992.

Boccaccio, Giovanni (1313–75). *Famous Women*. Ed. and trans. Virginia Brown. The I Tatti Renaissance Library. Cambridge, MA: Harvard University Press, 2001.

———. *Corbaccio or the Labyrinth of Love*. Trans. Anthony K. Cassell. Second revised edition. Binghamton, NY: Medieval and Renaissance Texts and Studies, 1993.

Booy, David, ed. *Autobiographical Writings by Early Quaker Women*. Aldershot and Brookfield: Ashgate Publishing Co., 2004.

Brown, Sylvia. *Women's Writing in Stuart England: The Mother's Legacies of Dorothy Leigh, Elizabeth Joscelin and Elizabeth Richardson*. Thrupp, Stroud, Gloceter: Sutton, 1999.

Bruni, Leonardo (1370–1444). "On the Study of Literature (1405) to Lady Battista Malatesta of Moltefeltro." In *The Humanism of Leonardo Bruni: Selected Texts*. Trans. and Introd. Gordon Griffiths, James Hankins, and David Thompson. Binghamton, NY: Medieval and Renaissance Studies and Texts, 1987, 240–51.

Castiglione, Baldassare (1478–1529). *The Book of the Courtier*. Trans. George Bull. New

York: Penguin, 1967; *The Book of the Courtier*. Ed. Daniel Javitch. New York: W. W. Norton & Co., 2002.

Christine de Pizan (1365–1431). *The Book of the City of Ladies*. Trans. Earl Jeffrey Richards. Foreword Marina Warner. New York: Persea Books, 1982.

———. *The Treasure of the City of Ladies*. Trans. Sarah Lawson. New York: Viking Penguin, 1985. Also trans. and introd. Charity Cannon Willard. Ed. and introd. Madeleine P. Cosman. New York: Persea Books, 1989.

Clarke, Danielle, ed. *Isabella Whitney, Mary Sidney and Aemilia Lanyer: Renaissance Women Poets*. New York: Penguin Books, 2000.

Couchman, Jane, and Ann Crabb, eds. *Women's Letters Across Europe, 1400–1700*. Aldershot and Brookfield: Ashgate Publishing Co., 2005.

Crawford, Patricia and Laura Gowing, eds. *Women's Worlds in Seventeenth-Century England: A Source Book*. London and New York: Routledge, 2000.

"Custome Is an Idiot": Jcobean Pamphlet Literature on Women. Ed. Susan Gushee O'Malley. Afterword Ann Rosalind Jones. Chicago and Urbana: University of Illinois Press, 2004.

Daybell, James, ed. *Early Modern Women's Letter Writing, 1450–1700*. Houndmills, England and New York: Palgrave, 2001.

De Erauso, Catalina. *Lieutenant Nun: Memoir of a Basque Transvestite in the New World*. Trans. Michele Ttepto and Gabriel Stepto; foreword by Marjorie Garber. Boston: Beacon Press, 1995.

Elizabeth I: Collected Works. Ed. Leah S. Marcus, Janel Mueller, and Mary Beth Rose. Chicago: University of Chicago Press, 2000.

Elyot, Thomas (1490–1546). *Defence of Good Women: The Feminist Controversy of the Renaissance*. Facsimile Reproductions. Ed. Diane Bornstein. New York: Delmar, 1980.

Erasmus, Desiderius (1467–1536). *Erasmus on Women*. Ed. Erika Rummel. Toronto: University of Toronto Press, 1996.

Female and Male Voices in Early Modern England: An Anthology of Renaissance Writing. Ed. Betty S. Travitsky and Anne Lake Prescott. New York: Columbia University Press, 2000.

Ferguson, Moira, ed. *First Feminists: British Women Writers 1578–1799*. Bloomington, IN: Indiana University Press, 1985.

Galilei, Maria Celeste. *Sister Maria Celeste's Letters to her father, Galileo*. Ed. and trans. Rinaldina Russell. Lincoln, NE, and New York: Writers Club Press of Universe.com, 2000; *To Father: The Letters of Sister Maria Celeste to Galileo, 1623–1633*. Trans. Dava Sobel. London: Fourth Estate, 2001.

Gethner, Perry, ed. *The Lunatic Lover and Other Plays by French Women of the 17ᵗʰ and 18ᵗʰ Centuries*. Portsmouth, NH: Heinemann, 1994.

Glückel of Hameln (1646–1724). *The Memoirs of Glückel of Hameln*. Trans. Marvin Lowenthal. New Introd. Robert Rosen. New York: Schocken Books, 1977.

Harline, Craig, ed. *The Burdens of Sister Margaret: Inside a Seventeenth-Century Convent*. Abridged ed. New Haven: Yale University Press, 2000.

Henderson, Katherine Usher, and Barbara F. McManus, eds. *Half Humankind: Contexts and Texts of the Controversy about Women in England, 1540–1640*. Urbana: University of Illinois Press, 1985.

Hoby, Margaret. *The Private Life of an Elizabethan Lady: The Diary of Lady Margaret Hoby 1599–1605*. Phoenix Mill: Sutton Publishing, 1998.

Humanist Educational Treatises. Ed. and trans. Craig W. Kallendorf. The I Tatti Renaissance Library. Cambridge, MA: Harvard University Press, 2002.

Hunter, Lynette, ed. *The Letters of Dorothy Moore, 1612–64.* Aldershot and Brookfield: Ashgate Publishing Co., 2004.

Joscelin, Elizabeth. *The Mothers Legacy to her Unborn Childe.* Ed. Jean leDrew Metcalfe. Toronto: University of Toronto Press, 2000.

Kaminsky, Amy Katz, ed. *Water Lilies, Flores del agua: An Anthology of Spanish Women Writers from the Fifteenth Through the Nineteenth Century.* Minneapolis: University of Minnesota Press, 1996.

Kempe, Margery (1373–1439). *The Book of Margery Kempe.* Trans. and ed. Lynn Staley. A Norton Critical Edition. New York: W. W. Norton, 2001.

King, Margaret L., and Albert Rabil, Jr., eds. *Her Immaculate Hand: Selected Works by and about the Women Humanists of Quattrocento Italy.* Binghamton, NY: Medieval and Renaissance Texts and Studies, 1983; second revised paperback edition, 1991.

Klein, Joan Larsen, ed. *Daughters, Wives, and Widows: Writings by Men about Women and Marriage in England, 1500–1640.* Urbana, IL: University of Illinois Press, 1992.

Knox, John (1505–72). *The Political Writings of John Knox: The First Blast of the Trumpet against the Monstrous Regiment of Women and Other Selected Works.* Ed. Marvin A. Breslow. Washington: Folger Shakespeare Library, 1985.

Kors, Alan C., and Edward Peters, eds. *Witchcraft in Europe, 400-1700: A Documentary History.* Philadelphia: University of Pennsylvania Press, 2000.

Krämer, Heinrich, and Jacob Sprenger. *Malleus Maleficarum* (ca. 1487). Trans. Montague Summers. London: Pushkin Press, 1928; reprinted New York: Dover, 1971.

Larsen, Anne R., and Colette H. Winn, eds. *Writings by Pre-Revolutionary French Women: From Marie de France to Elizabeth Vigée-Le Brun.* New York and London: Garland Publishing Co., 2000.

de Lorris, William, and Jean de Meun. *The Romance of the Rose.* Trans. Charles Dahlbert. Princeton: Princeton University Press, 1971; reprinted University Press of New England, 1983.

Marcus, Leah S., Janel Mueller, and Mary Beth Rose, eds. *Elizabeth I: Collected Works.* Chicago: University of Chicago Press, 2000.

Marguerite d'Angoulême, Queen of Navarre (1492–1549). *The Heptameron.* Trans. P. A. Chilton. New York: Viking Penguin, 1984.

Mary of Agreda. *The Divine Life of the Most Holy Virgin.* Abridgment of *The Mystical City of God.* Abr. by Fr. Bonaventure Amedeo de Caesarea, M.C. Trans. from French by Abbé Joseph A. Boullan. Rockford, IL: Tan Books, 1997.

Mullan, David George. *Women's Life Writing in Early Modern Scotland: Writing the Evangelical Self, c. 1670–c. 1730.* Aldershot and Brookfield: Ashgate Publishing Co., 2003.

Myers, Kathleen A., and Amanda Powell, eds. *A Wild Country Out in the Garden: The Spiritual Journals of a Colonial Mexican Nun.* Bloomington: Indiana University Press, 1999.

Russell, Rinaldina, ed. *Sister Maria Celeste's Letters to Her Father, Galileo.* San Jose and New York: Writers Club Press, 2000.

Teresa of Avila, Saint (1515–82). *The Life of Saint Teresa of Avila by Herself.* Trans. J. M. Cohen. New York: Viking Penguin, 1957.

———. *The Collected Letters of St. Teresa of Avila. Volume One: 1546–1577,* trans. Kieran Kavanaugh. Washington, DC: Institute of Carmelite Studies, 2001.

Travitsky, Betty, ed. *The Paradise of Women: Writings by Entlishwomen of the Renaissance.* Westport, CT: Greenwood Press, 1981.

Weyer, Johann (1515–88). *Witches, Devils, and Doctors in the Renaissance: Johann Weyer, De praestigiis daemonum.* Ed. George Mora with Benjamin G. Kohl, Erik Midelfort, and Helen Bacon. Trans. John Shea. Binghamton, NY: Medieval and Renaissance Texts and Studies, 1991.

Wilson, Katharina M., ed. *Medieval Women Writers.* Athens: University of Georgia Press, 1984.

———, ed. *Women Writers of the Renaissance and Reformation.* Athens: University of Georgia Press, 1987.

———, and Frank J. Warnke, eds. *Women Writers of the Seventeenth Century.* Athens: University of Georgia Press, 1989.

Wollstonecraft, Mary. *A Vindication of the Rights of* Men *and a Vindication of the Rights of* Women. Ed. Sylvana Tomaselli. Cambridge: Cambridge University Press, 1995. Also *The Vindications of the Rights of Men, The Rights of Women.* Ed. D. L. Macdonald and Kathleen Scherf. Peterborough, Ontario, Canada: Broadview Press, 1997.

Woman Defamed and Woman Defended: An Anthology of Medieval Texts. Ed. Alcuin Blamires. Oxford: Clarendon Press, 1992.

Women Critics 1660–1820: An Anthology. Edited by the Folger Collective on Early Women Critics. Bloomington, IN: Indiana University Press, 1995.

Women Writers in English 1350–1850: 15 published through 1999 (projected 30-volume series suspended). Oxford University Press.

Women's Letters Across Europe, 1400–1700. Ed. Jane Couchman and Ann Crabb. Aldershot and Brookfield: Ashgate Publishing Co., 2005.

Wroth, Lady Mary. *The Countess of Montgomery's Urania.* 2 parts. Ed. Josephine A. Roberts. Tempe, AZ: MRTS, 1995, 1999.

———. *Lady Mary Wroth's "Love's Victory": The Penshurst Manuscript.* Ed. Michael G. Brennan. London: The Roxburghe Club, 1988.

———. *The Poems of Lady Mary Wroth.* Ed. Josephine A. Roberts. Baton Rouge: Louisiana State University Press, 1983.

de Zayas Maria. *The Disenchantments of Love.* Trans. H. Patsy Boyer. Albany: State University of New York Press, 1997.

———. *The Enchantments of Love: Amorous and Exemplary Novels.* Trans. H. Patsy Boyer. Berkeley: University of California Press, 1990.

SECONDARY SOURCES

Abate, Corinne S., ed. *Privacy, Domesticity, and Women in Early Modern England.* Aldershot and Brookfield: Ashgate Publishing Co., 2003.

Ahlgren, Gillian. *Teresa of Avila and the Politics of Sanctity.* Ithaca: Cornell University Press, 1996.

Akkerman, Tjitske, and Siep Sturman, eds. *Feminist Thought in European History, 1400–2000.* London and New York: Routledge, 1997.

Allen, Sister Prudence, R.S.M. *The Concept of Woman: The Aristotelian Revolution, 750 B.C. – A.D. 1250.* Grand Rapids, MI: William B. Eerdmans Publishing Company, 1997.

————. *The Concept of Woman: Volume II: The early Humanist Reformation, 1250–1500.* Grand Rapids, MI: William B. Eerdmans Publishing Company, 2002.

Altmann, Barbara K., and Deborah L. McGrady, eds. *Christine de Pizan: A Casebook.* New York: Routledge, 2003.

Ambiguous Realities: Women in the Middle Ages and Renaissance. Ed. Carole Levin and Jeanie Watson. Detroit: Wayne State University Press, 1987.

Amussen, Susan D, and Adele Seeff, eds. *Attending to Early Modern Women.* Newark: University of Delaware Press, 1998.

Andreadis, Harriette. *Sappho in Early Modern England: Female Same-Sex Literary Erotics 1550–1714.* Chicago: University of Chicago Press, 2001.

Architecture and the Politics of Gender in Early Modern Europe. Ed. Helen Hills. Aldershot and Brookfield: Ashgate Publishing Co., 2003.

Armon, Shifra. *Picking Wedlock: Women and the Courtship Novel in Spain.* New York: Rowman and Littlefield Publishers, Inc., 2002.

Attending to Early Modern Women. Ed. Susan D. Amussen and Adele Seeff. Newark: University of Delaware Press, 1998.

Backer, Anne Liot. *Precious Women.* New York: Basic Books, 1974.

Ballaster, Ros. *Seductive Forms.* New York: Oxford University Press, 1992.

Barash, Carol. *English Women's Poetry, 1649–1714: Politics, Community, and Linguistic Authority.* New York and Oxford: Oxford University Press, 1996.

Barker, Alele Marie, and Jehanne M. Gheith, eds. *A History of Women's Writing in Russia.* Cambridge: Cambridge University Press, 2002.

Battigelli, Anna. *Margaret Cavendish and the Exiles of the Mind.* Lexington: University of Kentucky Press, 1998.

Beasley, Faith. *Revising Memory: Women's Fiction and Memoirs in Seventeenth-Century France.* New Brunswick: Rutgers University Press, 1990.

————. *Salons, History, and the Creation of Seventeenth-Century France.* Aldershot and Brookfield: Ashgate Publishing Co., 2006.

Becker, Lucinda M. *Death and the Early Modern Englishwoman.* Aldershot and Brookfield: Ashgate Publishing Co., 2003.

Beilin, Elaine V. *Redeeming Eve: Women Writers of the English Renaissance.* Princeton: Princeton University Press, 1987.

Bennett, Lyn. *Women Writing of Divinest Things: Rhetoric and the Poetry of Pembroke, Wroth, and Lanyer.* Pittsburgh: Duquesne University Press, 2004.

Benson, Pamela Joseph. *The Invention of Renaissance Woman: The Challenge of Female Independence in the Literature and Thought of Italy and England.* University Park: Pennsylvania State University Press, 1992.

———— and Victoria Kirkham, eds. *Strong Voices, Weak History? Medieval and Renaissance Women in their Literary Canons: England, France, Italy.* Ann Arbor: University of Michigan Press, 2003.

Berry, Helen. *Gender, Society and Print Culture in Late-Stuart England.* Aldershot and Brookfield: Ashgate Publishing Co., 2003.

Beyond Isabella: Secular Women Patrons of Art in Renaissance Italy. Ed. Sheryl E. Reiss and David G. Wilkins. Kirksville, MO: Turman State University Press, 2001.

Beyond Their Sex: Learned Women of the European Past. Ed. Patricia A. Labalme. New York: New York University Press, 1980.

Bicks, Caroline. *Midwiving Subjects in Shakespeare's England*. Aldershot and Brookfield: Ashgate Publishing Co., 2003.

Bilinkoff, Jodi. *The Avila of Saint Teresa: Religious Reform in a Sixteenth-Century City*. Ithaca: Cornell University Press, 1989.

—————. *Related Lives: Confessors and Their Female Penitents, 1450–1750*. Ithaca, NY: Cornell University Press, 2005.

Bissell, R. Ward. *Artemisia Gentileschi and the Authority of Art*. University Park: Pennsylvania State University Press, 2000.

Blain, Virginia, Isobel Grundy, and Patricia Clements, eds. *The Feminist Companion to Literature in English: Women Writers from the Middle Ages to the Present*. New Haven: Yale University Press, 1990.

Blamires, Alcuin. *The Case for Women in Medieval Culture*. Oxford: Clarendon Press, 1997.

Bloch, R. Howard. *Medieval Misogyny and the Invention of Western Romantic Love*. Chicago: University of Chicago Press, 1991.

Bogucka, Maria. *Women in Early Modern Polish Society, Against the European Background*. Aldershot and Brookfield: Ashgate Publishing Co., 2004.

Bornstein, Daniel, and Roberto Rusconi, eds. *Women and Religion in Medieval and Renaissance Italy*. Trans. Margery J. Schneider. Chicago: University of Chicago Press, 1996.

Brant, Clare, and Diane Purkiss, eds. *Women, Texts and Histories, 1575–1760*. London and New York: Routledge, 1992.

Briggs, Robin. *Witches and Neighbours: The Social and Cultural Context of European Witchcraft*. New York: HarperCollins, 1995; Viking Penguin, 1996.

Brink, Jean R., ed. *Female Scholars: A Traditioin of Learned Women before 1800*. Montréal: Eden Press Women's Publications, 1980.

—————, Allison Coudert, and Maryanne Cline Horowitz. *The Politics of Gender in Early Modern Europe*. Sixteenth Century Essays and Studies, 12. Kirksville, MO: Sixteenth Century Journal Publishers, 1989.

Broude, Norma, and Mary D. Garrard, eds. *The Expanding Discourse: Feminism and Art History*. New York: HarperCollins, 1992.

Brown, Judith C. *Immodest Acts: The Life of a Lesbian Nun in Renaissance Italy*. New York: Oxford University Press, 1986.

————— and Robert C. Davis, eds. *Gender and Society in Renaisance Italy*. London: Addison Wesley Longman, 1998.

Burke, Victoria E. Burke, ed. *Early Modern Women's Manuscript Writing*. Aldershot and Brookfield: Ashgate Publishing Co., 2004.

Burns, Jane E., ed. *Medieval Fabrications: Dress, Textiles, Cloth Work, and Other Cultural Imaginings*. New York: Palgrave Macmillan, 2004.

Bynum, Carolyn Walker. *Fragmentation and Redemption: Essays on Gender and the Human Body in Medieval Religion*. New York: Zone Books, 1992.

—————. *Holy Feast and Holy Fast: The Religious Significance of Food to Medieval Women*. Berkeley: University of California Press, 1987.

Campbell, Julie DeLynn. "Renaissance Women Writers: The Beloved Speaks her Part." Ph.D diss., Texas A&M University, 1997.

Catling, Jo, ed. *A History of Women's Writing in Germany, Austria and Switzerland*. Cambridge: Cambridge University Press, 2000.

Cavallo, Sandra, and Lyndan Warner. *Widowhood in Medieval and Early Modern Europe.* New York: Longman, 1999.

Cavanagh, Sheila T. *Cherished Torment: The Emotional Geography of Lady Mary Wroth's Urania.* Pittsburgh: Duquesne University Press, 2001.

Cerasano, S. P., and Marion Wynne-Davies, eds. *Readings in Renaissance Women's Drama: Criticism, History, and Performance 1594–1998.* London and New York: Routledge, 1998.

Cervigni, Dino S., ed. *Women Mystic Writers. Annali d'Italianistica* 13 (1995) (entire issue).

———— and Rebecca West, eds. *Women's Voices in Italian Literature.* Special issue. *Annali d'Italianistica* 7 (1989).

Charlton, Kenneth. *Women, Religion and Education in Early Modern England.* London and New York: Routledge, 1999.

Chojnacka, Monica. *Working Women in Early Modern Venice.* Baltimore: Johns Hopkins University Press, 2001.

Chojnacki, Stanley. *Women and Men in Renaissance Venice: Twelve Essays on Patrician Society.* Baltimore: Johns Hopkins University Press, 2000.

Cholakian, Patricia Francis. *Rape and Writing in the* Heptameron *of Marguerite de Navarre.* Carbondale and Edwardsville: Southern Illinois University Press, 1991.

————. *Women and the Politics of Self-Representation in Seventeenth-Century France.* Newark: University of Delaware Press, 2000.

Christine de Pizan: A Casebook. Ed. Barbara K. Altmann and Deborah L. McGrady. New York. Routledge, 2003.

Clogan, Paul Maruice, ed. *Medievali et Humanistica: Literacy and the Lay Reader.* Lanham, MD: Rowman & Littlefield, 2000.

Clubb, Louise George (1989). *Italian Drama in Shakespeare's Time.* New Haven: Yale University Press

Clucas, Stephen, ed. *A Princely Brave Woman: Essays on Margaret Cavendish, Duchess of Newcastle.* Aldershot and Brookfield: Ashgate Publishing Co., 2003.

Conley, John J., S.J. *The Suspicion of Virtue: Women Philosophers in Neoclassical France.* Ithaca, NY: Cornell University Press, 2002.

Crabb, Ann. *The Strozzi of Florence: Widowhood and Family Solidarity in the Renaissance.* Ann Arbor: University of Michigan Press, 2000.

The Crannied Wall: Women, Religion, and the Arts in Early Modern Europe. Ed. Craig A. Monson. Ann Arbor: University of Michigan Press, 1992.

Creative Women in Medieval and Early Modern Italy. Ed. E. Ann Matter and John Coakley. Philadelphia: University of Pennsylvania Press, 1994.

Crowston, Clare Haru. *Fabricating Women: The Seamstresses of Old Regime France, 1675–1791.* Durham, NC: Duke University Press, 2001.

Cruz, Anne J. and Mary Elizabeth Perry, eds. *Culture and Control in Counter-Reformation Spain.* Minneapolis: University of Minnesota Press, 1992.

Datta, Satya. *Women and Men in Early Modern Venice.* Aldershot and Brookfield: Ashgate Publishing Co., 2003.

Davis, Natalie Zemon. *Society and Culture in Early Modern France.* Stanford: Stanford University Press, 1975.

————. *Women on the Margins: Three Seventeenth-Century Lives.* Cambridge, MA: Harvard University Press, 1995.

DeJean, Joan. *Ancients against Moderns: Culture Wars and the Making of a Fin de Siècle*. Chicago: University of Chicago Press, 1997.

———. *Fictions of Sappho, 1546–1937*. Chicago: University of Chicago Press, 1989.

———. *The Reinvention of Obscenity: Sex, Lies, and Tabloids in Early Modern France*. Chicago: University of Chicago Press, 2002.

———. *Tender Geographies: Women and the Origins of the Novel in France*. New York: Columbia University Press, 1991.

———. *The Reinvention of Obscenity: Sex, Lies, and Tabloids in Early Modern France*. Chicago: University of Chicago Press, 2002.

D'Elia, Anthony F. *The Renaissance of Marriage in Fifteenth-Century Italy*. Cambridge, MA: Harvard University Press, 2004.

Dictionary of Russian Women Writers. Ed. Marina Ledkovsky, Charlotte Rosenthal, and Mary Zirin. Westport, CT: Greenwood Press, 1994.

Dixon, Laurinda S. *Perilous Chastity: Women and Illness in Pre-Enlightenment Art and Medicine*. Ithaca: Cornell University Press, 1995.

Dolan, Frances, E. *Whores of Babylon: Catholicism, Gender and Seventeenth-Century Print Culture*. Ithaca: Cornell University Press, 1999.

Donovan, Josephine. *Women and the Rise of the Novel, 1405–1726*. New York: St. Martin's Press, 1999.

Early [English] Women Writers: 1600–1720. Ed. Anita Pacheco. New York and London: Longman, 1998.

Eigler, Friederike and Susanne Kord, eds. *The Feminist Encyclopedia of German Literature*. Westport, CT: Greenwood Press, 1997.

Engendering the Early Modern Stage: Women Playwrights in the Spanish Empire. Ed. Valeria (Oakey) Hegstrom and Amy R. Williamsen. New Orleans: University Press of the South, 1999.

Erdmann, Axel. *My Gracious Silence: Women in the Mirror of Sixteenth-Century Printing in Western Europe*. Luzern: Gilhofer and Rauschberg, 1999.

Erickson, Amy Louise. *Women and Property in Early Modern England*. London and New York: Routledge, 1993.

Extraordinary Women of the Medieval and Renaissance World: A Biographical Dictionary. Ed. Carole Levin, et al. Westport, CT: Greenwood Press, 2000.

Ezell, Margaret J. M. *The Patriarch's Wife: Literary Evidence and the History of the Family*. Chapel Hill: University of North Carolina Press, 1987.

———. *Social Authorship and the Advent of Print*. Baltimore: Johns Hopkins University Press, 1999.

———. *Writing Women's Literary History*. Baltimore: Johns Hopkins University Press, 1993.

Farrell, Michèle Longino. *Performing Motherhood: The Sévigné Correspondence*. Hanover, NH and London: University Press of New England, 1991.

Feminism and Renaissance Studies. Ed. Lorna Hutson. New York: Oxford University Press, 1999.

The Feminist Companion to Literature in English: Women Writers from the Middle Ages to the Present. Ed. Virginia Blain, Isobel Grundy, and Patricia Clements. New Haven: Yale University Press, 1990.

Feminist Encyclopedia of Italian Literature. Edited by Rinaldina Russell. Westport, CT: Greenwood Press, 1997.

Feminist Thought in European History, 1400–2000. Ed. Tjitske Akkerman and Siep Sturman. London and New York: Routledge, 1997.

Ferguson, Margaret W. *Dido's Daughters: Literacy, Gender, and Empire in Early Modern England and France.* Chicago: University of Chicago Press, 2003.

————, Maureen Quilligan, and Nancy J. Vickers, eds. *Rewriting the_Renaissance: The Discourses of Sexual Difference in Early Modern Europe.* Chicago: University of Chicago Press, 1987.

Ferraro, Joanne M. *Marriage Wars in Late Renaissance Venice.* Oxford: Oxford University Press, 2001.

Fletcher, Anthony. *Gender, Sex and Subordination in England 1500–1800.* New Haven: Yale University Press, 1995.

Franklin, Margaret. *Boccaccio's Heroines.* Aldershot and Brookfield: Ashgate Publishing Co., 2006.

French Women Writers: A Bio-Bibliographical Source Book. Ed. Eva Martin Sartori and Dorothy Wynne Zimmerman. Westport, CT: Greenwood Press, 1991.

Frye, Susan and Karen Robertson, eds. *Maids and Mistresses, Cousins and Queens: Women's Alliances in Early Modern England.* Oxford: Oxford University Press, 1999.

Gallagher, Catherine. *Nobody's Story: The Vanishing Acts of Women Writers in the Marketplace, 1670–1820.* Berkeley: University of California Press, 1994.

Garrard, Mary D. *Artemisia Gentileschi: The Image of the Female Hero in Italian Baroque Art.* Princeton: Princeton University Press, 1989.

Gelbart, Nina Rattner. *The King's Midwife: A History and Mystery of Madame du Coudray.* Berkeley: University of California Press, 1998.

Giles, Mary E., ed. *Women in the Inquisition: Spain and the New World.* Baltimore: Johns Hopkins University Press, 1999.

Gill, Catie. *Somen in the Seventeenth-Century Quaker Community.* Aldershot and Brookfield: Ashgate Publishing Co., 2005.

Glenn, Cheryl. *Rhetoric Retold: Regendering the Tradition from Antiquity Through the Renaissance.* Carbondale and Edwardsville, IL: Southern Illinois University Press, 1997.

Goffen, Rona. *Titian's Women.* New Haven: Yale University Press, 1997.

Going Public: Women and Publishing in Early Modern France. Ed. Elizabeth C. Goldsmith and Dena Goodman. Ithaca: Cornell University Press, 1995.

Goldberg, Jonathan. *Desiring Women Writing: English Renaissance Examples.* Stanford: Stanford University Press, 1997.

Goldsmith, Elizabeth C. *Exclusive Conversations: The Art of Interaction in Seventeenth-Century France.* Philadelphia: University of Pennsylvania Press, 1988.

————, ed. *Writing the Female Voice.* Boston: Northeastern University Press, 1989.

———— and Dena Goodman, eds. *Going Public: Women and Publishing in Early Modern France.* Ithaca: Cornell University Press, 1995.

Grafton, Anthony, and Lisa Jardine. *From Humanism to the Humanities: Education and the Liberal Arts in Fifteenth-and Sixteenth-Century Europe.* London: Duckworth, 1986.

The Graph of Sex and the German Text: Gendered Culture in Early Modern Germany 1500–1700. Ed. Lynne Tatlock and Christiane Bohnert. Amsterdam and Atlanta: Rodolphi, 1994.

Grassby, Richard. *Kinship and Capitalism: Marriage, Family, and Business in the English-Speaking World, 1580–1740.* Cambridge: Cambridge University Press, 2001.

Greer, Margaret Rich. *Maria de Zayas Tells Baroque Tales of Love and the Cruelty of Men.* University Park: Pennsylvania State University Press, 2000.

Grossman, Avraham. *Pious and Rebellious: Jewish Women in Medieval Europe.* Trans. Jonathan Chipman. Brandeis/University Press of New England, 2004.

Gutierrez, Nancy A. *"Shall She Famish Then?" Female Food Refusal in Early Modern England.* Aldershot and Brookfield: Ashgate Publishing Co., 2003.

Habermann, Ina. *Staging Slander and Gender in Early Modern England.* Aldershot and Brookfield: Ashgate Publishing Co., 2003.

Hacke, Daniela. *Women Sex and Marriage in Early Modern Venice.* Aldershot and Brookfield: Ashgate Publishing Co., 2004.

Hackel, Heidi Brayman. *Reading Material in Early Modern England: Print, Gender, Literacy.* Cambridge: Cambridge University Press, 2005.

Hackett, Helen. *Women and Romance Fiction in the English Renaissance.* Cambridge: Cambridge University Press, 2000.

Hall, Kim F. *Things of Darkness: Economies of Race and Gender in Early Modern England.* Ithaca, NY: Cornell University Press, 1995.

Hamburger, Jeffrey. *The Visual and the Visionary: Art and Female Spirituality in Late Medieval Germany.* New York: Zone Books, 1998.

Hampton, Timothy. *Literature and the Nation in the Sixteenth Century: Inventing Renaissance France.* Ithaca, NY: Cornell University Press, 2001.

Hannay, Margaret, ed. *Silent But for the Word.* Kent, OH: Kent State University Press, 1985.

Hardwick, Julie. *The Practice of Patriarchy: Gender and the Politics of Household Authority in Early Modern France.* University Park: Pennsylvania State University Press, 1998.

Harris, Barbara J. *English Aristocratic Women, 1450–1550: Marriage and Family, Property and Careers.* New York: Oxford University Press, 2002.

Harth, Erica. *Ideology and Culture in Seventeenth-Century France.* Ithaca: Cornell University Press, 1983.

———. *Cartesian Women. Versions and Subversions of Rational Discourse in the Old Regime.* Ithaca: Cornell University Press, 1992.

Harvey, Elizabeth D. *Ventriloquized Voices: Feminist Theory and English Renaissance Texts.* London and New York: Routledge, 1992.

Haselkorn, Anne M., and Betty Travitsky, eds. *The Renaissance Englishwoman in Print: Counterbalancing the Canon.* Amherst: University of Massachusetts Press, 1990.

Hawkesworth, Celia, ed. *A History of Central European Women's Writing.* New York: Palgrave Press, 2001.

Hegstrom (Oakey), Valerie, and Amy R. Williamsen, eds. *Engendering the Early Modern Stage: Women Playwrights in the Spanish Empire.* New Orleans: University Press of the South, 1999.

Hendricks, Margo, and Patricia Parker, eds. *Women, "Race," and Writing in the Early Modern Period.* London and New York: Routledge, 1994.

Herlihy, David. "Did Women Have a Renaissance? A Reconsideration." *Medievalia et Humanistica* 13 n.s. (1985): 1–22.

Hill, Bridget. *The Republican Virago: The Life and Times of Catharine Macaulay, Historian.* New York: Oxford University Press, 1992.

Hills, Helen, ed. *Architecture and the Politics of Gender in Early Modern Europe.* Aldershot and Brookfield: Ashgate Publishing Co., 2003.

A History of Central European Women's Writing. Ed. Celia Hawkesworth. New York: Palgrave Press, 2001.

A History of Women in the West.
Volume 1: *From Ancient Goddesses to Christian Saints.* Ed. Pauline Schmitt Pantel. Cambridge, MA: Harvard University Press, 1992.
Volume 2: *Silences of the Middle Ages.* Ed. Christiane Klapisch-Zuber. Cambridge, MA: Harvard University Press, 1992.
Volume 3: *Renaissance and Enlightenment Paradoxes.* Ed. Natalie Zemon Davis and Arlette Farge. Cambridge, MA: Harvard University Press, 1993.

A History of Women Philosophers. Ed. Mary Ellen Waithe. 3 vols. Dordrecht: Martinus Nijhoff, 1987.

A History of Women's Writing in France. Ed. Sonya Stephens. Cambridge: Cambridge University Press, 2000.

A History of Women's Writing in Germany, Austria and Switzerland. Ed. Jo Catling. Cambridge: Cambridge University Press, 2000.

A History of Women's Writing in Italy. Ed. Letizia Panizza and Sharon Wood. Cambridge: University Press, 2000.

A History of Women's Writing in Russia. Edited by Alele Marie Barker and Jehanne M. Gheith. Cambridge: Cambridge University Press, 2002.

Hobby, Elaine. *Virtue of Necessity: English Women's Writing, 1646–1688.* London: Virago Press, 1988.

Horowitz, Maryanne Cline. "Aristotle and Women." *Journal of the History of Biology* 9 (1976): 183–213.

Howell, Martha. *The Marriage Exchange: Property, Social Place, and Gender in Cities of the Low Countries, 1300–1550.* Chicago: University of Chicago Press, 1998.

Hufton, Olwen H. *The Prospect before Her: A History of Women in Western Europe, 1: 1500–1800.* New York: HarperCollins, 1996

Hull, Suzanne W. *Chaste, Silent, and Obedient: English Books for Women, 1475–1640.* San Marino, CA: Huntington Library, 1982.

Hunt, Lynn, ed. *The Invention of Pornography: Obscenity and the Origins of Modernity, 1500–1800.* New York: Zone Books, 1996.

Hutner, Heidi, ed. *Rereading Aphra Behn: History, Theory, and Criticism.* Charlottesville: University Press of Virginia, 1993.

Hutson, Lorna, ed. *Feminism and Renaissance Studies.* New York: Oxford University Press, 1999.

The Invention of Pornography: Obscenity and the Origins of Modernity, 1500–1800. Ed. Lynn Hunt. New York: Zone Books, 1996.

Italian Women Writers: A Bio-Bibliographical Sourcebook. Edited by Rinaldina Russell. Westport, CT: Greenwood Press, 1994.

Jaffe, Irma B., with Gernando Colombardo. *Shining Eyes, Cruel Fortune: The Lives and Loves of Italian Renaissance Women Poets.* New York: Fordham University Press, 2002.

James, Susan E. *Kateryn Parr: The Making of a Queen.* Aldershot and Brookfield: Ashgate Publishing Co., 1999.

Jankowski, Theodora A. *Women in Power in the Early Modern Drama.* Urbana, IL: University of Illinois Press, 1992.

Jansen, Katherine Ludwig. *The Making of the Magdalen: Preaching and Popular Devotion in the Later Middle Ages.* Princeton: Princeton University Press, 2000.

Jed, Stephanie H. *Chaste Thinking: The Rape of Lucretia and the Birth of Humanism.* Bloomington: Indiana University Press, 1989.

Jones, Ann Rosalind and Peter Stallybrass. *Renaissance Clothing and the Materials of Memory*. Cambridge: Cambridge University Press, 2000.

Jordan, Constance. *Renaissance Feminism: Literary Texts and Political Models*. Ithaca: Cornell University Press, 1990.

Kagan, Richard L. *Lucrecia's Dreams: Politics and Prophecy in Sixteenth-Century Spain*. Berkeley: University of California Press, 1990.

Kehler, Dorothea and Laurel Amtower, eds. *The Single Woman in Medieval and Early Modern England: Her Life and Representation*. Tempe, AZ: MRTS, 2002.

Kelly, Joan. "Did Women Have a Renaissance?" In her *Women, History, and Theory*. Chicago: University of Chicago Press, 1984. Also in Renate Bridenthal, Claudia Koonz, and Susan M. Stuard, eds., *Becoming Visible: Women in European History*. Third edition. Boston: Houghton Mifflin, 1998.

———. "Early Feminist Theory and the *Querelle des Femmes*." In *Women, History, and Theory*.

Kelso, Ruth. *Doctrine for the Lady of the Renaissance*. Foreword by Katharine M. Rogers. Urbana: University of Illinois Press, 1956, 1978.

Kendrick, Robert L. *Celestical Sirens: Nuns and their Music in Early Modern Milan*. New York: Oxford University Press, 1996.

Kermode, Jenny, and Garthine Walker, eds. *Women, Crime and the Courts in Early Modern England*. Chapel Hill: University of North Carolina Press, 1994.

King, Catherine E. *Renaissance Women Patrons: Wives and Widows in Italy, c. 1300–1550*. New York and Manchester: Manchester University Press (distributed in the U.S. by St. Martin's Press), 1998.

King, Margaret L. *Women of the Renaissance*. Foreword by Catharine R. Stimpson. Chicago: University of Chicago Press, 1991.

Krontiris, Tina. *Oppositional Voices: Women as Writers and Translators of Literature in the English Renaissance*. London and New York: Routledge, 1992.

Kuehn, Thomas. *Law, Family, and Women: Toward a Legal Anthropology of Renaissance Italy*. Chicago: University of Chicago Press, 1991.

Kunze, Bonnelyn Young. *Margaret Fell and the Rise of Quakerism*. Stanford: Stanford University Press, 1994.

Labalme, Patricia A., ed. *Beyond Their Sex: Learned Women of the European Past*. New York: New York University Press, 1980.

Lalande, Roxanne Decker, ed. *A Labor of Love: Critical Reflections on the Writings of Marie-Catherine Desjardina (Mme de Villedieu)*. Madison, NJ: Fairleigh Dickinson University Press, 2000.

Lamb, Mary Ellen. *Gender and Authorship in the Sidney Circle*. Madison: University of Wisconsin Press, 1990.

Laqueur, Thomas. *Making Sex: Body and Gender from the Greeks to Freud*. Cambridge, MA: Harvard University Press, 1990.

Larsen, Anne R., and Colette H. Winn, eds. *Renaissance Women Writers: French Texts/American Contexts*. Detroit, MI: Wayne State University Press, 1994.

Laven, Mary. *Virgins of Venice: Enclosed Lives and Broken Vows in the Renaissance Convent*. London: Viking, 2002.

Ledkovsky, Marina, Charlotte Rosenthal, and Mary Zirin, eds. *Dictionary of Russian Women Writers*. Westport, CT: Greenwood Press, 1994.

Lehfeldt, Elizabeth A. *Religious Women in Golden Age Spain: The Permeable Cloister*. Aldershot and Brookfield: Ashgate Publishing Co., 2005.

Lerner, Gerda. *The Creation of Patriarchy* and *Creation of Feminist Consciousness, 1000–1870*. Two vols. New York: Oxford University Press, 1986, 1994.

Levack. Brian P. *The Witch Hunt in Early Modern Europe*. London: Longman, 1987.

Levin, Carole, and Jeanie Watson, eds. *Ambiguous Realities: Women in the Middle Ages and Renaissance*. Detroit: Wayne State University Press, 1987.

Levin, Carole, Jo Eldridge Carney, and Debra Barrett-Graves. *Elizabeth I: Always Her Own Free Woman*. Aldershot and Brookfield: Ashgate Publishing Co., 2003.

Levin, Carole, et al. *Extraordinary Women of the Medieval and Renaissance World: A Biographical Dictionary*. Westport, CT: Greenwood Press, 2000.

Levy, Allison, ed. *Widowhood and Visual Culture in Early Modern Europe*. Aldershot and Brookfield: Ashgate Publishing Co., 2003.

Lewalsky, Barbara Kiefer. *Writing Women in Jacobean England*. Cambridge, MA: Harvard University Press, 1993.

Lewis, Gertrud Jaron. *By Women for Women about Women: The Sister-Books of Fourteenth-Century Germany*. Toronto: University of Toronto Press, 1996.

Lewis, Jayne Elizabeth. *Mary Queen of Scots: Romance and Nation*. London: Routledge, 1998.

Lindenauer, Leslie J. *Piety and Power: Gender and Religious Culture in the American Colonies, 1630–1700*. London and New York: Routledge, 2002.

Lindsey, Karen. *Divorced Beheaded Survived: A Feminist Reinterpretation of the Wives of Henry VIII*. Reading, MA: Addison-Wesley Publishing Co., 1995.

Lochrie, Karma. *Margery Kempe and Translations of the Flesh*. Philadelphia: University of Pennsylvania Press, 1992.

Longino Farrell, Michèle. *Performing Motherhood: The Sévigné Correspondence*. Hanover, NH: University Press of New England, 1991.

Lougee, Carolyn C. *Le Paradis des Femmes: Women, Salons, and Social Stratification in Seventeenth-Century France*. Princeton: Princeton University Press, 1976.

Love, Harold. *The Culture and Commerce of Texts: Scribal Publication in Seventeenth-Century England*. Amherst: University of Massachusetts Press, 1993.

Lowe, K. J. P. *Nuns' Chronicles and Convent Culture in Renaissance and Counter-Reformation Italy*. Cambridge: Cambridge University Press, 2003.

Lux-Sterritt, Laurence. *Redefining Female Religious Life: French Ursulines and English Ladies in Seventeenth-Century Catholicism*. Aldershot and Brookfield: Ashgate Publishing Co., 2005.

MacCarthy, Bridget G. *The Female Pen: Women Writers and Novelists 1621–1818*. Preface by Janet Todd. New York: New York University Press, 1994. (Originally published by Cork University Press, 1946–47).

Mack, Phyllis. *Visionary Women: Ecstatic Prophecy in Seventeenth-Century England*. Berkeley: University of California Pres, 1992.

Maclean, Ian. *Woman Triumphant: Feminism in French Literature, 1610–1652*. Oxford: Clarendon Press, 1977.

———. *The Renaissance Notion of Woman: A Study of the Fortunes of Scholasticism and Medical Science in European Intellectual Life*. Cambridge: Cambridge University Press, 1980.

MacNeil, Anne. *Music and Women of the Commedia dell'Arte in the Late Sixteenth Century*. New York: Oxford University Press, 2003.

Maggi, Armando. *Uttering the Word: The Mystical Performances of Maria Maddalena de' Pazzi, a Renaissance Visionary*. Albany: State University of New York Press, 1998.

Maids and Mistresses, Cousins and Queens: Women's Alliances in Early Modern England. Ed. Susan Frye and Karen Robertson. Oxford: Oxford University Press, 1999.

Marshall, Sherrin, ed. *Women in Reformation and Counter-Reformation Europe: Public and Private Worlds.* Bloomington: Indiana University Press, 1989.

Masten, Jeffrey. *Textual Intercourse: Collaboration, Authorship, and Sexualities in Renaissance Drama.* Cambridge: Cambridge University Press, 1997.

Matter, E. Ann, and John Coakley, eds. *Creative Women in Medieval and Early Modern Italy.* Philadelphia: University of Pennsylvania Press, 1994.

McGrath, Lynette. *Subjectivity and Women's Poetry in Early Modern England.* Aldershot and Brookfield: Ashgate Publishing Co., 2002.

McIver, Katherine A. *Women, Art, and Architecture in Northern Italy, 1520–1580.* Aldershot and Brookfield: Ashgate Publishing Co., 2006.

McLeod, Glenda. *Virtue and Venom: Catalogs of Women from Antiquity to the Renaissance.* Ann Arbor: University of Michigan Press, 1991.

McTavish, Lianne. *Childbirth and the Display of Authority in Early Modern France.* Aldershot and Brookfield: Ashgate Publishing Co., 2005.

Medieval Women's Visionary Literature. Ed. Elizabeth A. Petroff. New York: Oxford University Press, 1986.

Medwick, Cathleen. *Teresa of Avila: The Progress of a Soul.* New York: Doubleday, 1999.

Meek, Christine, ed. *Women in Renaissance and Early Modern Europe.* Dublin and Portland: Four Courts Press, 2000.

Mendelson, Sara, and Patricia Crawford. *Women in Early Modern England, 1550–1720.* Oxford: Clarendon Press, 1998.

Merchant, Carolyn. *The Death of Nature: Women, Ecology and the Scientific Revolution.* New York: HarperCollins, 1980.

Merrim, Stephanie. *Early Modern Women's Writing and Sor Juana Inés de la Cruz.* Nashville, TN: Vanderbilt University Press, 1999.

Messbarger, Rebecca. *The Century of Women: The Representations of Women in Eighteenth-Century Italian Public Discourse.* Toronto: University of Toronto Press, 2002.

Miller, Nancy K. *The Heroine's Text: Readings in the French and English Novel, 1722–1782.* New York: Columbia University Press, 1980.

Miller, Naomi J. *Changing the Subject: Mary Wroth and Figurations of Gender in Early Modern England.* Lexington: University Press of Kentucky, 1996.

——— and Gary Waller, eds. *Reading Mary Wroth: Representing Alternatives in Early Modern England.* Knoxville: University of Tennessee Press, 1991.

Monson, Craig A. *Disembodied Voices: Music and Culture in an Early Modern Italian Convent.* Berkeley: University of California Press, 1995.

———., ed. *The Crannied Wall: Women, Religion, and the Arts in Early Modern Europe.* Ann Arbor: University of Michigan Press, 1992.

Moore, Cornelia Niekus. *The Maiden's Mirror: Reading Material for German Girls in the Sixteenth and Seventeenth Centuries.* Wiesbaden: Otto Harrassowitz, 1987.

Moore, Mary B. *Desiring Voices: Women Sonneteers and Petrarchism.* Carbondale: Southern Illinois University Press, 2000.

Mujica, Bárbara. *Women Writers of Early Modern Spain.* New Haven: Yale University Press, 2004.

Musacchio, Jacqueline Marie. *The Art and Ritual of Childbirth in Renaissance Italy.* New Haven: Yale University Press, 1999.

Newman, Barbara. *God and the Goddesses: Vision, Poetry, and Belief in the Middle Ages.* Philadelphia: University of Pennsylvania Press, 2003.

Newman, Karen. *Fashioning Femininity and English Renaissance Drama.* Chicago: University of Chicago Press, 1991.

O'Donnell, Mary Ann. *Aphra Behn: An Annotated Bibliography of Primary and Secondary Sources.* Aldershot and Brookfield: Ashgate Publishing Co., 2nd ed., 2004.

Okin, Susan Moller. *Women in Western Political Thought.* Princeton: Princeton University Press, 1979.

Ozment, Steven. *The Bürgermeister's Daughter: Scandal in a Sixteenth-Century German Town.* New York: St. Martin's Press, 1995.

————. *Flesh and Spirit: Private Life in Early Modern Germany.* New York: Penguin Putnam, 1999.

————. *When Fathers Ruled: Family Life in Reformation Europe.* Cambridge, MA: Harvard University Press, 1983.

Pacheco, Anita, ed. *Early [English] Women Writers: 1600–1720.* New York and London: Longman, 1998.

Pagels, Elaine. *Adam, Eve, and the Serpent.* New York: Harper Collins, 1988.

Panizza, Letizia, and Sharon Wood, eds. *A History of Women's Writing in Italy.* Cambridge: University Press, 2000.

Panizza, Letizia, ed. *Women in Italian Renaissance Culture and Society.* Oxford: European Humanities Research Centre, 2000.

Parker, Patricia. *Literary Fat Ladies: Rhetoric, Gender and Property.* London and New York: Methuen, 1987.

Pernoud, Regine, and Marie-Veronique Clin. *Joan of Arc: Her Story.* Rev. and trans. Jeremy DuQuesnay Adams. New York: St. Martin's Press, 1998.

Perry, Mary Elizabeth. *Crime and Society in Early Modern Seville.* Hanover, NH: University Press of New England, 1980.

————. *Gender and Disorder in Early Modern Seville.* Princeton: Princeton University Press, 1990.

————. *The Handless Maiden: Moriscos and the Politics of Religion in Early Modern Spain.* Princeton: Princeton University Press, 2005.

Petroff, Elizabeth A., ed. *Medieval Women's Visionary Literature.* New York: Oxford University Press, 1986.

Perry, Ruth. *The Celebrated Mary Astell: An Early English Feminist.* Chicago: University of Chicago Press, 1986.

The Practice and Representation of Reading in England. Ed. James Raven, Helen Small, and Naomi Tadmor. Cambridge: University Press, 1996.

Quilligan, Maureen. *Incest and Agency in Elizabeth's England.* Philadelphia: University of Pennsylvania Press, 2005.

Rabil, Albert. *Laura Cereta: Quattrocento Humanist.* Binghamton, NY: MRTS, 1981.

Ranft, Patricia. *Women in Western Intellectual Culture, 600–1500.* New York: Palgrave, 2002.

Rapley, Elizabeth. *A Social History of the Cloister: Daily Life in the Teaching Monasteries of the Old Regime.* Montreal: McGill-Queen's University Press, 2001.

————. *The Devotés: Women and Church in Seventeenth-Century France.* Kingston, Ontario: Mc-Gill-Queen's University Press, 1989.

Raven, James, Helen Small, and Naomi Tadmor, eds. *The Practice and Representation of Reading in England.* Cambridge: University Press, 1996.

Reading Mary Wroth: Representing Alternatives in Early Modern England. Ed. Naomi Miller and Gary Waller. Knoxville: University of Tennessee Press, 1991.

Reardon, Colleen. *Holy Concord within Sacred Walls: Nuns and Music in Siena, 1575–1700.* Oxford: Oxford University Press, 2001.

Recovering Spain's Feminist Tradition. Ed. Lisa Vollendorf. New York: MLA, 2001.

Reid, Jonathan Andrew. "King's Sister—Queen of Dissent: Marguerite of Navarre (1492 1549) and Her Evangelical Network." Ph.D diss., University of Arizona, 2001.

Reiss, Sheryl E,. and David G. Wilkins, ed. *Beyond Isabella: Secular Women Patrons of Art in Renaissance Italy.* Kirksville, MO: Turman State University Press, 2001.

The Renaissance Englishwoman in Print: Counterbalancing the Canon. Ed. Anne M. Haselkorn and Betty Travitsky. Amherst: University of Massachusetts Press, 1990.

Renaissance Women Writers: French Texts/American Contexts. Ed. Anne R. Larsen and Colette H. Winn. Detroit, MI: Wayne State University Press, 1994.

Rereading Aphra Behn: History, Theory, and Criticism. Ed. Heidi Hutner. Charlottesville: University Press of Virginia, 1993.

Rheubottom, David. *Age, Marriage, and Politics in Fifteenth-Century Ragusa.* Oxford: Oxford University Press, 2000.

Richardson, Brian. *Printing, Writers and Readers in Renaissance Italy.* Cambridge: University Press, 1999.

Riddle, John M. *Contraception and Abortion from the Ancient World to the Renaissance.* Cambridge, MA: Harvard University Press, 1992.

———. *Eve's Herbs: A History of Contraception and Abortion in the West.* Cambridge, MA: Harvard University Press, 1997.

Roper, Lyndal. *The Holy Household: Women and Morals in Reformation Augsburg.* New York: Oxford University Press, 1989.

Rose, Mary Beth. *The Expense of Spirit: Love and Sexuality in English Renaissance Drama.* Ithaca, NY: Cornell University Press, 1988.

———. *Gender and Heroism in Early Modern English Literature.* Chicago: University of Chicago Press, 2002.

———, ed. *Women in the Middle Ages and the Renaissance: Literary and Historical Perspectives.* Syracuse: Syracuse University Press, 1986.

Rosenthal, Margaret F. *The Honest Courtesan: Veronica Franco, Citizen and Writer in Sixteenth-Century Venice.* Foreword by Catharine R. Stimpson. Chicago: University of Chicago Press, 1992.

Rublack, Ulinka, ed. *Gender in Early Modern German History.* Cambridge: Cambridge University Press, 2002.

Russell, Rinaldina, ed. *Feminist Encyclopedia of Italian Literature.* Westport, CT: Greenwood Press, 1997.

———. *Italian Women Writers: A Bio-Bibliographical Sourcebook.* Westport, CT: Greenwood Press, 1994.

Sackville-West, Vita. *Daughter of France: The Life of La Grande Mademoiselle.* Garden City, NY: Doubleday, 1959.

Sage, Lorna, ed. *Cambridge Guide to Women's Writing in English.* Cambridge: University Press, 1999.

Sánchez, Magdalena S. *The Empress, the Queen, and the Nun: Women and Power at the Court of Philip III of Spain.* Baltimore: Johns Hopkins University Press, 1998.

Sartori, Eva Martin, and Dorothy Wynne Zimmerman, eds. *French Women Writers: A Bio-Bibliographical Source Book*. Westport, CT: Greenwood Press, 1991.

Scaraffia, Lucetta, and Gabriella Zarri. *Women and Faith: Catholic Religious Life in Italy from Late Antiquity to the Present*. Cambridge, MA: Harvard University Press, 1999.

Scheepsma, Wybren. *Medieval Religious Women in the Low Countries: The 'Modern Devotion', the Canonesses of Windesheim, and Their Writings*. Rochester, NY: Boydell Press, 2004.

Schiebinger, Londa. *The Mind has no sex?: Women in the Origins of Modern Science*. Cambridge, MA: Harvard University Press, 1991.

———. *Nature's Body: Gender in the Making of Modern Science*. Boston: Beacon Press, 1993.

Schutte, Anne Jacobson, Thomas Kuehn, and Silvana Seidel Menchi, eds. *Time, Space, and Women's Lives in Early Modern Europe*. Kirksville, MO: Truman State University Press, 2001.

Schofield, Mary Anne, and Cecilia Macheski, eds. *Fetter'd or Free? British Women Novelists, 1670–1815*. Athens: Ohio University Press, 1986.

Schutte, Anne Jacobson. *Aspiring Saints: pretense of Holiness, Inquisition, and Gender in the Republic of Venice, 1618–1750*. Baltimore: Johns Hopkins University Press, 2001.

———, Thomas Kuehn, and Silvana Seidel Menchi, eds. *Time, Space, and Women's Lives in Early Modern Europe*. Kirksville, MO: Truman State University Press, 2001.

Seifert, Lewis C. *Fairy Tales, Sexuality and Gender in France 1690–1715: Nostalgic Utopias*. Cambridge, UK: Cambridge University Press, 1996.

Shannon, Laurie. *Sovereign Amity: Figures of Friendship in Shakespearean Contexts*. Chicago: University of Chicago Press, 2002.

Shemek, Deanna. *Ladies Errant: Wayward Women and Social Order in Early Modern Italy*. Durham, NC: Duke University Press, 1998.

Silent But for the Word. Ed. Margaret Hannay. Kent, OH: Kent State University Press, 1985.

The Single Woman in Medieval and Early Modern England: Her Life and Representation. Ed. Dorothea Kehler and Laurel Amtower. Tempe, AZ: MRTS, 2002.

Smarr, Janet L. *Joining the Conversation: Dialogues by Renaissance Women*. Ann Arbor: University of Michigan Press, 2005.

Smith, Hilda L. *Reason's Disciples: Seventeenth-Century English Feminists*. Urbana: University of Illinois Press, 1982.

———. *Women Writers and the Early Modern British Political Tradition*. Cambridge: Cambridge University Press, 1998.

Snook, Edith. *Women, Reading, and the Cultural Politics of Early Modern England*. Aldershot and Brookfield: Ashgate Publishing Co., 2005.

Sobel, Dava. *Galileo's Daughter: A Historical Memoir of Science, Faith, and Love*. New York: Penguin Books, 2000.

Sommerville, Margaret R. *Sex and Subjection: Attitudes to Women in Early-Modern Society*. London: Arnold, 1995.

Soufas, Teresa Scott. *Dramas of Distinction: A Study of Plays by Golden Age Women*. Lexington: The University Press of Kentucky, 1997.

Spencer, Jane. *The Rise of the Woman Novelist: From Aphra Behn to Jane Austen*. Oxford: Basil Blackwell, 1986.

Spender, Dale. *Mothers of the Novel: 100 Good Women Writers Before Jane Austen*. London and New York: Routledge, 1986.

Sperling, Jutta Gisela. *Convents and the Body Politic in Late Renaissance Venice.* Foreword by Catharine R. Stimpson. Chicago: University of Chicago Press, 1999.

Steinbrügge, Lieselotte. *The Moral Sex: Woman's Nature in the French Enlightenment.* Trans. Pamela E. Selwyn. New York: Oxford University Press, 1995.

Stephens, Sonya, ed. *A History of Women's Writing in France.* Cambridge: Cambridge University Press, 2000.

Stephenson, Barbara. *The Power and Patronage of Marguerite de Navarre.* Aldershot and Brookfield: Ashgate Publishing Co., 2004.

Stocker, Margarita. *Judith, Sexual Warrior: Women and Power in Western Culture.* New Haven: Yale University Press, 1998.

Straznacky, Marta. *Privacy, Playreading, and Women's Closet Drama, 1550–1700.* Cambridge: Cambridge University Press, 2004.

Stretton, Timothy. *Women Waging Law in Elizabethan England.* Cambridge: Cambridge University Press, 1998.

Strong Voices, Weak History: Early Women Writers and Canons in England, France, and Italy. Ed. Pamela J. Benson and Victoria Kirkham. Ann Arbor: University of Michigan Press, 2005.

Stuard, Susan M. "The Dominion of Gender: Women's Fortunes in the High Middle Ages." In Renate Bridenthal, Claudia Koonz, and Susan M. Stuard, eds. *Becoming Visible: Women in European History.* Third edition. Boston: Houghton Mifflin, 1998.

Summit, Jennifer. *Lost Property: The Woman Writer and English Literary History, 1380–1589.* Chicago: University of Chicago Press, 2000.

Surtz, Ronald E. *The Guitar of God: Gender, Power, and Authority in the Visionary World of Mother Juana de la Cruz (1481–1534).* Philadelphia: University of Pennsylvania Press, 1991.

———. *Writing Women in Late Medieval and Early Modern Spain: The Mothers of Saint Teresa of Avila.* Philadelphia: University of Pennsylvania Press, 1995.

Suzuki, Mihoko. *Subordinate Subjects: Gender, the Political Nation, and Literary Form in England, 1588–1688.* Aldershot and Brookfield: Ashgate Publishing Co., 2003.

Tatlock, Lynne, and Christiane Bohnert, eds. *The Graph of Sex* (q.v.).

Teaching Tudor and Stuart Women Writers. Ed. Susanne Woods and Margaret P. Hannay. New York: MLA, 2000.

Teague, Frances. *Bathsua Makin, Woman of Learning.* Lewisburg, PA: Bucknell University Press, 1999.

Thomas, Anabel. *Art and Piety in the Female Religious Communities of Renaissance Italy: Iconography, Space, and the Religious Woman's Perspective.* New York: Cambridge University Press, 2003.

Tinagli, Paola. *Women in Italian Renaissance Art: Gender, Representation, Identity.* Manchester: Manchester University Press, 1997.

Todd, Janet. *The Secret Life of Aphra Behn.* London, New York, and Sydney: Pandora, 2000.

———. *The Sign of Angelica: Women, Writing and Fiction, 1660–1800.* New York: Columbia University Press, 1989.

Tomas, Natalie R. *The Medici Women: Gender and Power in Renaissance Florence.* Aldershot and Brookfield: Ashgate Publishing Co., 2004.

Traub, Valerie. *The Renaissance of Lesbianism in Early Modern England.* Cambridge: Cambridge University Press, 2002.

Valenze, Deborah. *The First Industrial Woman*. New York: Oxford University Press, 1995.

Van Dijk, Susan, Lia van Gemert, and Sheila Ottway, eds. *Writing the History of Women's Writing: Toward an International Approach*. Proceedings of the Colloquium, Amsterdam, 9–11 September. Amsterdam: Royal Netherlands Academy of Arts and Sciences, 2001.

Vickery, Amanda. *The Gentleman's Daughter: Women's Lives in Georgian England*. New Haven: Yale University Press, 1998.

Vollendorf, Lisa. *The Lives of Women: A New History of Inquisitional Spain*. Nashville, TN: Vanderbilt University Press, 2005.

Walker, Claire. *Gender and Politics in Early Modern Europe: English Convents in France and the Low Countries*. New York: Palgrave, 2003.

Wall, Wendy. *The Imprint of Gender: Authorship and Publication in the English Renaissance*. Ithaca, NY: Cornell University Press, 1993.

Walsh, William T. *St. Teresa of Avila: A Biography*. Rockford, IL: TAN Books & Publications, 1987.

Warner, Marina. *Alone of All Her Sex: The Myth and Cult of the Virgin Mary*. New York: Knopf, 1976.

Warnicke, Retha M. *The Marrying of Anne of Cleves: Royal Protocol in Tudor England*. Cambridge: Cambridge University Press, 2000.

Watt, Diane. *Secretaries of God: Women Prophets in Late Medieval and Early Modern England*. Cambridge, England: D. S. Brewer, 1997.

Weaver, Elissa. *Convent Theatre in Early Modern Italy: Spiritual Fun and Learning for Women*. New York: Cambridge University Press, 2002.

Weber, Alison. *Teresa of Avila and the Rhetoric of Femininity*. Princeton: Princeton University Press, 1990.

Welles, Marcia L. *Persephone's Girdle: Narratives of Rape in Seventeenth-Century Spanish Literature*. Nashville: Vanderbilt University Press, 2000.

Whitehead, Barbara J., ed. *Women's Education in Early Modern Europe: A History, 1500–1800*. New York and London: Garland Publishing Co., 1999.

Widowhood and Visual Culture in Early Modern Europe. Ed. Allison Levy. Aldershot and Brookfield: Ashgate Publishing Co., 2003.

Widowhood in Medieval and Early Modern Europe. Ed. Sandra Cavallo and Lydan Warner. New York: Longman, 1999.

Wiesner, Merry E. *Working Women in Renaissance Germany*. New Brunswick, NJ: Rutgers University Press, 1986.

Wiesner-Hanks, Merry E. *Christianity and Sexuality in the Early Modern World: Regulating Desire, Reforming Practice*. New York: Routledge, 2000.

———. *Gender, Church, and State in Early Modern Germany: Essays*. New York: Longman, 1998.

———. *Gender in History*. Malden, MA: Blackwell, 2001.

———. *Women and Gender in Early Modern Europe*. Cambridge: Cambridge University Press, 1993.

———. *Working Women in Renaissance Germany*. New Brunswick, NJ: Rutgers University Press, 1986.

Willard, Charity Cannon. *Christine de Pizan: Her Life and Works*. New York: Persea Books, 1984.

Wilson, Katharina, ed. *Encyclopedia of Continental Women Writers*. 2 vols. New York: Garland, 1991.

Winn, Colette, and Donna Kuizenga, eds. *Women Writers in Pre-Revolutionary France*. New York: Garland Publishing, 1997.

Winston-Allen, Anne. *Convent Chronicles: Women Writing about Women and Reform in the Late Middle Ages*. University Park: Pennsylvania State University Press, 2004.

Women and Monasticism in Medieval Europe: Sisters and Patrons of the Cistercian Reform, ed. Constance H. Berman. Kalamazoo: Western Michigan University Press, 2002.

Women, Crime and the Courts in Early Modern England. Ed. Jenny Kermode and Garthine Walker. Chapel Hill: University of North Carolina Press, 1994.

Women in Italian Renaissance Culture and Society. Ed. Letizia Panizza. Oxford: European Humanities Research Centre, 2000.

Women in Reformation and Counter-Reformation Europe: Public and Private Worlds. Ed. Sherrin Marshall. Bloomington, IN: Indiana University Press, 1989.

Women in Renaissance and Early Modern Europe. Ed. Christine Meek. Dublin-Portland: Four Courts Press, 2000.

Women in the Inquisition: Spain and the New World. Ed. Mary E. Giles. Baltimore: Johns Hopkins University Press, 1999.

Women in the Middle Ages and the Renaissance: Literary and Historical Perspectives. Ed. Mary Beth Rose. Syracuse: Syracuse University Press, 1986.

Women Players in England, 1500–1660: Beyond the All-Male Stage. Ed. Pamela Allen Brown and Peter Parolin. Aldershot and Brookfield: Ashgate Publishing Co., 2005.

Women, "Race," and Writing in the Early Modern Period. Ed. Margo Hendricks and Patricia Parker. London and New York: Routledge, 1994.

Woodbridge, Linda. *Women and the English Renaissance: Literature and the Nature of Womankind, 1540–1620*. Urbana: University of Illinois Press, 1984.

Woodford, Charlotte. *Nuns as Historians in Early Modern Germany*. Oxford: Clarendon Press, 2002.

Woods, Susanne. *Lanyer: A Renaissance Woman Poet*. New York: Oxford University Press, 1999.

——— and Margaret P. Hannay, eds. *Teaching Tudor and Stuart Women Writers*. New York: MLA, 2000.

Writing the Female Voice. Ed. Elizabeth C. Goldsmith. Boston: Northeastern University Press, 1989.

Writing the History of Women's Writing: Toward an International Approach. Ed. Susan Van Dijk, Lia van Gemert and Sheila Ottway Proceedings of the Colloquium, Amsterdam, 9–11 September. Amsterdam: Royal Netherlands Academy of Arts and Sciences, 2001.

INDEX OF FIRST LINES

GENERAL INDEX

Italicized page numbers indicate references in the poetry.